WOODBR

David Thomson was born in India of Scottish parents in 1914. Much of his childhood was spent in the country, in Derbyshire and at Nairn in Scotland where his grandparents lived. After leaving Oxford University, he took a job at Woodbrook in Ireland, and stayed there for almost ten years. *Woodbrook*, first published in 1974, grew out of that time. Later he joined the BBC, where he wrote and produced many distinguished programmes, including *The Irish Storyteller* series, *The Great Hunger* and a number of other programmes on animal folklore. During his secondment to UNESCO he worked in France, Liberia and Turkey. His much-loved book about seals and their legends, *The People of the Sea*, appeared in 1954. *In Camden Town*, a study of the place where he lived for the last thirty-two years of his life appeared in 1983. David Thomson's memoir, *Nairn in Darkness and Light*, won the McVitie's Prize for the Scottish Writer of the year in 1987, and the NCR Book Award for Non-Fiction in 1988. He died in 1988.

David Thomson

WOODBROOK

VINTAGE

Published by Vintage 1991

Reprinted 1994, 1996, 1997, 2002

10

Copyright © David Thomson 1974

First published by Barrie & Jenkins 1974
Arena edition 1988

Vintage
Random House, 20 Vauxhall Bridge Road,
London SW1V 2SA

Random House Australia (Pty) Limited
20 Alfred Street, Milsons Point, Sydney,
New South Wales 2061, Australia

Random House New Zealand Limited
18 Poland Road, Glenfield
Auckalnd 10, New Zealand

Random House (Pty) Limited
Endulini, 5A Jubilee Road, Parktown 2193,
South Africa

The Random House Group Limited Reg. No. 954009

www.randomhouse.co.uk

A CIP catalogue record for this book
is available from the British Library

ISBN 0 09 935991 X

Printed and bound in Great Britain by
Bookmarque Ltd, Croydon, Surrey

I acknowledge assistance from the Arts Council of Great Britain. I also wish to thank all those who helped me personally with the book: among them Mrs I.M. Kirkwood, the Maxwell brothers, Leo Corduff, James Delaney, Séamus Delargy, Shane Flynn, Michael Molloy, and Seán Ó Súilleabháin. I am grateful to the staff of the Department of Irish Folklore, University College, Dublin, and the staff of the London Library for their kindness and the trouble they took.

Part One

Chapter One

I was eighteen when I first saw Woodbrook. The children excitedly pulled me towards the right-hand window of the car and I saw its slate roof from the turn of the road at the top of Hughestown Hill. It was about midday and sunny. The slates shone for a moment between the leaves of beech trees and we descended rattling towards the house, looking out from the window of this old Fiat which had fetched us from the station three miles away. Major Kirkwood, their father, drove mostly on the right, not, as I later found out, because that is the rule of the road in Ireland, but to find a smoother surface – on his way back to the station he would drive mostly on the left – and coming down the hill we seemed to be on the grassy edge of a precipice. The sunken meadow between us and the house was covered with ground mist which made the house on its ridge above look larger than it really was. We descended fast and grinding to the level of its roof, of its upstairs windows, of its wide front door and a moment later, after glancing at rough pastures on our left, I was looking up to it across a brook which ran parallel with the flat stretch of the road. We drove on until the house was out of sight and then turned sharply back through a white gateway over a bridge and up the drive. The children, their mother and I had left London on the previous evening, by train to Holyhead, and come three hours by boat and four by train from Broadstone station, Dublin.

I was then reading History at Oxford, making journeys by old books into the details of the past, and though I absorbed through the window of the Fiat the present only, strongly flying, I found in the days and years that followed that I had begun to uncover a physical past, which lives in my memory now where the details academically learnt have sunk. For example, as I

9

walked on the pastures of Woodbrook watching the horses graze, on that first day, I observed many low curved undulations of the turf, straight and regularly spaced, the valleys between them three feet apart, the ridges sloping upwards with the hill, never across it, all obviously made by men, but it did not occur to me for years that they were potato beds abandoned with their rotten crop by the starving people who fled or died in the Great Famine eighty-five years before. And when I met the Maxwell brothers, who lived with their parents on Woodbrook farm and worked there, I did not know that they were the great-great-grandchildren of the only survivors in that townland, nor that their little house had been one of thirty at that time, each standing in its own plot of several acres, every one of which except theirs had been pulled down in the years of the famine, nor that they felt ashamed because they knew why their house had been spared, nor that they secretly cherished hatred for the Major, their present landlord and employer whom in day to day relationships they loved – cherished this hatred because of his ancestors and theirs, and because it might help their advancement.

I think of these examples, one lodged in the soil and the other in the mind, because they led me gradually beneath the surface of the soil and mind. My mind was then always on the surface of what I saw or heard and I owned nothing durable except a watch which soon fell into the lake. It was years before I understood what land means to a peasant people, that love of it can be more jealous than love of a woman and more steadfast because it is embedded in the past. None of my friends thought much about possessions. One had a car, it is true, and one a motor-bicycle, but these they treated like toys to be swapped or sold at a whim.

My feeling for Woodbrook was more like friendship than love, and now as I look back I can see that it began unconsciously like friendship. When two people meet and take to each other, they start gradually to uncover one another's past, and the slower the process the deeper the friendship becomes. It is like falling in love, without the torment, and although you do not find each other layer by layer in the archaeologists' way, you see after months or years a whole being who contains his past and present merged with the lives of his forebears. You see the whole of him and he sees you, the present surface always near and the layers of the past melted into one. In modern history the layers are jumbled in the ground and buildings, and in the minds of the people.

The car drew up before the building – Woodbrook House – but I did not then look at it because the house servants and the farm servants, all except Tom, were standing before the front door to greet us, in a group as though they were posing for a photograph. I saw them through my window first, the one on the left of the car, which would not open and was cloudy, and then face to face when I got out, and I felt embarrassed and shy. But the two children scrambled after me, holding their Welsh sheepdog puppies in their arms and for a time no one looked at me – the new curiosity from England. I do not know which of the servants was first to speak but perhaps it was James, the old horseman, with his long grey face and baggy breeches who said, 'Welcome home, Miss Phoebe. Welcome home, Miss Tony.' Phoebe was eleven years old and Tony about four. Tony's real name was Antoinette. She was always called Tony.

Beside him stood Winnie, the cook, in an apron, which was all I saw of her at that moment, and beside her a boy who cleaned the floors and fetched the turf and coal and sawed logs for the fires – even at the height of summer fires were needed in the evenings and all the cooking and hot water was done by an old kitchen range burning coal. I remember him well, but not his name. He was thin and emotional and wore a tattered wide-brimmed hat that hid his face. There were also two girls, but I cannot remember them because they only stayed for a few months that first summer and were replaced in the succeeding years by others from the neighbouring small farms where daughters of huge families took any temporary job they could find. One worked in the dairy and kitchen and the other as a housemaid. I suppose that is why I have forgotten them, for except at meal-times and night, and the two hours a day that I taught the children, I did not keep to the house.

Beside the girls stood Willie Maxwell, the oldest of the servants of the farm, a grave and solid man about thirty years of age, with a square impassive face, reserved and dignified, who looked calmly at us in turn and smiled only when he was spoken to. His smile, when it came, crinkled up his face, transformed him in a second and vanished. I came to know later that his smile showed more of himself than the self-protective look which covered him on that peculiar occasion. He belonged to the old Ireland of his father and grandfathers, and was nearer to them than to his younger brothers. He did not show his mobility of mind until you got to know him well. He was not a bit like his young brother Johnny who was by him. Johnny was light and small with a thin boyish face and eyes that never stayed still. He was the herd and could run after cattle and leap walls like a boy. Almost everything he saw and heard amused him and he could respond to solemn talk or a carelessly trite remark with intelligent wit or a glance that was disconcerting. His style of dress was unusual too and unsuited to the rough, hard-weather work of a herd. He always wore a formal blue suit, too faded and tattered for Mass, and sometimes he put on a tie.

Jimmy Maxwell, a good bit taller than Johnny and some years older – there was a sister, in between them, at home – came forward to help with the suitcases. I thought old James Currid reproved him for this in an undertone, but am not sure. Jimmy always helped other people unobtrusively and if he resented the old horseman's possessive grip on the family he did not show it as his brothers did.

All these people greeted us separately, as we struggled out of the car, with the words 'Welcome home'. They addressed Mrs Kirkwood as 'Mistress' and when they spoke about her they always said 'The Mistress'. She had been living in London for the past six months and they were pleased to see her. They greeted me warmly too and called me 'Master David' from the start. They said 'Welcome home, Master David', as though I were one of the family and Woodbrook my home, which later it became. I felt happy and flattered like a dog that is patted by an agreeable stranger. I could not think how they even knew my name, but of course Major Kirkwood had met me often during his visits to London and must have told them about me.

The men straggled off and we went into the house led by Winnie and followed by the girls who stepped shyly through the carpeted hall and ran giggling with echoey footfalls into the darkness of a stone-flagged corridor which led, curved and windowless, towards the kitchen. Winnie, who was speaking rapidly to Mrs Kirkwood, broke off with a deprecating glance, apologizing for them, and then began to say even more quickly, pointing out this and that, that this had got broken in the spring cleaning by Peter and that had been moved over there. The children put down their puppies, one of which immediately made a puddle on the carpet, and went to explore their old familiar house.

The hall was a large square room with white walls and dark furniture, black leather armchairs which had once been green, some upright chairs with seats the same, a round mahogany table and a smaller, oblong one on which stood a china vase of marigolds and daisies. It seemed dark and unlived in on that first day. Indeed the whole house except the servants' quarters and Major Kirkwood's bedroom had been unlived in for six months; when his family was in London he spent most of his time in the kitchen or out of doors. But a faded Indian carpet, Persian rugs torn in places and the brass rail of a fender by the empty fireplace were light.

The front door opened into the hall, not in the middle but at its right-hand side, so that the first thing I saw amid the confusion of people was the little vase of flowers which stood on the table before us. To the right of the front door before you came to this table was a room which they called the office where Major Kirkwood used to store a vast heap of bills and letters that were dealt with, if his creditors were lucky, on one or two winter evenings every year. The room was also a repository for shoes, boots, fishing rods and a seldom used gun, tennis rackets, most of them with broken strings, golf clubs and old coats, croquet hoops and mallets, riding-crops and walking-sticks and several kinds of balls. I remember with nostalgia the faded colours of the croquet balls, blue, yellow, green and black, and the feel of them, although I cannot remember any of us ever playing croquet.

Across the hall, opposite the office, a door opened into the drawing-room. It was spacious and beautiful, with three large sash windows, two looking out from the front of the house across the lawn and the sunken meadow called 'The Bottoms', and across the 'Canal' which was really a brook, to the road and Hughestown Hill, the other looking out on a huge copper beech, whose leaves with the sun shining through them were luminous that day like dragon-flies' wings or bits of stained-glass window. From here, at the side of the house, you could see part of the drive up which we had come curving away beneath a high bushy bank until it went out of sight and gave place to a piece of the long, low meadow, which stretched from the bottom of Hughestown Hill as far as the gate lodge to the west. By the time I looked out through this window the ground mist had gone and I saw deep grass in flower almost ready to be mown.

The old part of the house had two storeys, but the drawing-room and dining-room had no bedrooms above them; they had been built later of the same grey blocks of stone, forming low wings of beautiful proportions with flat roofs. One of the windows of the dining-room opened on to a rough sloping garden with more shrubs in it than flowers, beyond which lay a tennis court and paddock, and beyond those the lake with the Leitrim mountains blue in the distance to the east. On the way from the station I had seen neither mountains nor lake and this view from the window as we went in to dinner was a shock of delight; but a moment later, hovering round the long dining table which was laid for five, I was beset by anxiety. Where were they going to ask me to sit? I glanced at the plentiful silver and knives looking for small ones which would be for the children. I knew that wherever I sat now would be my place at meals for the rest of my stay and I wanted to sit beside Phoebe. When she was out of sight in those days she caused me no anxiety at all but as soon as she entered a room I needed her by me; I was jealous of everyone, even of her puppy.

I was shown to the chair beside hers, facing the front windows, with no one between me and the view of the lake on my left, her father at the head of the table next to her, her mother and little sister opposite us. He was always the last to sit down; he stood at the sideboard behind me at the beginning of each meal, carving meat or dishing out helpings of pie which he handed to me to pass on. His slicing of the meat and sharpening of the blade on a long old-fashioned steel was always accompanied by heavy breathing of a happy kind which is hard to describe. I mean he expelled the air through his throat making a sound at each breath. You have to imagine a contented groan. He talked with blithe exhilaration at that first dinner referring to people and places and using words which meant nothing to me but were soon to be part of my language. He had tremendous vitality and warmth of heart, a largeness of spirit unique in my experience. I never met anyone who did not love him, although some might laugh at his eccentric ways or nurture a grudge of ancient origin.

'When the Summers come,' he said, 'I don't know how to mount us all, unless Phoebe is able for one of the long-tails.'

'Castor and Pollux,' said Tony spilling gravy and potatoes down her shirt.

'They've lost their milk teeth,' said the Major. 'They are both doing well, but Castor still has a bad habit of poking her nose.'

'Can't I ride Smuggler?' said Phoebe, but Smuggler had cut his pastern on some wire and the cut would not heal in the ordinary way and the vet would not treat him because when he drove into the stableyard he found the horse doctor there, stooping over Smuggler's leg with herbs and mumbo-jumbo. He had not even got out of his car; just turned it round noisily scaring the horse, shouted a brief insult about quacks and driven away.

'What colour was the car?'

'Green.'

By the time it came to second helpings they had decided who should ride what and Major Kirkwood went to the sideboard again saying, 'What about David? He'd better get up on Molly till we see how he does,' which made everybody laugh because Molly was the Maxwells' cob, used for ploughing and all sorts of jobs and somewhat thick and sleepy.

'Eat up,' said Major Kirkwood then, 'or Winnie won't give us so much next time.' It was something he always said as he dished the lavish portions out and the children often joined in or said it for him.

He was over six-foot tall, his body perfectly proportioned, athletic but without the exaggerated chest and muscles of an athlete; his face was big and longish, the forehead high and bony, the outlines of the cheek and chinbones clearly showing – though no one would have thought of him as lean – the eyes a bit too small for it and blue, the mouth large and humorous but straight. He was then in his fifties, fair-headed, with slightly darker eyebrows and moustache. Like many men whose cheekbones are high, he left unshaven tufts of hair beneath each eye. He usually wore a bow-tie, jodhpurs and a tweed riding coat fawn-coloured, with black and dull red checks, loosely cut and long with huge pockets full of pipes and tobacco tins and a slit at the back for the rim of the saddle. A monocle dangled from his collar on a black cord and he liked silk handkerchiefs with spots on. He was in every way what country women call 'a fine man'.

Suddenly, during the pudding (a suet one with raisins and custard) Phoebe shouted 'Bullocks!', her sister screamed 'Look at the lawn', and we ran down the stone passage and out through the hall, seizing sticks or golf clubs on the way, to drive them back to their field. Mrs Kirkwood, who had stayed at the table, watched us return to our pudding, breathless, sweating and excited, with amusement. Perhaps she was pleased that life at Woodbrook had not changed during her long absence.

When Major Kirkwood had finished eating, he placed his monocle in his eye, pushed his chair back, began to fill a pipe, and said rather loudly, 'Well, you people, what's the programme?', which again made the children laugh because he said it every day while they were there and they had not heard him say it for six months.

The programme for the mornings was never in question; it began with lessons, first Phoebe's, then Tony's while Phoebe practised her violin, after which we went out riding. Their mother had given up riding; she started her day with housework, sometimes followed us on foot or came to meet us as we

16

returned and always spent at least an hour by herself at the piano, singing scales and exercises. She was still at that time a professional singer and although hér public engagements were rare she practised for two or three hours every day. Phoebe, I remember, was supposed to practise for three hours but in fine weather did not always do so.

But the programme for the afternoons was varied. We could swim or fish in the lake, go for long bicycle rides untroubled by cars, or in the Fiat to distant places, fifteen or even thirty miles away. The names of these places, familiar to the others, struck my imagination newly. They were as mysterious as milk teeth and long-tails and never became commonplace to me. Throughout all the years, while I grew to know what they stood for, they excited my curiosity revealing origins little by little; but neither by reading nor by listening to people could I ever dig deep enough.

There was a road called Stirabout Road that we searched for, always thinking, 'This must be it' as we bicycled along a narrow lonely way, and another called Green Road, which was covered with grass, the people said. 'Stirabout' meant porridge. (The wages of the men who made the road during the famine were bowls of porridge.) The Green Road was built for the same reason – to keep a few of the starving alive but not harm their morals by presenting them with food. It is likely that neither road led anywhere, so as to avoid competing with those that did. Perhaps that is why we could not find them.

There was a holy well – Saint Lasair's well – on a cliff-like bank that sloped steeply to the waters of Lough Key, often rough, often still as a mirror. Phoebe and I went there on bicycles and sometimes I went alone. It became holy to me, but in a private way. Others worshipped there together, crawling under a flat rock to be cured of madness or toothache or anything. It was a tiny Lourdes once a year and they shared the same religion, not knowing that the well and rock were holy long before Christ. And we, without their community, and as ignorant as they were of the distant past, with no religious tradition of our own, were suddenly silenced when we came there.

In Kilronan graveyard nearby there was the lichened tomb of

the last of the great Irish harpers, Carolan – 'Born at Nobber 1670, died at Alderford 1738'.

The tomb and the well were surrounded by mountains and lakes with euphonic names – Lough Allen, Lough Arrow, Lough Skean, Lough Meelagh, Lough Gara, Lough Key, Seltannasaggart (often called the Corry Mountain), Kilronan Mountain, Arigna, Moytirra, the Curlew Mountains (an old and fearful battlefield), the Cuilcagh Mountains where the river Shannon starts.

It was the borderland of one of the last strongholds the Irish held against the English. Roads came late in its history; pack animals carried goods; and until the middle of the twentieth century it remained unsought by strangers. When the road was made they travelled through it to Sligo and the coast. I have never been able to find a travel book earlier than the nineteenth century that gives any account of it at all. Historians describe the strategic position of its main town, Boyle, and centuries of fighting in the mountain passes that led down to it, but say nothing of the lives of its people in peacetime. Travellers from many countries throughout the sixteenth, seventeenth and eighteenth centuries left accounts of more remote parts of Ireland where customs have changed little and the native language is spoken to this day – Counties Kerry, Galway and Donegal for instance. The borderland which I had come to live in, between the towns of Carrick-on-Shannon and Boyle, was unheard of then to all my friends in England.

Chapter Two

It surprises me now to find myself thinking of the downstairs bathroom as one of the memorable places in the house. Its door was where the passage ended, almost opposite the dining-room door beside an unopenable window that gave light to the grey flagstones and made one or two of them glisten in damp weather when shallow films of condensed water lay in the hollows of their rough-cut surface. From this window and from the smaller one in the bathroom you could see the lake. The bathroom, like the passage, had whitewashed walls which left marks on your clothes if you brushed against them, marks that were easy to dust off. It was oblong and narrow. There was a basin and a looking-glass beside the window, an old wooden towel-horse painted creamy white but chipped, and at the back, beside the head of the bath, a w.c. with a cistern high above it near the ceiling and a plug to pull, which needed a special knack, made sometimes of an old dog-chain, sometimes of string or galvanized wire from the fields, and for a time (by me) of rabbit snares tied together – of whatever one could find when the old thing broke. But the best bit of furniture was the bath itself, a long narrow one sunk deep into the ground, its curved rim forming a slight camber, pleasurable to naked toes, just above the level of the floor. I cannot remember the floor, I suppose it was covered with linoleum of some sort. But I do remember the sensation of stepping down from it into the bath, my warm bed beneath the earth, my warm and temporary grave. I never have been inclined to have baths very often which, like not having drinks very often, makes each a sensuous luxury, and at Woodbrook the fewer you had the better for the household, because every gallon of water had to be pumped up to a tank on the roof from a pool four or five hundred yards away.

The sunken bath had been made for Nina Kirkwood, an old maiden aunt of the Major's, who was almost paralysed by arthritis for many years and could not have climbed into a bath above the floor. The shape into which the rigid joints of her legs and hips had set was peculiar to her, for never since childhood had she walked more than four steps outside a house, three to a mounting block and one up on to it, or three to the groom who stood by the door and gave her a leg up on to her horse. She rode everywhere, even to the gate lodge or across the one field to the Maxwells' house only five minutes' walk from the stable-yard; and of course she always rode side-saddle and rode all day except for church and meal-times, enjoying most of her social life and conversation in the open air with friends who sat on horses more often than chairs. So it happened that after arthritis began during her middle age, her legs became gradually immovable from the position they were accustomed to and when not on a horse she had at last to be held up or carried, because she was like a crane in shallow water with one leg curled and the other straight. Her right leg raised, as though to tuck itself about the pummel, was lost and unsteady without the comfort of pressure below the knee. When her straight leg rested on the ground she longed for the give and movement of a stirrup. She looked like any other woman when she was in the saddle and more graceful than most.

In her old age, until she consented to use a bathchair, James used to carry her in this posture from her bedroom on the ground floor – the room we used as a dining-room – and lift her on to her horse. She fitted the side-saddle perfectly and, although she was always in pain, she felt comparatively easy when she was on it. They say she was cheerful, witty and imperturbable until her end.

One of the difficulties of mounting a horse that medieval knights and soldiers experienced after being encased by mechanics in their heavy armour was the stiffness of the metal joints. They had to be hoisted aloft and dropped on to their horses. James, as I remember, loved mechanical improvisation and could easily have invented a hoist for Miss Nina; but she was light enough to lift. She could lower herself alone into her sunken bath. A maid within calling distance was needed to help her out and that was all. She had a chair and a towel nearby for discretion and was able to dry herself. Then she would be helped across the passage to her room.

I soon began to call the children's parents by their first names – Charles and Ivy – and shall do so here from now on. Ivy, who is always extremely sensitive to her surroundings, used often to speak about the aura of a house. If there had been cruelty or much unhappiness in it she would feel it, she said, as soon as she came in, before being told what had gone on there in the past, and the opposite in houses where people had lived happily. Perhaps such emanations do persist. A battlefield remains sick land for many generations and a garden made and kept with love does not lose its beauty after it goes wild. Nor, Ivy thought, does a house whose people loved each other.

The aura of the downstairs bathroom, then, must be mixed for those who use it now. A confusion of spirits must float in it, tense with emotion and chiefly male and adolescent, for the only woman to use it after Nina's death was Winnie, and the only mature and calm man Charles himself.

Tony Trevor-Roper, a pupil of mine, would lock himself in and brood for two or three hours at a time; Leslie Summers, forlornly in love with the parson's daughter Deirdre, could there, and there only, hold his restless body quiet and still – even if you rattled at the door and told him to hurry he would make no sound; I would nurse my black thoughts there or luxuriate in hopeful dreams; the actor Gerry MacLarnon, from MacMaster's touring company, who used to stay at Woodbrook, would rehearse to himself in an undertone before the shaving mirror; the melancholy slim Tom Crowe, who during my last years at Woodbrook came in his vacations from Trinity College, Dublin to teach Greek and Latin to the children, would step into the downstairs bathroom lightly, a bowl of hot water in his hand, filled from one of the great black kettles that always stood hot on the kitchen range, and shave quickly, groaning at every thought that came into his mind. And then for some time there was a real crow in the bathroom, which had been domesticated by Leslie Summers, who was able like Saint Francis of Assisi to draw wild creatures to him unafraid. He had removed the towels from the towel-horse and put it to roost on the wooden top rail, but he went in to talk to it frequently and to feed and caress it and after a few days he let it free to hop and fly in the garden, knowing that it would approach him when he called it and come back to sleep on the towel-horse at night. It would stare at me out of its left eye as I shaved in the mornings and I watched it preening its feathers whenever I lay in the bath. I liked the way it moved and the sheen of its feathers and its dusky curled feet which were above mine and above the old bath taps which had four fingers each. I missed it when Leslie had trained it to live a wild life again.

A bathroom is for many people the only solitary place, the only room in a house whose door may be locked without people saying, 'Why does he lock himself in?' Out of doors, however lonely the countryside appears to be, you soon find out that you are always being watched. The herdsman or the woman at her hidden window on the mountain sees and reports your actions, and your thoughts belong not to yourself but to the land about you. No wonder then that bathrooms are fit for contemplation. In shape, size and in their bare walls, they resemble monastic cells.

In the country at that time only the landlords had bathrooms. They were a mark of rank as well as money, for the upper class of servants were allowed to use them too, female servants that is. The mistress could offer a bath to the cook as a privilege, like a bottle of scent, a share in the luxuries she enjoyed herself.

Winnie had a bath on occasional Sunday mornings while the family were at church. By the time she got into it, at about half past ten, she had cycled to Early Mass and back, cooked breakfast and washed up the things and prepared the vegetables for lunch. She stayed in the bathroom for an hour, singing quietly to herself from time to time and splashing a bit. I knew, because I did not always go to church. I liked to read or write on Sunday mornings and soon discovered that she would wait till I was out of the house or in my bedroom upstairs, for fear of being seen in déshabille, and though I gave her what seemed ample time to get back to her room unobserved, I once or twice confronted her in the narrow passage dressed in white drapery of very strange shapes with ribbons and parts that hung from her like streamers, her hair in curlers, pink, yellow and black, her arms full of soap and flannels and things, and in her right hand the kitchen clock, a round alarm clock with a bell on top. She took it to the bathroom, I suppose, to make sure of getting back to the kitchen in time to put the meat into the oven and the pot of potatoes on to the hottest part of the range. The bath was like a little, secret holiday to her, fraught with nerves on the journey to and from it and with excited thoughts about the afternoon, her few hours off each week away from the house, when she would go rambling, as the country people call it – that is visiting the houses of several friends by turn. Winnie went rambling on her bicycle however wet or cold the weather. On almost every Sunday she bicycled home, twelve miles there and twelve miles back, and went to see her friends along side roads or beyond.

It never occurred to me in those days that she could want to make herself beautiful or that the dresses and hats she put on after clearing up the lunchtime débris would appeal to men. She was, after all, rather old, thirty or more, her eyes were obscured like mine by spectacles, and though hers were not so thick they had black speckled frames like tortoiseshell which I thought added to the disfigurement we shared. The rims of mine were made of blackened wire. But a few years later when pretty girls with perfect eyes began to buy horn-rimmed spectacles with plain glass lenses to look smart, as people now buy dark lensed ones, I saw it was unnecessary to feel sad about Winnie's. Her face, unmasked or not, held everyone's attention by its astonishing vitality, but if she met me in the bathroom passage it went flat as though it belonged to a bride in a wedding photograph on a mantelpiece, impossible to remember or to distinguish from the face of any other bride on any other mantelpiece. Yet when she spoke to me or laughed or got in a rage, one of which she was doing almost all the time, for she really was vivacious, her face shone with individuality. I have not forgotten her vivacity, nor her strong bare arms churning butter, but my clearest memory of her appearance is of her Sunday clothes which depressed my spirits as Salvation Army uniforms have since childhood, and that is unfair because she dressed in the fashion of her time and place more carefully than most. The clothes she wore at work in summer were beautiful – blue linen and white apron.

Although I did not want to see her naked any more than I would my aunt or an old iron bedstead stripped of its mattress – 'An iron bedstead!' she would say if we met now. 'Oh, Master David – after I looked after you so well!' – I used to imagine her body when the steamy scent of unfamiliar soap pervaded the passage to Aunt Nina's room and I used to imagine her solitary daydreams. I thought her pleasant ones were about puddings and cakes, the rarest and richest she could make, and about the children, how they would praise her for them and even kiss her; and her nasty ones, I thought, were about James who ate in the kitchen and so spoke a lot to her, how he did the wrong things all the time in his fastidious way and spoke crossly to the maids, which was not for a man to do, and would not often eat dainties or show enjoyment when he did.

After his death, which happened about ten years later, a visitor said, 'Ah, James Currid – he was known all over. He had a cure for horses, for a sprain.' And an old man answered, 'He had! And he had a cure for women too. He was great with the girls, but he held back the cure till he died, God rest him' – meaning that he never would commit himself to marriage.

I was too shy to ask Winnie about her private life, but it now seems to me that twenty years of giving James his meals in the kitchen cannot have passed without a thought of marriage in his mind. Perhaps in hers. So maybe her daydreams were romantic and about him. He seemed ancient to me, and was in fact nearly twice her age, and I thought he had left it too late. But it was not too late. It was too late for James of course who, partly from devotion to the Kirkwoods and their horses, and mostly because he thought women a nuisance, postponed marriage long after he had obtained land and a house to get married in, so long that he only moved into it to die; but not a bit too late for other men who, because of rules about dowries and land, seldom began to look for a wife until they were fifty or sixty years old.

There were several who would have married Winnie then had

circumstances allowed it. Having left home to 'go into service' when she was in her 'teens, she was comparatively free of her parents' demands; she was popular with those who were old and brave enough to face her bossiness, and was strong for work and capable. But so many years in the big house had given her expensive tastes, such as cake and meat, and no doubt she hated the prospect of life on a small farm. She was considered snobbish. She did get married when she was over forty, but not locally – her man lived twelve miles away – and by then she had accumulated enough savings and things to do for a dowry.

Sometimes, when I knew she was out of the bath and dressed, I would go and sit on the kitchen table. She would talk over her shoulder leaning back from the hot range, or from different parts of the room, as she carried pots about. The kitchen was a tranquil place for me, in spite of the slap of her shoes on the stone floor and the clatter of dishes and fire-irons. It must have been twenty feet long and fifteen wide. Its walls were white, its ceiling smokey yellow in stripes between warped and knotty rafters from which hung hooks for ham and bacon. It had long narrow windows and an enormous dresser bright with crockery. No one could feel sad for Winnie in the kitchen. She moved strongly and precisely as people do in workshops and when visitors came she was confident and warm in manner.

I liked to hear her talk about her first years in the house, of how she had arrived frightened at the age of fifteen with a little suitcase specially bought by her mother. She was thirsty after carrying it for twelve miles along the dusty roads, but as soon as she sat down with the others in the servants' hall her hand shook and she could not drink her tea. She could not eat either, so lonely she was for her family. Later on, by herself in the kitchen, she tried the tap but had never used one before and the water rushed out with such force that it splashed from the sink to the floor. The water tasted muddy. The cook came to tell her she would die if she drank it and to scold her for the mess on the floor. Her sharp reply caused a war between them that did not end till the cook got married three years later and left. She used to tell me repeatedly, with too much vehemence, that she never was afraid of that cook, but when she told me how she feared

Miss Nina I believed her. It took years, she said, before she grew accustomed to the way she spoke, and this was because Nina had what Winnie called an English accent, the accent of the educated Anglo-Irish which seems to English people as Irish as can be.

But she often spoke of Nina with affection and of her sister Topsy. 'It's wonder they never were married,' she said. 'It is true they were orphaned scarce past thirty years of age, but their brother had good dowries for them.' I thought that they might not have wanted to be married or that perhaps they were forbidding in their ways and looks, and once I said, 'Perhaps they seldom met men.' She laughed at that and said there were plenty of gentlemen in and out of the house, many from Dublin and some from the 'far side', which means England. 'But they had no father,' she said. 'It's what their brothers thought always of the horses and did nothing to help them.'

Winnie had lived with the gentry all those years without learning that they thought it no disgrace to let their children die unmarried. Behaviour and manners of speech were more relaxed between the classes than they are in England, but ignorance of each others' ways was absolute. Like Africans under European rule, the Irish people had lived apart for generations. In some ways, they were more detached from their rulers than the people of Africa were. Their social customs, dances, games, the stories they enjoyed, their food, furniture, sex-life did not even arouse the curiosity of anthropologists. Only their music was noticed. By nature, they lack the spontaneity of African people, the free expression of emotion, and centuries of poverty and subjection have made them cautious.

It never occurred to me that Winnie might have resented my visits to the kitchen. She had accepted a new custom by then. Charles spent hours there, chatting, and the rest of the family drifted in and out. But once when she spoke of his father she said, 'Colonel James was very good. He never would come in to the kitchen. He'd stand by the end of the passage and call, "Where's my Winnie? Is my Winnie there?" And he'd have a little envelope in his hand and give it to me.' (A present of money, I think.) Nowadays, a cook in such a household would have a self-contained flat. To Winnie the kitchen and servants' quarters were the nearest approach to that.

Aunt Nina outlived her brother. She died eight years before I came to Woodbrook, but if ever a stranger's spirit lived on in my mind it is hers. Yet I know very little about her – scraps of talk, that is all, one or two anecdotes, the sunken bath and the huge bathchair with a black hood which was pulled by a pony during her last years when she could no longer sit in the saddle. She drove herself about in that until a few days before her death. The pony went soon after her but the bathchair remained in the coach house and was often used by Phoebe and Tony, who harnessed their donkey into it and trotted up and down the drive.

Chapter Three

Not counting the farm carts, Nina's bathchair and a trap were the only horse-drawn vehicles to survive the First World War. When Ivy first visited Woodbrook there were seven, a black brougham, smelly, dusty and dark, which brought her very slowly from the station, a landau, a phaeton, a governess cart, an outside-car, a dog-cart, faded yellow, and a two-wheeled market cart. All were somewhat dangerous to ride in on account of their advanced age and the nature of the horses that pulled them, but the market cart was the most dangerous of all. It was shaped like a tumbril, but smaller and lighter and fitted with springs to make it suitable for trotting. It had a cross-bench for people to sit on and a place for things behind, but as the bench was loosely fitted and removable it used to slip backwards imperceptibly as the cart went along until suddenly everyone was tilted out on to the road. Even in those old grander days there was no attempt at grandeur, none of the rivalry one reads of in stories of the English gentry who competed with each other's showy equipages.

The choice of which army to join was unshowy too. (The Kirkwoods had not thought of any other career for generations.) They joined the Indian army without question. My father and his friends found themselves in the Indian army because they could not afford the uniforms and accoutrements British army officers had to buy, nor the splendid life they were expected to lead with the help of a private income. The Kirkwoods of Charlie's generation had not enough money either, but he and his brother Billy really chose the Indian army, so they told me. It seemed more adventurous and the polo grounds were not like city parks. Also the prospect of learning languages appealed to them. They were both gifted in that way and besides Hindustani and Pushtu, which every officer needed in the north, Billy was sent to Moscow and St Petersburg to study Russian and Charlie became an official interpreter in Persian, Arabic and Turkish.

Ivy first met them in India when she was eighteen, soon after she had been transported from England much against her will. You could not then introduce anyone suddenly into the bizarre society of the English in India; there was the gradual sea journey among passengers who worked there. But it seemed sudden to Ivy. She had been taken away from school. She knew no world beyond the English countryside. The transition was extreme.

Her father, now a colonel, had lived in India since long before her birth. She hardly knew him. Her mother had died before she was two and he had only been to see her twice for a few days, once when she was ten and once when he took her to a hunt ball at the age of twelve, as though he was impatient for her to grow up. When he next saw her, near the end of one of his 'home leaves', he decided she was old enough to act as hostess for him in India. Arrangements had by then been made for her to study music in Salzburg as soon as she left school, but now she could not even complete her ordinary education. Her aunt said she should be sorry for her father, alone out there without a woman at his table. All her hopes were blasted and she went.

When the ship stopped at Port Said her most horrible imaginings of the East came true. Even the seawater was putrid. 'You couldn't touch the ground with your bare foot,' she said during an outburst so strong that her father relented. 'But I can't leave you here alone,' he said. 'If the next ship for England comes before ours leaves you may go home on it.' At the shipping agent's they heard she would have an hour to wait. He did not dare leave her even so long in a strange Port Said agent's care and they went on board again. The home-bound steamer passed them as they approached the Suez Canal. This chance of timing settled the course of the rest of her life.

The year was 1912 or thereabouts. E. M. Forster had begun to write *A Passage to India*, which shocked the English community when it was published twelve years later, and the older people in the Punjab where she was to live were still annoyed by the different kind of impropriety shown by Kipling in *Plain Tales from the Hills*, which had been selling like hot cakes since 1888. But Ivy, who knew nothing of society of any kind, accepted the peculiarity of Anglo-Indians. She thought all grown-ups behaved and thought like them. Only the Kirkwood brothers seemed abnormal and if anyone had asked her why she enjoyed being with them she could not have thought of a reason. Perhaps it was their complete freedom from any kind of anxiety. Perhaps it was their kindness.

She had heard a lot about Woodbrook before she met them. Several of her father's friends had stayed there on leave. The most lively talker among them was a man of sixty-five, Sir Garrett O'Moore Creagh, commander-in-chief, India. When she was first told to invite him and his entourage to dinner she was somewhat alarmed. He had won the V.C. in the Afghan war which made him seem very old indeed and he was now at the top of the whole military hierarchy. But socially he was easy going. He liked her very much and showed it at once. They met on many occasions and became friends.

In spite of his name, his upbringing had been entirely English and he spoke of Woodbrook and the Irish people in the half envious, half deprecatory way the Swedish bourgeoisie laugh at Norwegians and their household life. The Norwegians are amusing and talented, charming and dirty and lazy and you cannot rely on anything they say or do. So are the Irish to the English. It is fun to be there for a holiday, an experience like camping in a marsh amongst a colony of interesting birds below a barren mountain, but it is not possible to think of living there. The birds themselves go regularly on migration if they can.

The general told Ivy about the ancient carriages and the leaking roof, and how the butler seldom turned up in time to wait at table – they had to sit there till he came to serve the soup – because something usually happened to delay him in the stables and when he did come the smell of horse-dung from his boots was mingled with the food. The butler, as she discovered when she went to Woodbrook, was James Currid, who had been kicked on the knees, could ride no more and was given a job in the house. The general said that the chimneys were cleaned with a blackthorn bush instead of brushes. The boiler of the kitchen range burst once while he was there and flooded the kitchen and the stone flagged passages with sooty water, ankle deep. He said the windows were dangerous and heavy. They were sash windows made without cords. In damp weather, when the frames were swollen, they might stay open for a while without support and then crash down like guillotines. The one in his bedroom was propped open with a dumb-bell.

Such talk at drinks and dinner parties sometimes ended solemnly. Guests said that in spite of the sentimental movement towards Home Rule, the murmurs of armed rebellion, the occasional arson and murder, the Irish people were fundamentally loyal – look how they flocked to join the British army. They were a friendly people and knew which side their bread was buttered on – the English side. There were troublemakers among them, a few extremists, said the guests, but those would be powerless against the sense of humour, and the laziness, of the majority. Billy Kirkwood, when he began to join their parties, thought the same was true of Russia. He had been there after the revolution of 1905, at a time when the fervour of its huge population was working up towards the final boiling point, yet he saw nothing but a friendly and contented people – poverty of course, but poverty was everywhere.

And here they were, talking with this absolute self-confidence in India, with two hundred million people seething underneath them whose thousand aspirations conflicted with each other and with the demands of their rulers. The administration, civil and military, was extraordinarily efficient. It could never have been so without that self-confidence.

In contrast to the reports of Woodbrook the Indian servants were efficient too, though they needed constant supervision, and all the bungalows that Ivy stayed in were perfectly appointed; windows, doors, punkahs worked as they should; gardens and tennis courts were beautifully kept. Sometimes at night one or two of the men who sat outside the bedrooms pulling ropes that kept the punkahs moving would doze off. She would wake up when the soft flapping sound stopped and the still air in the room grew stifling. Then she would hear a shout from another bedroom, a movement in the corridor outside, and the fanning motion would begin again. She never learned to shout.

Her first spell of freedom came when her father went away on manoeuvres and allowed her to stay, for her safety, with Billy and his wife. Billy was married to a painter, a pretty girl called Peta, with coppery hair and big eyes and a beautiful wide mouth, who soon became one of her closest friends. They were both in their early twenties and all their friends were young. The weight of authority was lifted and they whirled Ivy with them through weeks of reckless activity that seemed to be over as soon as they began. Billy often spoke of his elder brother Charles, talking about him as though he was a twin. They had never been separated until they came to India, but then Charles had joined the 23rd Cavalry Frontier Force and was always far away.

Then her father came to be stationed at Quetta, near the border of Afghanistan. Wherever he was stationed she was stationed, and though life went on in much the same way – the constantly moving groups of English people meeting each other again and again in different centres – the climate and the beauty of the mountains were exhilarating. Quetta is over five thousand feet above sea level and within sight of snow-capped peaks on every side. Charles Kirkwood's regiment was there.

'Hadn't we better invite the other Kirkwood?'

'If you like,' her father said, forgetting for a moment that the other Kirkwood was not married.

Charles came to dinner with some other people. He was two years older than Billy, but really seemed like a twin – the same eyes and voice, fair hair, an agile face, the same height, about six foot two. He was probably more thoughtful. The things he said at dinner were funny, but in a different way. Wiser? That idea was dispelled by some silliness. Steadier and more reliable? No one could know.

Next morning at breakfast her father said, 'What did you think of Kirkwood?' And she answered lightly, 'A nice man for someone to get married to.' She meant nothing by that, or thought she meant nothing. It just came out of her mouth, so she thought.

Then his thank-you letter came. It was the custom there, where telephones were few, to send a note of thanks by a servant; but in his, below the formal message there was something in military code. She did not need to show the letter to her father. She puzzled it out after he had gone for the day. She had seen many things in code and this one was simple. It said, 'You don't know yet, but we are going to get married.' It made her laugh, all by herself on the veranda.

That evening when her father came home to dinner he asked her to sign a sheet of paper he had written on – a promise not even to get engaged till she was twenty-one. This annoyed her, but she signed it without any other qualm; the last thing she wanted was to get married. If ever she escaped to Europe she would resume her music.

She did not escape until 1914. The war began a few months after she reached home and the idea of studying in Germany was abandoned for ever. Only part of the 23rd Cavalry was ordered to sail for France. The officers drew lots to decide who should go and Charlie was one of the lucky ones; they thought it lucky. He had less than a year in France before his home leave was due. Ivy's father knew this and approached his commanding officer saying 'Don't give young Kirkwood leave, whatever you do. He'll only marry my daughter.' Which was exactly what happened. It was 1915 and she was over twenty-one. A year later Charlie was in a prison camp in Turkey. She did not see him again for three years.

Chapter Four

It was after the news of his capture that she went to Woodbrook for the first time. His parents had kindly invited her, but no degree of kindness could assuage the sense of desolation that opened wider and wider about her on the journey there in the rain. She floated from one intention to another, private or public, just as she had been propelled by other people from nursing in one hospital to nursing in another, thinking with half her mind that the only glimmer of hope lay in waiting for the war to end as one waited in childhood for the rage of adults to subside, as survivors of flood or famine waited, as the beggars waited on the Dublin pavements, as the whole of India seemed to be waiting for nothing anyone could define. The war was indefinable, its end out of sight. (Had there not been a thirty years' war and a hundred years' war?) The numbers killed were enormous already and every month brought the names of people she knew. I don't know whether her brother had been killed by then, but he was among the ten million counted after peace came. And it was said that the chances of survival in a Turkish prison camp were low. The Turkish government could not even feed its own army. The diseases that followed malnutrition were usually mortal.

She was met at the station of Carrick-on-Shannon and the black brougham dragged her slowly to the house. And of course the house and the positivity of the people in it sealed down these fears and emotions for a time. The outlandish servants headed by James Currid, if you could call him a head, would have distracted any patient's attention from an incurable disease. The Master and the Mistress, Charlie's parents, and Topsy and Nina, his aunts, four strong contrasting personalities, pulled her towards four points of the emotional compass and let her go again.

Outside the house, she could not go a hundred yards without seeing something the boys had told her of in India. The longest lasting thing they had made together was a bridge of tree-trunks across the 'canal', to save walking down to the gate-lodge and back along the road. It was still firm in my day. Riding about the country or going in the market cart to Carrick on a shopping expedition she explored the large scene of their idyllic childhood, but never in the sun. She stayed six weeks and it rained every day.

Their childhood had been almost as parentless as hers. Although both their mother and father were alive, they only saw them every few years when home leave came. They had lived with an aunt in England, spending term time at schools in London and nearby and their holidays running wild at Woodbrook in the happy lack of care of their bachelor uncle Tom – Colonel Thomas Yaden Lloyd Kirkwood, the well known owner whose horses, bred at Woodbrook, had won the Grand National, the Ascot Gold Vase, the Gold Cup, the Coronation Cup and so on. He taught them to ride, first on donkeys – they raced about the countryside on donkeys – then on ponies, then when their legs were long enough he trusted them with the job of schooling young horses. Horses became their main preoccupation and remained so all their lives. The seeds of Charlie's financial misfortunes were gaily sown by Uncle Tom.

Old people spoke of the boys as inseparable, forgetting which was which, because no one remembered ever seeing them apart. They rode together, swam in the lake together, explored the river, climbed trees, built bridges and secret camps. They had always shared bedrooms and been to the same schools. Billy entered Sandhurst before Charles left it. The entrance exams were as easy as pie Charlie had said; it was the medical certificates that took time. They had to be signed by one's own doctor, and theirs, who lived in Carrick-on-Shannon, was unable to hold a pen. Having no telephone at Woodbrook, they could not make an appointment and would ride to the town to catch him early before he went out for the day. With a glance at their faces he would rightly diagnose an excellent state of health, then tell them to fetch a bowl of water from the rain-butt outside his back door. One held the bowl while the other steeped the doctor's hand in it. Then they dried him with a towel and fetched the pen. He would try to catch hold of it and fail, send them for another bowl and another and another until at last he was able to grip the pen and sign. Charlie, being the eldest, was the one who dipped it in the ink. Cold water, it seems, restored the circulation of the doctor's blood which failed to reach his extremities without the help of alcohol, and knowing nothing about that the boys never thought of following him on their ponies with their forms and catching him later in the day when his sight had been restored and his hand steadied. Drunkards, especially if they were doctors or schoolmasters, were looked on by the country people with something more than the tolerance we show to a dissolute poet. Like those prodigious drinkers, the old harpers such as Carolan, they were thought to be unable to practise without the water of life. The burden of their talents, the stresses on their souls, could not be borne without it.

The boys' old uncle Tom had died in 1910 and as the estate was entailed in the male line it passed to his brother James, Colonel James Kirkwood, I.A., retired, the father of Charlie and Billy. Nina, Topsy and Isobel, his three sisters, all in their sixties when Ivy arrived, passed to him too in the terms of the will which required him to support them. Nina and Topsy lived at Woodbrook, but Isobel was married and away. Each had an allowance of £300 a year.

Most women hated Woodbrook. However much they loved the beauty of the countryside or of the house itself in spite of its dampness, the rats on the ground floor, the bats in the bedrooms at night, they could find nothing of interest to do. The houses of the gentry were many miles apart. Even in peacetime, when friends and relations in Dublin or England enjoyed the prosperous gaiety their money brought, in a fashion of so-called immorality hallowed by their King, the country ladies of Ireland had felt like prisoners. It took a whole day to make the nearest call, and if you wanted to go farther it meant writing letters and staying the night. In wartime their isolation was complete. The young men of their own class were all away, many older men and women went to England and even the rare ones who owned cars had not enough petrol for long journeys.

Aunt Topsy was intensely interested to hear about India and London, and Ivy, telling her all she could at every moment of those rainy days, was sad when she saw she had built a dream palace, woven a rope of sand for her to catch hold of. Aunt Topsy began to disclose her loneliness and longings. Ever since she grew up there had only been one thing worth living for at Woodbrook – hunting – and the season was too short, the dark evenings in the house too long and cold. Even when there was room near the fire you got chilblains and spoiled your complexion, and playing cards was soporific, just with one's family, and, besides, the Boyle Harriers, their local pack, had become the laughing stock of Connaught. The Roscommon Hunt with whom she occasionally went were better, but that meant staying with friends and riding a strange horse. The Galway Blazers would have been perfect if only she lived near them, but who could afford the cap, three times as much as the local hunt, or the train journey with a railway horsebox that took all day because of shunting at junctions? Topsy did not like riding except with a hunt. The spring and summer time at Woodbrook bored her literally to tears from the age of sixteen until she was over sixty, because when the hunting season ended she saw no one and did nothing. She knew all about the bridge parties that were going on in Dublin; she had enjoyed them sometimes for a fortnight or a week and had been on yachting trips in Dublin Bay, and to dances and parties and made many friends who seldom even wrote.

Her longings had not died when Ivy came and the talks they had together strengthened her till at last at the age of sixty-something she had the courage to persuade her brother to let her go. Three hundred a year was then a large income, especially to her, who had no dependants, and from the day she left Carrick-on-Shannon station until the day she died she lived in Dublin, playing bridge and going about in yachts and motor cars. She came home to Woodbrook only for the hunting.

Ivy was too young to foresee her own discontent. She liked being with other people and was full of curiosity about them and their furniture and houses; she had a distinctive kind of beauty and enough reserve to make her seem mysterious. Everyone wanted to get to know her better and her engagement book, like her card at every ball, was filled too quickly for her liking, but she was less dependent on all that than Topsy had ever been. She had had a better education, her musical talents had been fostered, she could read with enjoyment and knew how to choose books that were not boring or stupid. Her loneliness in childhood and the unhappiness that grew between her and her father had uncovered resources within her which did not need stimulation from outside. The dances, games and rushing about that Topsy always longed for were to Ivy, who had too much of them, a tempting distraction from activities she valued more. As she listened to Topsy's forlorn expression of hope, she thought how unfair it was, this dispensation of fate.

Her mother-in-law to be was bored at Woodbrook too. The only pursuits she followed with zeal were golf and tennis and even if the rain stopped there were no facilities nearby. She had been brought up in the lowlands of Scotland where even working men play golf as the English play football. She longed wistfully for Scotland all the time and continually reminded Ivy of the games they had played together there when, soon after their first meeting, Ivy had stayed with James and her at their other house in Fifeshire. She remembered scores and handicaps, lost balls and naughty caddies. Ivy, trying to join in, could only remember silently, with shame, how the tireless energy of this woman who was twice her age had exhausted her daily at tennis and golf until she felt sleepy and cross in the evenings.

'Do you know,' said Ivy on one of her sallies against such talk, 'Billy's C-in-C often spoke about Woodbrook. He said his bedroom window was propped open by a dumb-bell.'

'What better thing could you have?' said Mrs Kirkwood. 'James has cut bits of wood of different lengths according to the weather. A dumb-bell has wide round ends.'

Ivy kicked over a jam-jar on her way to bed. Her paraffin lamp cast a shadow on the floor, and it was then dim because you had to turn the wick down when you carried it to stop it smoking or blowing out. She had forgotten about this jam-jar near the door. The rooms were dotted with jars, pots and pans exactly placed to catch drips from the ceilings and emptied once a day by a maid who went round with a slop-pail. She thought of the pools of water on the way to Nina's room, of the mildewed books – not many readable ones to get mildewed, but rows and rows of volumes of *The Racing Calendar* which sometimes she disturbed in idleness – and she wondered how her Bechstein would get on. She would have to bring it here if ever the war ended because she and Charlie would have nowhere else to live. But the upright piano his parents had was warped by damp, its notes gone this way and that beyond recognition, and when she told them what had happened to it they explained that the piano-tuner lived in Dublin, ninety miles away and that while they had guests there was no bed to offer him.

The men of the Kirkwood family did not think of themselves as farmers, but from the day they retired from the army at the age of about forty-five they lived in the style of the poorer gentlemen farmers in England. Their land was not a pleasure ground like the beautiful park of an English great house, their house not a place of repose like the ones that businessmen retire to but the focal point of the work which they and their employees did. The women of the family could only be happy if they took part in the work as farmers' wives do, and few of them were apt and willing to do that. Nina was the exception. She devoted herself to horses not merely as a pastime. She knew as much as her father and uncle about breeding, training, diet, the quality of oats and hay, rich grasses and poor, the care of saddlery, veterinary skill. After hunting she never went straight indoors, as Topsy would as soon as the groom took her horse away; when the racehorses were in training she attended all the gallops; she liked to be the first to handle foals and yearlings, and when they grew older to help in their education. And so she was fully occupied winter and summer with work she loved. Even after she was crippled these interests did not fail.

For the men of the family, the conduct of horses had for generations been a career. They learned to keep their balance astride donkeys and ponies before they could walk and as soon as they left school they started training for the cavalry. Their only hope of making money lay in breeding racehorses and the ordinary keep of their house and land depended partly on the sale of heavy half-bred hunters which Russian people bought for pulling carriages and sleighs and English people for jumping thick hedges in pursuit of the fox. The half-breds were completely schooled at Woodbrook and the thoroughbreds were trained there too before going on to a racing stable. When Charlie and Billy were boys, the gatelodge was the jockey's house. He was not a very good one, but managed the gallops and local races and held his job for years.

Uncle Tom had won the Grand National with a horse called Woodbrook in 1881, a year before Charlie's birth. It sustained him and the people who worked for him throughout a decade of agricultural depression and saved his tenants from eviction. His were few because his father had evicted almost all the small farmers when he and James were little boys. He knew all about the horrors of eviction and how lucky he was to escape the temptation to complete the operation his father had begun. His father had managed the distressing business rather quietly. But evictions enforced in 1880 only fifty miles away by a retired army officer, Captain Charles Boycott, had caused organized reprisals. Captain Boycott, agent for the absentee landlord, Lord Erne, had been driven from the country after months of misery. No one would work for him or buy his produce. No shop would sell him food. Even a large gang of Protestant labourers sent from Ulster failed to save him. The people cut off the tails of all his cattle one night and no dealer would buy them. The steamboat companies, being warned by the Land League, refused to ship them and although he did get them away in the end on a special boat chartered by the Belfast Association, he soon had to follow them. The mental torture and loss of money were impossible to bear.

And then, in 1884, Lord Cloncurry, one of the richest and most powerful landlords, had been exposed to unpleasant publicity by a peaceful demonstration on his estates in Limerick. He had evicted seventy families under the surveillance of a large escort of police and about fifty soldiers. 'A good deal of mud and good many stones' were thrown at the police, but there was no serious resistance and the soldiers stood idle. 'In each house, the whole family lay on the ground and refused to move. Two policemen then took men, women and children, in succession, and gently deposited them on the manure heap; then they carried all the furniture outside, and lastly the landlord's agent took possession.'[1] Until then it was like any other eviction, though without bloodshed. But before the troops of police and military had retired dozens of carts laden with prefabricated wooden huts drew up and all the tenants had new houses by the roadside before dark. The Land League supported the seventy families for years and boycotted their old farms. Lord Cloncurry did manage to graze cattle unmutilated there, but only because he had enough influence to keep armed police stationed in some of the empty farms.

His people had asked for a ten per cent reduction in their rents. Thousands of others all over Ireland were earning too little to pay any rent at all and thousands offered rent that was refused because it was much more profitable to put them out, knock down their houses and the walls of their potato gardens and sow wide stretches of grass for sheep and cattle. The greatest number of evictions took place at times when the landowners' resources were reduced by famine or economic depression, at the very times when neighbours could not feed the destitute evicted. Hatred and distress were exacerbated.

The crisis the rural population of all Europe went through in the 1880s was intensified in Ireland by the failure of the potato crop in 1879 which caused famine in some parts of the country and near-starvation everywhere. Even in good circumstances recovery would have been slow. Also, the oppression suffered by the Irish people was not due merely to class. Even fifty years after Catholic emancipation, Baron de Mandat-Grancy, himself a powerful landowner with enormous properties in Normandy, felt on his tour of Ireland that the country was under enemy occupation. Contrasting England with Spain and Portugal, 'who used the most abominable means to conquer their colonies', he said of England, 'Neither in Canada, in India nor anywhere else has she ever been able to assimilate the conquered race ... It is certain that the Irish people are in a state of war or of rebellion, whichever you like, against England. This is incontestable.'² He was writing in 1887.

Of course English landowners oppressed their own poor too. The country schools of that time had to close and let their pupils go wherever a rich local farmer required child labour on his land.³ Whenever a family struck lucky and called attention to themselves by wearing new boots and clothes at an unusual time of the year – the only acceptable time was after harvest when most people's money was better – they could expect the parson or squire to stride into their house after church and lift the lid off the pot in which Sunday's dinner was cooking to make sure they were not living above their station on meat bought from the butcher or poached from the woods.⁴

But these powerful men did not go about in fear of their lives, nor did their children play Landlord and Tenant, a game like Cowboys and Indians. 'I'll show you a capital game,' said a little boy of six, on holiday from Ireland, to a Parisian girl of seven. 'You shall be landlord and I'll kill you with my gun.'⁵

No Irish landowner would have looked into a pot. The Victorian parent–child discipline had no place there and anyway only about one third of their number lived on their estates. Those that did, and the agents of the absentees, carried loaded pistols, always visible, and many never left their houses without an armed escort. In the twelve months before the Grand National of 1881 a thousand cases of boycotting had been reported from the thirty-two counties of Ireland and two hundred of these, a fifth of the total, happened in Co. Roscommon where Woodbrook was. These figures were included in the sum of nearly three thousand 'agrarian outrages', an expression used to include every act from murder to resisting eviction.

Colonel Tom lived near three of the most hated men in Ireland, Colonel King-Harman of Rockingham, a mile away, Lord Kingston of Kilronan, and the Earl of Leitrim, colonel of the Leitrim regiment, who had a lot of land and made a lot of fuss near Carrick. Leitrim was ambushed and shot dead on his way to evict tenants on his distant estates in Donegal. King-Harman, though a supporter of Home Rule, was one of those who tried to rouse Westminster to a policy of indiscriminate revenge. The draconian punishments he inflicted on his tenants remain a local legend. The young Lord Kingston allowed his agent, Tatlow, to enforce evictions by the cruellest methods Wilfred Scawen Blunt, the English poet, ever witnessed in his travels through Ireland.[6]

I cannot find out whether Colonel Tom evicted people from his part of the Plains of Boyle nearby – the plains were certainly cleared of inhabitants long before Charlie inherited the estate – or from his distant lands in Co. Sligo, but on the home farm he was certainly not as unpopular as his surviving neighbour. Nor had his forebears ever been, in spite of several cruel acts. Their estates were small and everybody living on them knew them personally. But none, before or after him, could rival the popularity of Uncle Tom. He was, they say, by nature kindly and amusing, but so were other members of the family. Tom's glorious distinction was on the racecourses of England. The whole district basked in its reflection. Their little stable repeatedly beat all the dukes and princes on the 'far side'. Everyone for miles around put money on the Woodbrook horses and names now long forgotten by the rest of the racing world are still remembered by their grandchildren – Paddy Maher, Apollo Belvedere, Phaeton, Knight of Usna, and, best of all, The White Knight.

It seems now like a record of continuous success, but the quarter of a century between 'Woodbrook' and 'The White Knight' included many years of failure, and at the end of the century Uncle Tom's fortunes, instead of leaping, sagging, sinking, rising as they always had, began to flicker towards bankruptcy. When 'The White Knight', a rather ugly foal, was born in 1903 it seemed as if the stables, house and land would have to be sold before he was reared. Creditors, kept off for years by the promise of another win, began their work of rapine and none of the family dreamt that the foal could save them. Even its pedigree seemed likely to stand in the way of success. 'Buckshot', its maternal grandsire, was 'a fearfully bad tempered animal' and 'Pella', its dam, was of 'unfashionable breeding'. Tom would have sold it as a yearling for ten or twenty pounds if a friend whose judgement he respected had not offered fifty. This made him keep it. In 1905, the White Knight won the Curragh Grand Prize for two-year-olds; in 1906, the Ascot Gold Vase and the Newmarket Autumn Handicap; in 1907, the Ascot Gold Cup, the Goodwood Cup, the Epsom Coronation Cup and the Newmarket March Stakes; and in 1908, the Epsom Coronation Cup and the Ascot Gold Cup again. His subscription list at stud for 1909 was almost full by July 1908.[7] So Woodbrook's house and land were saved.

And so an eternal phoenix of hope made its nest in the hearts of Uncle Tom's successors.

Chapter Five

The heart of Woodbrook was a natural spring called by some the spring well or the boiling well and by those who used its water daily the Well. It boiled very cold and seemed to me holy and secret long before I thought about the meaning of the Holy Wells of Ireland. It was hidden from strangers by a low wall and even if they knew to look over that they would only see a rocky ledge half covered with grass. The yellow flag-lilies beside it made them think it was a patch of marshy ground and however clearly you described its position they would step across the stream which flowed from it and search higher on the hill. I passed by it walking alone on the day of our arrival and sat for a while by the washing place where the stream had been widened and deepened to form a pool. The grassy bank on which I sat, cropped close by sheep, was used for bleaching linen whenever the sheep were on other pastures, and while they were there or their droppings too wet to be swept away the sheets and tablecloths would be spread over clumps of hawthorn nearby. The women used to pound their washing on an outcrop of white limestone which formed the upper edge of the pool. I rested my feet on it as I sat looking down across the lake and at the distant mountains. I stared into the washing pool too, at its stony bottom and slight green weeds and at the swirling current curving through it, and though its clarity delighted me I did not think its source could be so near. A few feet to my left, between it and the hidden well, a hut about five feet high had been built into the hillside, out of rough-hewn limestone, without mortar, each block a different size and shape. It was something like an old Scottish cairn, a beehive hut with the top cut off or one of those ancient shrines you see beside mountainy roads. I thought it might have been a hermit's cell, but there was no room to lie down in it – less than four feet from the entrance to the back wall. Its narrow door had long since been taken away, probably for a field gate before iron bedsteads were available, but the jambs were still there, flat limestone posts, slightly fallen, one with rusty iron hinge-hooks still in it and the other bored for hasp and lock. The roof was made of enormous flagstones, whitish-grey with crooked ledges on their surface where they had been cut. They were much lichened and marked with birds' droppings, and their underpart, which formed a ceiling, was blackened by smoke. Flat stones about a foot high had been placed on the floor to hold pots over a fire. But I wondered why a boiler for washing, or a hermit's cell, had been built as strongly as a fortress. Low structures like that always please me as boulders do in heather or bright grass – I mean dry-stone walls, cowsheds, pigsties or long single-storeyed houses – perhaps because they are usually made of local stone and fit in to their landscape naturally, perhaps because in childhood I had happier times on old farms where corners were irregular and every wall bulged than in suburbs of London where smooth rectangles predominate.

At supper I described the stone hut.

'That's Molly's House,' said Phoebe, as though the name explained everything.

Next morning after breakfast we went for our first ride. The path from the woodshed at the back of the stable yard led across a rushy lowland known as Shanwelliagh, through a thin coppice of alder trees and up to the Maxwells' house where it turned right towards the lake. On our left from there on was the low dry-stone wall of the Bull's Paddock, a roughly oblong enclosure of about twenty acres of beautiful grass sloping up towards the Hill of Usna. Near Molly's House it crossed a stream through a shallow, stony ford and the sound of the horses' hooves changed musically as they stepped through it and out on to the sheep-cropped grass. Riders know where they are in mist or dark by the sound of hooves, and the changing tones are to my senses the most distinct of all the memories my riding days have left me. They range from fear, while being run away with in a wood or rocky place, to the safe idyllic joy of that first morning on the Maxwells' fat and sleepy cob. I remember the smell of the air too.

Past Molly's House we went at a walk by the short lower end of the Bull's Paddock, but still I did not notice the boiling well across the wall. Then we turned left, away from the lake and cantered uphill, jumping banks if the horse would jump, but mine climbed.

We stopped, before we reached the top of the hill, to look at a tumbled heap of monoliths known as the Giants' Graves. It was like a miniature Stonehenge, but diamond-shaped, and all its stones askew or lying flat, except the small ones that marked its outline. Two or three old ragged bushes grew out of it.

'There's supposed to be gold underneath,' Phoebe said, 'and people knocked the gravestones down to search for it. Something terrible happens to anyone who looks.'

The graves – if they are graves – had never been excavated, though a huge black stone, the only black one, had been broken and several holes dug by men looking for the gold. So their mystery remained. Some called the place Leaba Dhiarmuda, which means McDermot's Bed, the last resting place of the old kings of Connaught whose descendants still lived nearby. Some thought it held the bones of Danish chieftains and their gold, and others that the Sons of Usna were buried in it – Naoise and his brothers who rescued Deirdre from her solitary upbringing as bride-to-be of an old man and were treacherously killed by him at last.

'You could easily recognize Deirdre's bones,' said Phoebe. 'If you dug. And all those giants.'

'I don't think she'd be buried with them.'

'She'd want to be, if she killed herself when she heard about Naoise.'

The rounded summit of Usna was fenced from the adjoining townland by a thick old hedge, fifteen feet high in places, the 'mearing' or boundary of the Kirkwoods' land. This was on our right as we rode up, and on our left a steep slope gradually flattened to the level of the road. The glory of this half-mile slope and the undulating plains beyond, broken once by the railway and marked with hedges, trees and low stone walls, was in varying shades of green that changed in the lights of the extraordinary west of Ireland sky that is much sought by painters. The racing gallops, long disused, were distinguishable across the road by a lighter green got from years of hard tread, and beyond, for miles into the distance, you could see nothing but pastures with a white house here or there. All were overnourished by rain except the Hill of Usna which, being drained by its limestone base, was as rich as the rest, but dry and ideal for horses. As we went down it cautiously, almost falling over our horses' heads, Charlie said not to walk so slowly because to walk fast was 'good for their hocks' – another phrase that had become a family catchword, because he said it every time anyone looked nervous going down a hill.

We cantered up to the top again, breathless and hot, the horses sweating too, and went at a walk back the way we had come, past the Giants' Graves, downhill by the side of the Bull's Paddock until we reached the well. Usually I forget what must have been the pleasant aspects of the past, but the exhilarating pleasure of that morning is vivid to me now. Perhaps I have combined with it in my memory many other morning rides.

Phoebe and I stopped at the well because we were so hot and thirsty. Our cheeks, pale from London, were burning in the sun. Her father was, as usual, on a nervous young horse – steady ones bored him just as walking bored him – and kept well ahead. By the stream we dismounted and she went to drink while I held her horse with mine. She was wearing light jodhpurs and a sleeveless shirt, the one I liked her best in at that time, the one I always think of as the 'strawberry' shirt, not only because of its colour but because the material was puckered into small pointed sections rounded at the base, each with a fleck of yellow in it, like a segment of a strawberry. In sunlight the colour glowed faintly on her cheek. It had a round neck rather low, no collar, no buttons. It left the whole of her shoulders bare except a piece two inches wide, and was close and fragile enough to show the full outline of her growing breasts. It made her seem more like a woman than a child. Perhaps that is why I liked her strawberry shirt. Her hair at that time was short.

She called it bobbed. It was fair, but not yellow. Perhaps it would have been called mousy if she had gone to school and made enemies, but I have never seen a mouse with hair that seems blond in the sun and brown under clouds, and hers was not sleek like a mouse's or a filmstar's; it was loosely curly and on some days, especially when it had dried quickly after swimming or a hairwash, it was fuzzy, which she did not like.

I told her to ask her mother to let it grow to her shoulders but she said it would 'always be getting in the way'. I suppose she was thinking of climbing trees and playing the fiddle and so on. Anyway, it remained as it was for a year or two, trimmed level with the lobes of her ears, and that day as she walked towards the well, suddenly I saw the back of her neck as if I had never seen it before. As I let the horses graze, holding both pairs of reins in one hand, I watched her as though she were a strange girl I longed for but dared not even speak to. She stood on top of the wall for a moment, then jumped down out of sight.

I know now that several people, half lovingly, half jeering, called her a tomboy. She seemed tireless and certainly was adventurous and agile. But when she dressed up for charades or a homemade play, although she was tall for her age, she could not disguise her femininity as her young sister could. She was too slightly built. She was better padded with cushions as Falstaff than without them as Prince Hal, because whenever she moved freely she moved like a girl.

She came back drying her face with the backs of her hands and took the horses from me.

'Did you see where I crossed the wall?' she said. 'You can reach the water with your mouth lying down. It's nicer. But if you want to scoop it up, your hands don't matter. New water comes all the time and flows out.'

'I'll do it like you.'

'All right. Your shirt'll soon dry. The ground's wet.'

The well was about two feet across, just wide and deep enough to allow a bucket to be filled without stirring the bottom or touching the sides. As I leant over it, it was like a lake in miniature seen from a plane. Each shore of the lake was lapped by rippling waves, not strong enough to break. They

spread gently from the middle in concentric rings, pushed by
the pulse of the well which I watched below me swelling and
falling, swelling and falling, with lesser pulses around it, forming bubbles constantly like a wide pan boiling on a narrow
flame. Once or twice, later on, in very warm weather when the
air was still, I saw steam rise from the boiling well.

I found enough space between the lilies to lie down. They
were in flower. I got rid of the reflection of my face by taking
off my spectacles and staring closely through the water at the
sandy floor. The sand had been carried there, I think, to keep
the water clean. There were no weeds. The dark place, shadowy
and overhung, where the water looked almost black and where
I would have chosen to drink, was beyond my reach and I put
my lips to the bright part near me. Phoebe called. I did not
answer, but sentimentally tried to reckon how long the water
she had touched would take to reach the washing place, to flow
along the stream past the Maxwells' house, along to her house,
under the avenue and into the brook. It was probably lost in the
big lake already, I thought. I climbed the wall and walked
quickly to her.

'You were ages.'

'Sorry.' She was leaning against the stone hut with the two
pairs of reins looped over her arm.

'Why is it called Molly's House?'

'It used to be a well till my great-great-great-great – ' she said
about twenty 'greats' until her breath ran out on the word
grandfather. 'He built it in and locked it with an iron-barred
gate to keep Molly and all the women from coming for water
and dipping their black cans in. Molly's real house was just over
the wall and next morning the boiling well began bubbling in
her garden. And when the landlord came for water his well was
dry. Is that called an act of God?'

'Yes.'

'Give me a leg up then.'

She knelt her left knee in my hand and jumped on to the
saddle. Her horse began to turn and fidget, as she waited for me
to mount Molly, and she burst out laughing.

'Do I look like a pea on a drum?' It was her father's expression. The horse was far too big for her. 'I'd be much better on Castor and Pollux. You tell Daddy.'

'Which are they?'

'The long-tails. He won't let me. I christened them the day they were born.'

'He wouldn't listen to me,' I said.

'There they are, look!'

She pointed to two slim chestnut ponies, which were grazing with the cows on the low rushy land between us and the stables. The house was hidden by leafy trees, tall elms, three beeches and a copse of little alders, several shades of green. The green of the grass varied too – light on the upland, dark below us as we rode along – and on its poorer patches thistles and buttercups were flowering. I counted ten cows, mostly white with brown markings, only two of them pure bred – an Ayrshire and a Kerry, dark grey which the people called blue.

'Shall I tell you the names of the cows?' said Phoebe.

'Yes.'

'Pookey, Bawneen, Ruby, Daisy, Jessie, Rosie, Darkie, Nanny, and Nelly. And Long Horns.'

'Can you tell which is which from here?'

'Yes.'

It was a scene from my childhood as well as hers.

Chapter Six

In my later years at Woodbrook, I often fetched water from the well in the two white enamelled buckets that were used for nothing else. They held two gallons each – enough for cooking and drinking water for a day – but once a week, when Winnie was churning, an extra journey had to be made for water to wash the butter with. The full buckets were too heavy for me, though not for the other men, to carry the whole way back without a rest; you had to hold your arms out a bit to prevent them from bumping and spilling water down your legs, which added to the strain; and I always used to stop outside the Maxwells' house which was about half-way.

Old Michael Maxwell would have stopped me anyway. Except when the rain was very heavy he was always by their wicket gate in his wide old hat and long top coat, resting against the wall of the potato-garden as though he was built into it, a walking stick in either hand and a lidded pipe in his mouth. When the air was still, the smoke from his pipe rose up like the smoke from the chimney behind him in the same position every day for, by the time I got to know him, he had long been immobilized by rheumatism, and could only manage the walk between his door and this chosen place on the outer side of the wall, ten yards at about a yard a minute. After a long active life as a herd to the Kirkwoods, he was in the same case as Aunt Nina of whom he often used to speak with sympathy, but his lack of company was worse and he would hail anyone who came in sight, raising one of his sticks with a shout.

He made a joke of the rheumatism often when he saw Charlie because 'first shot' from Jameson's whiskey distillery where Billy worked was supposed to ease the stiffness if rubbed into his legs, and Billy sent a bottle from Dublin now and then – a raw spirit in the first stage of distillation – knowing well that it would not be wasted on the surface of the body. Charlie and old Michael kept up the pretence in an exchange that kept its pattern like folklore.

'How's the rheumatism?'

'Well now Major, it eased a bit after Christmas, and that's no word of a lie.'

'Do you think does the first shot do any good?'

'Why wouldn't it, why wouldn't it?'

'If it's rubbed in well.'

'My arms was tired rubbing it and I wouldn't put you to the trouble of a letter to Dublin all them miles and the bottle to be lost – Dieu knows it might – on the railway coming home.'

Their voices could be heard half a mile away, Charlie shouting from his horse and Michael from his place by the wall, and even when I was alone with him, having found a level place to rest the buckets on the ground, he would speak at the top of his voice. I don't think he was deaf; it was just that his enormous vigour, having no other outlet any more, released itself through his lungs. He was not tall, but very strongly built, rather square-faced with eyes that seemed too young for it and a bushy moustache brownish grey which gave him the look of an old cavalry man, which he was not.

He used to comment on the water as people do on precious drinks calling it the sweetest water in all Ireland in fine weather when it was perfectly clear, and consoling me after a rainy night with, 'There's no loss on it. Them [the specks in it] will settle one hour after ye bringing it into the dairy.' He seldom drank water himself, he said, only tea, but when he was young they never saw tea except at Christmas when some drank so much of it they made themselves sick, and though his parents were well off enough to keep a cow, he never had a taste of sweet milk [fresh milk] till he was married and came to Woodbrook as the Kirkwood's herd. In the old times all the cream was kept for butter and the skimmed milk for the calf, but they never tasted butter either unless they stole some on their fingers; it all went to the fair of Boyle to pay the rent. 'Buttermilk and potatoes was our meat and drink and there's no better in the world,' he would say, but next day. if he knew his wife was cooking it, bacon and cabbage would be the best in the world. Bacon was boiled with cabbage more as a flavouring than the main part of the dish, but in spite of his fondness for superlatives I think he liked it better than a plate of mutton or beef, which had by then taken the place of tea as a Christmas treat. Whenever he spoke of food he said something about the shortage of it – the 'hungry months' every year of his youth from June to September when the old potatoes were finished and the new not ripe, and the 'Great Hunger', as he called the famine, when his grandfather, the only man strong enough, 'brought fifty and sixty corpses on a barrow one by one', two miles from Cootehall near his home to the graveyard at Ardcarne, and 'the people were lying dead by the roadside with green on their mouths where they had been eating grass'.

Like many old people he repeated himself, sometimes for emphasis but more often because he thought repetition enjoyable as it is to children, who ask for the same story again and again. The repetition I liked best was about his courting days: how he swam across the lake to Woodbrook and back every evening with his clothes tied on to his head. When Tony heard this she was much impressed, and asked what he did with his hat, but his sons used to laugh at him and say, 'The most swimming he ever did was in porter on a Fair Day.' We were his best listeners, I suppose, we and the people who occasionally came to be cured of skin diseases by him. For he 'had the cure', as they called it, a knowledge of herbal remedies which had been passed secretly for generations from father to a chosen son, and which he passed on when he died to his youngest son Tommy. He could no longer gather the herbs himself when I knew him, but still prepared and mixed them into an ointment with lard or unsalted butter.

One of the pleasant things about Irish country life is that any passer-by, except on the main roads where few wish to stop, is welcomed into every house. In remote places it is a slight not to go in for a cup of tea or buttermilk if you are a stranger, as bad as passing someone on the road without a greeting. I was shy of this at first and Nanny Maxwell, Michael's wife, had to press me, but I soon became a frequent visitor and got to know her well.

Their house was a curiosity, its merits and demerits much discussed. Like Nina's bath and the tap-water pump it had been bought out of The White Knight's winnings when the old stone house on lower ground behind it began to crumble in a morass of mud. It had been brought over from England as a pre-fab in about 1910 by three English workmen who put it up before a large audience. It was the same size as most of the country people's houses, a single storey of three rooms, but was made of corrugated iron instead of stone, and lined with wood, and it looked much the same as the others because the Maxwells whitewashed it inside and out every year. But it was a different shape which, as Nanny several times explained to me, turned out to be a blessing during the civil war. The half door that opened into the kitchen was at a corner of the gable end, not in the centre of the long front wall, and you could not see the back door from it as you walked in. Some of her sons were on different sides in that war and when one came home unexpectedly her husband could delay him at the front while she smuggled the enemy son out.

There was a good woman living in the big house in the troubled times, she said, a Scotch woman by the name of Miss MacDonald, who was nurse and companion to Miss Nina. She was one who cared nothing for politics but only for the safety of the men that were 'in hide'. And she was thought to be a mad old spinster by them that did not know, for she would stand with her bicycle outside the protestant rectory of Ardcarne shouting and raging at the parson within doors and she would be out rowing on the lake and up the Boyle river at first light in the morning. 'But what she was doing alone with the boat in all weathers, with her veil on like as if she was on her way to church, was she was bringing the men that were in hide by the Salmon Hole up the Boyle Water their feed and tobacco.' I never heard what she looked like, but imagined a thin body like the tongue of a bell in waterproof cape, and a purple straw hat with cherries on it, such as I had seen in church, held down with grey gauze that was tied below a sharp chin. I often rowed home from the Salmon Hole after fishing, just as it was getting dark, and imagined her wetting the rowlocks to stop them squeaking in the silence. The water would be black in the early light, as at dusk, and her cape black and glistening.

It is difficult after all these years to distinguish between what I saw in my mind's eye and what I saw outside me, but I grew to know Nanny so well and to like her so much that I believe I remember her as she really was – about five foot four, light, quick and very thin. She was well over sixty then and I suppose there were small wrinkles at the corners of her eyes, but the skin of her forehead and cheeks was smooth like a young woman's and the eyes as bright and alert as her youngest son's. They were almost black like his. Her hair still had strands of black in it and was beautifully glowing and healthy. She wore it pinned loosely in a bun. Her face, neck and arms were dark from the weather. She was always dressed completely in black – a black cotton blouse, buttoned up to her neck with small white buttons, a wide skirt which almost reached the ground, small black boots that showed only when she sat down. Except for Mass or visits to the town, she had never worn anything on her feet until she got married and she still preferred to be barefoot, she said, but young people did not like it and she had had to go with the new fashion.

Now that I am thinking of the melting together of inner and outer vision, I remember that the only hint I have ever heard of how Miss MacDonald dressed came from Willie Maxwell who once saw her ghost. I did not then believe that people can see ghosts, that inner vision can be so clear to some that a figure of a person appears in natural surroundings, but Willie was the oldest of the sons, except for one who lived in America, and his mind still worked in the old para-psychic way. 'She died,' he said, 'in or around the fifteenth of August. And I was very great with her. And I had been to the show in Boyle in the month of September. I was coming home in duskish in the evening. 'Twasn't anything like dark or anything, just falling dusky in the month of September, and I was cycling then on up ahead about three hundred yards from the big house. There was a tree growing up. And she walked out across from the tree, across the road – the avenue! And turned in on the other side o' the avenue, wearing a suit of plaid – she was a Scotchwoman – and she passed up, she walked up in front o' me. And when I didn't die after seeing her I never will die. Aye. With the fright. I got weak when I went home. And they wouldn't believe me.'

Willie is a pensioner of the old I.R.A. and I guess he was one of those she looked after in the troubled times.

Besides the men by the Salmon Hole, whose numbers varied week by week from two to six, she usually had four to look after in the hay barn near the house. These were the enemies of the Salmon Hole lot, some slightly wounded and some whom she imagined to be deserters, and they had to be kept secretly away from the others as well as from those who were hunting them. She had to cook for them too – make tea, boiled eggs and soup with lumps of meat in it, and potatoes sometimes, half of which they saved up and ate cold – because of course it was impossible for them to make a fire. Hay, as I knew from my own wanderings, is warm to sleep in, warmer than straw. If it has been stacked damp, which usually it is in Ireland, it can become unbearably hot or even go on fire. Miss MacDonald refused to give them cigarettes or tobacco until she caught one of them smoking and read at the end of the week in the *Roscommon Herald* that a shop thirty miles away had been raided at night. The thief was never caught but she spoke to him severely and showed him a disused pigsty where, if they dared risk being observed, he might take his comrades for a smoke. She said, in her sharp Fife accent, that she could not trust her own tongue when men did wrong. She might without meaning it give them away. And from that day on she supplied them with matches, cigarettes and tobacco.

Their refuge was the high Dutch barn which I got to know so well and which is still there in the cow yard of Woodbrook set back from the byre, though now even in the autumn after haytime only quarter of it is filled. It has two long bays about twenty feet high and fifteen feet in width. You can always force your way between them when the barn is full and close the opening behind you with loose hay. By pressing the hay back with their shoulders the men had widened the passage between the two stacks and with a hay knife cut a circular room round the central upright girder which they then climbed, pulling after them the hay they had cut and storing it between the tops of the stacks and the curve of the iron roof. A fair amount of light came from under the roof in daytime and Miss MacDonald had supplied them with an electric torch. She only came to see them in the early morning, before the servants were awake, and their one hot meal a day was breakfast. Then she would carry her packages down to the boat and visit the Salmon Hole. She knew she was known as an eccentric and believed that the servants, who were usually kindling fires when she returned, thought she had been out for an early morning walk. One who was nearest when she opened the noisy front door would help her off with her galoshes and take them away to be washed and say, 'You are hardy, Miss MacDonald, this time in the morning. That's the truth.' But I think they knew what she did. In the country, especially in Ireland, everybody knows what everybody does and if necessary they keep quiet about it.

As soon as cloak and galoshes were off she would go to wake Aunt Nina, resuming the loud piercing voice that had become habitual through years of living with one so deaf.

Aunt Nina was by then unable to ride. She could no longer inspect the quality of the hay in the Dutch barn because her bathchair was too wide for the narrow gate that leads to it from the stable yard. She had attempted it one rainy day and her pony went through eagerly, seeing the hay before him. The shafts and little front wheels went through too, and down the shallow step, but the body of the chair, wider, newly varnished and lovingly polished every day by James Currid, scraped horribly along the gate-posts and came to a halt with a jerk.

Aunt Nina was not defeated yet. She tried one other way to reach the hay and again chose a time of day when none of the men were about. She drove her chair successfully round by the field without overturning it, but when she reached the cow gate all four wheels sank above their axles in the mud and she was stuck again. This, and an earlier adventure on the Hill of Usna she so much loved and longed to see again, when the bathchair overturned and threw her out, had induced her to keep to the drive and the nearby roads. The rest of the family were away and Miss MacDonald's secret was preserved.

A few years earlier she had suffered the injustice and indignity of being locked up in Aunt Nina's bedroom, with the rest of the household, by the I.R.A. It was in the summer of 1919 or 1920, during the war for independence. Charlie and Ivy, reunited, were back in India, his parents away at their house in Fifeshire and Topsy, as always in the season, yachting in the Bay of Dublin and attending balls in Merrion Square. Miss MacDonald, Nina and the servants were alone in the house and asleep.

The *Irish Times* came by post at lunchtime every day. It was always yesterday's. In it Nina read of the rebellion, but even after the raid she referred to the incident as a burglary. In the confusion of the moment she had misunderstood what was happening and she never quite believed Miss MacDonald's explanation. Miss MacDonald was fond of dramatics. That was evident.

The raiders, five of them it seems, were looking for shot-guns and petrol. They obviously knew the household well. Their first act was to rouse the stable lads, whose room was in the yard, and push them into the house; then they woke Miss MacDonald, James Currid and the maids and, without giving any of them time to dress, herded them at the point of their one gun down the stone-flagged passage into Nina's room. She heard nothing, but when they lit the paraffin lamp on her writing table and her bedside candle she woke up.

'What has happened?' said Miss Nina. 'Has the boiler burst?'

The raiding party went to search the house, leaving the man with the gun on guard inside the room. Winnie was afraid of him because, to her surprise, she did not know him and could not frighten him by hinting that she would tell.

'Ye've a right to let me fetch my gown. It isn't decent,' she said, trembling with the cold and fear.

'Sit down in the chair,' said the man with the gun.

'Well make up the fire, girls,' said Winnie. 'There is red in it yet, and Miss Nina feels the cold.'

The fire was usually lit on summer evenings. The girls were

whispering and giggling in one corner of the room and the stable lads, in another, pulling faces at them, imitated Winnie's gestures, clutching their nightshirts, pretending to shiver.

'If one of yiz stirs,' said the man with the rifle, 'I will shoot yiz. That's my orders.' He had a horrible Dublin accent which made them want to laugh and, though all except Winnie and James knew that he was laughing too, they remained where they had been put.

James feared the Dublin accent. He knew how rashly men away from home behaved. But that was not why he was standing with his face to the wall. The men had pushed him into the corner by Miss Nina's pillow, then lit the candle just behind him and he was overcome with shame.

'Tell me what has happened!' said Nina, louder this time, staring at the back of his nightshirt from the pillows.

Being unable to sit up unaided, she did not see his long underpants or stockinged feet. His earnest hope was not to see her in bed, nor any of the women in nightclothes, and facing the wall with his eyes lowered he kept on saying, 'I beg your pardon, Miss Nina, I beg your pardon', over and over again, raising his voice as much as he dared to in the presence of the guard.

'There is no use in praying,' said Miss Nina. 'If none of you can fix it, you must go for the smith. Where is Miss Mac-Donald? Wake her, Winnie, and bring her here at once.'

Miss MacDonald was sitting out of sight near the guard in the high-backed armchair he had offered to Winnie. Winnie felt safer standing and Miss MacDonald thought it wise to be silent, knowing no explanation that the guard might find acceptable especially if it had to be shouted across the room.

The phaeton and the landau had recently been replaced by a Daimler with brass lamps. It had been in the coach-house all winter, shrouded in dust sheets, and at last they heard the roar of its engine in the stable yard.

'Run off at once or you'll be left behind,' said Miss Mac-Donald.

He did. They all went away in the Daimler, with Colonel James's shot-guns and about five gallons of petrol in cans. Winnie lit the range and put a kettle on; then, with the girls for company, carried a lamp about the house to look for damage. There was none. Only the guns were missing from their place by the umbrella stand, and all the cartridges and an army revolver from a drawer.

'I know well who brought them here.'

'Who?' said the girls.

'Never mind who it is. But he'd leave the place tidy.'

When Willie came to the cow yard to work that morning, the gardener said, 'They done it last night.'

'What?'

'They raided the house. The arms is all taken away out of it.'

Willie, remembering that moment fifty years later – he is now in his seventies – says he 'got sort of hot' in himself. 'And the next thing, the District Inspector from Boyle and the police and military came out. I was in the I.R.A. and I had documents and a couple of guns in our house at the time. And I got a heavy questioning. But someone went down to our house before that and told them, and my father, the Lord have mercy on him, went and he took the two guns that was hid under the bed and hid them in a potato plot. And those few documents – they were in a box left within in the room I used to sleep in – those were taken out and all was hid.'

Fortunately it was August and the full-grown potato leaves completely covered the space between the ridges. Fortunately, too, it was the morning after the Carrick show. Willie had come home tired from the show and gone to bed early, and was able to tell the inspector the truth.

'He took me in and challenged me. And he had a policeman standing on one side, along with him, and when I'd all told him, he sent out the policeman. He gave him the nod. And the policeman went down to our house. And the first thing he wanted to know was what time I was home, from last night.

'So he was told. The correct time, d'ye see? And where did I go after that? They said, "He went to bed." '

'And, "I want to see his clothes." '

'The suit of clothes was brought down to him.

' "I want to see his shoes." '

'They were clean and span, and all to that. So he came back

again to the big house, and then I was let go when he came back. And they went down the road then, down the avenue.'

Four of the men were caught. Two went to jail and two who were young lads 'with no one at home belonging to them only an old mother to keep, an old woman, were let go – to be good behaviour' as Willie describes it, 'and represent England's King.'

Chapter Seven

I have tried to imagine what Ivy felt like near that time when she first became mistress of Woodbrook at the age of twenty-three. Events, which were described to me lightly long afterwards, were close to her. She was English, and the country she had come to live in had just won independence from hers in a war conducted with vicious cruelty by both sides. The civil war, which succeeded it, between those who agreed to the partition of Ireland and those who wanted to fight on, had split the people, not geographically but piecemeal; counties, villages, families were broken apart; and, though it was almost over by the time she settled at Woodbrook, she could never feel that she had moved into one territory or another, to live with the conquered or the conquerors and know how the people round her felt. The hatred engendered by the civil war survives to this day among old men and a few of the young. People hide it from strangers as much as they can, but Ivy was aware of the undercurrents, and even twelve years later when I arrived the emotional tension was evident to me. Then, too, she had come to a house that did not seem to be hers or even her husband's, for the Irish gentry had one thing in common with their tenants and workmen: when they married, they lived with parents. Sometimes the man would move to the house his wife had been brought up in, as Michael Maxwell had, but usually it was the girl who moved.

Ivy had no real home, it is true, because of her mother's early death and her father's absence in India. But she had always thought of marriage as a beginning for man and woman, not only in love but in a place where they could make their own new way of living. All her friends who got married set up house alone with their men. Usually, they chose their own furniture too. And the one who married a landowner, although she was stuck with the ancestral chairs, inherited a dower house half a mile away and kept her mother-in-law in that.

Ivy was accustomed to shortage of money. She was not accustomed to money at all. As a child she had never had any in her purse, except a new penny every Christmas, but was of course fed and clothed and given enough sweets, and when her father retired from the army and stared at her after his last sea voyage, saying, 'You've grown up, you'd better get some clothes at Harrods. Put it down to the account', she took the train to London and spent three hundred pounds in two days. He had given her her return fare, some letters to friends she might stay with, and ten shillings for pocket money for a week. She came home dressed like a debutante and until the bill came he was pleased.

Charlie's incaution about money exceeded hers. When they arrived at Woodbrook with luggage and the grand piano she at least made an effort to divide his army pension by the rates and wages. The rates seemed small to her – one visit to Harrods would have covered three years – but when she asked how much Winnie and the girls got her mother-in-law said, 'You just give them whatever they need.'

'But surely it's agreed, by the week.'

'What, dear Ivy?'

'Their wages. The week's money.'

Old Mrs Kirkwood was startled. 'Money!' she said. 'Every week! They wouldn't know what to do with it. They never had money at home.'

'But suppose they wanted clothes – a new dress.'

'They only have to ask me. We are four miles from the nearest shop and the things are hideous. Can you imagine Winnie bicycling in to Carrick for that? The shop people would cheat her and she'd come back looking a fright.'

'Still they must need money for some things . . . Stamps,' said Ivy loudly, having thought of a necessity at last.

'They put their letters on the hall table. I stamp them and give them to the postman with our own. They know that very well. Now don't start by making new problems for yourself, dear Ivy. You'll find quite enough as it is.'

Ivy decided not to talk about it any more, but not wishing to appear unique in a new foolish form of philanthropy, could not stop herself from saying that her father's maids got wages.

'We are in Ireland, dear Ivy. Just think of the jealousies. Of course, Charlie will give Christmas boxes just as his father does. In sealed envelopes.'

This duty fell to Charlie sooner than they thought. His father died that year, leaving all his money to Billy, and the three aunts together with the house and land to his eldest son. The income from the land, the lawyers said, was nearly £2,000 a year including, as their documents showed, rents from a little slum street in Sligo called Harmony Hill and the benefits of some square miles of luscious grasslands known as the Plains of Boyle. Even after the aunts had been paid, this seemed plentiful. They bought a small Fiat – the Daimler had never been replaced – and Ivy, not finding anything she liked in the Carrick-on-Shannon clothiers, asked Charlie to drive her to Sligo to choose dresses for the maids. She also bought brimless hats, with artificial berries on, which were in fashion. They looked with despair at Harmony Hill – even Charles had not seen it before – and drove home again through the Sligo mountains, thirty miles without meeting another car. It was beautiful, and an adventure. They were happy, and the maids and Winnie were delighted with the clothes. But Winnie had been troubled for some nights by a bronchial cough and Ivy as soon as she got into bed remembered that she had not given her her dose of cough mixture.

'Could you go down?' she said to Charlie who was not yet undressed. 'One tablespoonful in a glass. She sips it through the night.'

'I'll leave her the bottle,' he said. He hated measuring anything out. But she told him that Winnie believed that if a tablespoon helped her a half pint would cure her, so he measured it roughly and left the bottle on the kitchen table after she had gone to bed. The housemaid came up in the night to say she was dying. He had given her cow-drench, the same colour, from the same shelf. She cured herself by vomiting, but never forgot the experience as I found out years afterwards by the many times she related it laughing.

The house was full of women. Aunt Topsy had come to stay and did not disguise her boredom. Aunt Nina drove about in her bathchair, amusing some and exasperating others with her sharp wit. Aunt Isobel, safely married and away, sent a letter once a week, and old Mrs Kirkwood kept on saying wearily, 'What shall we do this afternoon?' She had had a tennis court made at the bottom of the flower garden, overlooking the paddock and lake, but it was seldom dry-enough to use. The nearest golf course was still at Sligo, thirty miles away. She said she would die of boredom, and meant it. But she died of golf, not boredom.

One summer she went as usual to her old home in Scotland intending to stay six weeks, perhaps two months if the weather was pleasant which it was, but within a month she sent a telegram asking them to meet her at Carrick station. She was pale and quiet, exhausted by games and disappointed, saying she had only been able to manage eighteen holes and three games of tennis a day.

'How could there be time for more?' said Ivy, kindly.

'The evenings are longer in the north.'

Three weeks later she died suddenly. She had strained her heart in Fife.

The house that had been too full of women soon seemed empty and they cherished Aunt Nina more than before, which may have been what made her flourish all that winter, driving her pony with new vigour up rocky slopes, through mud that looked impassable and in and out the trees. She was entertaining and kind, and to Ivy she was like a household spirit, sometimes capricious, often helpful, always wise. She seemed eternal too. She had lived at Woodbrook as long as most of the furniture and longer than many of the trees. Even if she only lived till she was ninety, Ivy would be middle-aged, which was an eternity away. So no one ever thought of Nina dying, except the old doctor who, said Charlie to explain it, began to think of death as soon as a new patient was born.

He was seldom called but took a special interest in Charlie and Ivy, stopping to give fatherly advice whenever they met him on the road.

'Ye are lucky to be married and find the land well stocked as well. How is the old lady? That's a terrible growth of rushes on the hill there since your uncle Tom died. £300 a year. Well, we all must die one day, God have mercy on us. It would go a long way to sweeten the land.'

'What did he mean?' said Ivy when he had gone, darkly imagining Nina's corpse as manure. But of course he meant her annuity to drain the slopes of the hill. And when she did die under the old doctor's care, Ivy was convinced that he had killed her thinking he was doing them a kindness, just as he was always telling them to shoot Lady Lucy, an old mare that was a beloved pet idle and at grass.

The cause of Aunt Nina's death was certainly unnameable. Except for arthritis, she had never been ill in her life and no one believed it at first when they heard she was dead.

'Did the bathchair turn over and crush her?' said the parson. No. She felt sick, that was all. Then she kept on being sick. On the Friday the doctor prescribed some pills and on the Monday she was dead.

Some weeks after this second funeral, Ivy somewhat guiltily felt elated and free. It was as though the new life could begin, and to make sure of it she pulled down part of the house. The front rooms in the centre had always been dark and cramped because in those days the front door opened into a narrow passage with a door on each side, one to the so-called office, the other to the dining-room as it then was, and the staircase at the end had no light until it curved towards a window on the upper floor. One morning she planned to pull down the dining-room wall and by two o'clock the men were called in from the fields and began to thump it joyfully with sledgehammers. The plaster flew, but even Tommy Maxwell, the horseman, who attacked it as though he were trying to break out of prison, could not dislodge one stone.

'Easy. Easy. Easy, Tom,' said James Currid, limping up and down the passage in a fuss. 'You will tumble the roof on the head of the mistress that way', which made them rest their hammers and turn towards her. She was in fact the only one who might escape if the roof fell. She was standing in the open front doorway. Old James had warned her that morning that this was a main wall not a partition of plaster and lath.

'Do you really think the roof could fall in?' she said, amused by the thought and showing it. 'There's the bedroom floor above this.'

'There is surely, mistress, the bedroom floor, and there's no doubt about it. But a man cannot stand without his feet. If ye take what's under him away, the whole will come down. And the hair of his head.'

'Oh please James – can't we try?'

The men started thumping again, to tease him, and the house shook. He looked so worried that she stopped them. But then he was always worried by anything unusual and, knowing nothing about building, she thought it was mainly because he hated to see the men inside the house. Even if the whole place was on fire, he would have made them wait outside, while he limped back and forwards with buckets from the kitchen.

She went to fetch Charlie, who was asleep in the drawing-room with the *Irish Times* open on his lap. He slept very little at night and like Napoleon took ten minute naps throughout the day, filling the rest of it with activity. He never planned a campaign but enjoyed other people's, especially Ivy's, which were bold and sudden, so now wide awake at her touch, with an animal sound of a yawn and a laugh together, he came to comfort James.

The men, never doubting he would let them go on with it, had now fetched cold-chisels and a pair of steps, intending to attack the wall more gently from the top, 'to give it a small little tip', they said, 'in one place and the next and ease the stones out singly'. Even James thought this better and went for logs of firewood to replace the stones as the ceiling sagged. They could then build it up again and no one would know the difference.

'That's right,' said Charlie, and immediately took Ivy to the garage asking where she would like to go till the work was done.

They drove to see friends twenty miles away and stayed out till dusk. On the way up the drive, coming home, they noticed that one of the elm trees had been felled and, looking through the window because the front door was jammed six inches open and somewhat warped, they saw the tree in the dining-room in a corner by the staircase holding the ceiling up. The wall was on the floor and bits of the staircase hung in splinters among rubble.

James Currid heard the car and came to tell them he had put the straw-stack ladder against their bedroom window when he saw the staircase was unsafe. He humbled himself, painfully to Ivy, about the front door, explaining that only after the ceiling fell he thought to open it and leave a free way to pass in. But then the staircase being broken a person would have to spend the night on the ground floor. No comfort in that. He had sent for Joe Fryer when the trouble began. Joe, the blacksmith and self-taught engineer who had put the first shoes on The White Knight, cut the tree-trunk to size, dragged it in by the window and erected it with his huge strength but little help from the others, so James said.

Ivy was the first to climb up to bed. James stood at the foot of the ladder saying, 'Hold it you, Major, for it might shake. And I'll be ready when the mistress puts a foot wrong,' but a glimpse of her stockings as she climbed made him turn his head away; he would have been too late to catch her if he dared look up at all.

As soon as Charles climbed into the bedroom, Ivy looked down and gasped, 'Why are you taking the ladder away?'

'I thought just in case we were raided, mistress.'

She turned to Charlie. 'What does he mean? The war is over.'

'It means burgled. Better let him take it or he'll stand there all night.'

In the end they had to get a steel girder from England to hold the upper floor up and send one of the farm carts with its side-boards off to draw it from the station. Crowds followed it and came back next day to watch the work. It is still there and so is the tree, encased in whitewashed plaster to form a beautiful pillar at the foot of the stairs.

Chapter Eight

Charlie's way with the men and women who worked for him was casual and friendly, without the forced intimacy or superior tone used by many of his class, and without religious prejudice. I was the only Protestant among them, my father and uncle like his had been Indian army officers, but his manner to me was the same as his manner to them, which pleased me. Ivy, whose warm-heartedness expressed itself more openly than his, was set apart from them – painfully for her because she had a loving curiosity and concern for other people that drew them towards her. Her kind actions were far more frequent than his. If someone was ill or had a roof that leaked, he might not notice though he spoke to most of them or rode past their houses every day. (His own roof leaked of course, and he was never ill.) But she would do something about it at once.

Betrothals, marriages and births were single occasions for him on which he behaved with extravagant generosity, making the neighbouring landowners laugh at him a bit, but for her they were also the beginning of new lives which she kept close to for years. So naturally she was loved. But because of the religion of the people who loved her she could not wholly return their love. She could not trust them. Doubt spoils love. She said to me more than once that Roman Catholic teaching was founded on deceit; for example that the high-ups of that Church thought of trans-substantiation as symbolically true, but taught it as though it were literally true. She believed that anyone brought up in an atmosphere of deceit must acquire a deceitful nature. It was impossible to trust a Roman Catholic. She distrusted those of her own class, especially doctors, and never thought as I did that she had merely found for herself a reason to explain the gap she so much wished to close between her ways and those of the people of Woodbrook.

My grandmother, a Scottish Presbyterian, not devout but rather gentle by nature, used to say without humour or shame that all the Irish should be hanged. A magistrate of Roscommon during Queen Anne's reign wrote that 'we shall never be safe and quiet till a wolf's head and a priest's head be at the same rate!'[1] In 1878 Lord Oranmore and Browne, that great enemy of his adopted country, said much the same thing in the House of Lords, but, wolves having been exterminated by then and priests protected, he proposed to hunt down the ordinary country people.[2]

I don't think the Kirkwoods knew much about the horrid legacy we had all inherited. English school books, or at least the ones I read as a boy, glossed over the atrocities of the Penal Laws or at best described them as over and done with, like the rack and thumbscrew, curiosities of a barbarous age. But the sins of the fathers can never be over and done with. The deceitfulness which Ivy saw in the Irish was a form of defence adopted by their fathers against one of the most brutal systems of oppression in the history of mankind, a defence that had become unnecessary and unconscious. I don't mean that the early Christians, the Huguenots, the Swedish Catholics, the witches, or the Jewish and gipsy peoples of my own time suffered less, but in most other religious persecutions I have read of the oppressors were in the majority. A long-lasting system was not needed, so the bout of sadism died out and though it might be succeeded by another its memory would be diffused among the scattered victims.

Charlie's authority over the little populace of Woodbrook was quite unconscious. For an army man his sense of discipline was faint. The only military exploit I ever heard him boast of was the peacetime ambush of a railway train loaded with hay intended for another regiment which he quickly captured for his own. But his forebears for nearly three hundred years after their arrival in Ireland had regarded themselves not as settlers but as a garrison in a hostile land, and even he and his friends, now subjects of the Irish Free State, felt unmixed loyalty to

England. When they spoke of the English they said 'we', unlike Canadians or Australians who had been in their new countries less than half the time. They wielded the moral power of a dominant race long after their legal powers had gone. They were feared by the natives and did not even know it.

So the source of Ivy's distrust was distinct from religion or class, though both fed the stream that was to swamp her. If she had married a Suffolk gentleman farmer she would have been shocked by the closely shut-in manner of the workers and their wives and children who will never commit themselves in speech and use silence or evasion with unconscious skill. If she had married a Highland landlord in Scotland she would have been annoyed and amused by the way people make appointments they know they cannot keep from a desire not to offend. But in Ireland such attitudes had been adopted longer ago as a matter of life or death. Dispossession and death by starvation were the consequences of the Penal Laws.

The first of these was enacted soon after the Treaty of Limerick which began with the assurance that 'the Roman Catholics of this Kingdom shall enjoy such privileges in the exercise of their religion as are consistent with the laws of Ireland, or as they did enjoy in the reign of Charles II' and went on to say that 'their Majesties . . . will endeavour to procure the said Roman Catholics such further security as may preserve them from any disturbance upon account of their said religion'.

Their Majesties were William and Mary, the Protestant rulers of England, exceptionally tolerant, whose parliament later violated the Treaty by an Act forbidding Catholics to sit in the parliament of Ireland which, thus freed from opposition, devised the rest of the Penal Code. Catholics were deprived of the vote, excluded from almost every profession, even from humble jobs such as constable or gamekeeper. They were not allowed to join the army or navy but had to pay towards the cost of the militia twice the tax paid by the Protestants. They could not pursue any trade outside their native cities and an exorbitant charge imposed on them but not on Protestant tradesmen put many of them out of business altogether. They were forbidden to move for any purpose to the important mercantile towns of Limerick and Galway. No Catholic could buy land, hold a lease of longer than thirty-one years, take out a mortgage or annuity.

As these laws applied to the whole population except a scattered few it is easy to see how they helped to destroy the economy of Ireland. The export to England of cattle, sheep, pigs, beef, mutton, pork, bacon, butter and cheese had been stopped in Charles II's reign. Irish ships were well placed for carrying goods to America but that trade was soon stifled too by an amendment to the Navigation Acts excluding Ireland from the shipping monopoly she had shared with England. The end of her overseas commerce came in 1696 by a law which prohibited all imports from the colonies unless they came in English ships via England.

Nations can recover from economic depression more quickly than from degradation of the spirit. In the eighteenth century it was possible to survive without owning a horse or wearing a sword, but the humiliation was deep. No Catholic could own a horse worth more than £5 and if a Protestant saw him with one he was entitled by law to stop him in the road, pay him £5 for it and leave him to walk. If such were the law in England now against Protestants' tractors, cars and lorries, trade would collapse but the angriest man would probably be the owner of a sports car or a Rolls. So it was in Ireland. Hundreds lost their means of earning a living and many of the rich were publicly shamed. At Mullingar, the largest town between Woodbrook and Dublin, on the Dublin road, a gentleman's carriage and pair was stopped by a Protestant who held ten pounds in his hand. The owner got out, with a pistol in each hand, which he also possessed in defiance of the law, and shot both horses dead. After that he drove scornfully in and out of Mullingar in the same carriage drawn by bullocks. In 1741, a book on the 'Enlargement of Tillage' refers to 'the rich Papists who have withdrawn themselves to other countries out of resentment, because the legislature would not permit them to carry arms'. A licence could be obtained, but only by individual petition to the Government and Privy Council who usually refused to grant it even to the great. Lord Gormanston and Richard Barnwell Esquire were arrested and indicted for wearing swords when they went to pay their respects to the judges and gentlemen at the County Meath Assizes. Yet to have appeared without swords would normally have been taken as an insult like not wearing a tie at a modern levee but more embarrassing than that, for the sword was indispensable not only to proper dress but as a mark of rank. Craftsmen and merchants were degraded and had to seek unskilled work, and the huge majority of Catholics – labourers and small farmers – were treated with contumely and physical abuse against which there was no legal redress.

The intention to demoralize the whole native population, the descendants of kings and of serfs, musicians, poets, scholars, teachers, artisans and workmen, was implicit in the Penal Code and publicly avowed.

Of all the people the country poor and small tenants such as Nanny Maxwell's ancestors were the most oppressed. Lord Chesterfield, who as Lord Lieutenant of Ireland in 1745 studied social conditions thoroughly, wrote that 'the poor people in Ireland are used worse than negroes by their lords and masters'. Arthur Young, who knew so much about the poor of England and was himself a Suffolk landowner, did not question the hard dividing lines that kept each class in its place, but was shocked by what he saw in Ireland. 'Speaking a language that is despised, professing a religion that is abhorred, and being disarmed, the poor find themselves in many cases slaves ... A landlord in Ireland can scarcely invent an order which a servant, labourer or cotter dares to refuse to execute. Nothing satisfies him but an unqualified submission.' He writes of the frequent use of canes and horsewhips. 'Knocking down is spoken of in the country in a way that makes an Englishman stare.'[3]

The most humiliating form of punishment is castration. One of the cardinal rules of persecution is break the mind as well as the body. What other motive would the Irish Privy Council have had in proposing to castrate unregistered priests of a Church that insisted on celibacy? The punishment had been in force in Sweden against Jesuits for several years. The English Parliament, often less ferocious than its Dublin underling, deleted the 'Castration clause' of the Bill Against Papists and put back an earlier suggestion from Dublin that unregistered priests should be branded on the cheek with a large 'P'. The Irish Parliament could not amend a bill after it had been returned from England but they could reject it as a whole, and because their House of Lords objected to some clauses about property this one did not become law. But it shows in one piece the hatred and cruelty of the government and its few but powerful supporters, amongst whom in a small way were the Kirkwood family.

Chapter Nine

In a different way I too was afraid of the Anglo-Irish – not of Charlie but his wealthier neighbours. I felt lost and shy in their huge and heavily furnished houses. However kind and friendly they might be, their public-school manners and clipped English speech kept me silent or made me burst out with a stupid remark, trembling in confusion. I have never made friends with an Englishman of that class and cannot imagine falling in love with one of their daughters. Their toneless speech makes it difficult for them to communicate even with each other. Its lack of rhythm does not suit warmth of feeling. Americans laugh at it and people of other nations think them impersonal and cold. Charlie spoke like an Irishman. Phoebe had inherited the softness of his speech, a little of his accent and all her mother's informality.

We often used to visit Rockingham, the nearest large demesne. Its nearest gatelodge – there were five, I think – was at Ardcarne by the church the Kirkwoods went to every Sunday, bringing me with them when I would go; but if you wanted to go down the most beautiful roadway in the country you had to enter by the main gate half a mile farther on and turn into the Beech Avenue, a tunnel of leaves in summer, a lovely long way lined by strong old beeches between which you saw acre upon acre of rich pasture wooded here and there. At the end of it Rockingham House came into view, a splendid house, built on rising ground beside the lake, of the most hideous architecture conceivable. Its portico had an unnecessary flight of wide stone stairs and an array of pseudo-Greek pillars that carried between them less weight than the wall Ivy had knocked down. On one side was a conservatory, well glazed and preserved, and ugly only because it was too tall for its length and breadth. The walls of the house, hugely solid and built of local limestone, towered above the park like some top-heavy mausoleum in a green graveyard.

I was astonished when I read of it as one of Nash's most beautiful houses, and so may he have been if he ever saw the changes that were made in it ten years after its completion. About 1805, Robert King, the first Lord Lorton, had commissioned him to build it and he went to Ireland to supervise the work. Four or five years later, he had created a beautiful two-storied house with a central dome, which made sense of the Ionic portico. But in 1822 Lorton, jealous of his brother's taller house at Michelstown, added two more storeys, and took away the dome, presumably because he could not find a way of sticking it on top.

But of course the site remained, and the windows gave access to all views that could have been seen by anyone standing on that high piece of ground. The views of the land and the lake – Lough Key with its many wooded islands – are beautiful. People travel miles to see them nowadays. From inside the house one could see them then, and that was the only agreeable thing about it – its tall wide windows which gave so much light to the rooms the King-Harman family occupied.

Their servants lived in what seemed to me to be a dungeon specially made for them.

An anonymous eighteenth-century book[1] says that it was 'not unusual in Ireland for the great landed proprietors to have regular prisons in their houses for the summary punishment of the lower orders'. The basement of Rockingham was not built for that purpose. It was no worse to live in than the attics and basements occupied by London servants but it was literally under ground, parts of it being roofed by lawns and flowerbeds. Nash built it on the site of an eighteenth-century house that had been burnt down. He may have based his idea on prisons he found in the old foundations, but his intention was merely to keep mess out of sight. Fuel brought across the lake in boats could be unloaded below the view from the windows and wheeled under the house through a tunnel. Goods came in by land through another tunnel whose entrance was a hundred yards away. Servants came and went through another dark tunnel and the whole arrangement appealed to young men in my time. Rockingham was known for miles around as a great place for girls.

The basement appealed very much to Isaac Weld who visited Rockingham about 1830.

'One of the most striking features of the house consists in its perfectly insulated position, no office of any kind being visible, but the whole being surrounded by smooth, shorn grass interspersed with beds of flowers and ornamental walks. This arrangement has been effected by having most of the offices of the basement story covered over, and subterranean passages carried from underneath the eminence on which the house stands, towards the stables, which stand at a considerable distance screened by trees; the covered passage however does not reach the whole way to the latter, but merely far enough to prevent the appearance of movement near the mansion.'[2]

This description remained true a hundred years later when I first went to tea there, and even to the smooth shorn grass it showed a continuity rare in Ireland, but it also shows how the landowners wished to keep apart from the people who served them.

The stables had survived the fire and kept their eighteenth-century beauty. They were shaped like the buildings of an Oxford quadrangle, large enough to turn a coach and four in, and I envied the stablemen who lived there with their families, whose windows looked out on the cobbles always swept and weeded and on the half doors of horse-boxes. The paintwork and whitewash were bright. I seem to remember pots of flowers on the upper windowsills but Irish countrymen seldom have flowers so perhaps it was a creeper. The entrance was a long archway underneath the upper storey, and could be completely closed with great wooden doors cut exactly to fit which, like the shining padlocks on the stable doors, seemed to me to be a sign of unnecessary fear. But as to the padlocks, I did not then know the dangers racehorses are subject to. The King-Harmans bred thoroughbreds. Opposite the entrance there was another gated archway, identical in strength and shape, which led to the old coach house. The loft above it was surmounted by a clock tower, delicate and somewhat French to look at. The clock was always right.

I have never liked the jumpy nature of thoroughbreds, their quick temper and sudden fears, but they were beautiful to watch, especially the lithe yearlings and the brood mares, and their foals who could run as fast as their mothers on slender legs that looked too long for their bodies. Phoebe loved them and her father spent hours by the stables and paddocks, often in the rain, listening to Cecil King-Harman or his racing friends. I remember him admiring, almost enviously, one brood mare and a bay yearling whose name I have forgotten that won several races later. Perhaps he thought sadly of the days of The White Knight. But it is likely that by the private chapel, a high, blunt edifice between the house and stables, and in the tidy stable yard, among aristocratic bloodstock and humble-seeming men, he dreaded Rockingham, as I did, with admiration and respect, and loved Woodbrook where the sounds and smells of the stables came in by the windows all the time.

I have never heard anyone say anything against the Kirkwoods or King-Harmans of the twentieth century. People spoke of them as good landlords and I found out what a compliment that was only gradually, for in England a country landowner may be popular or not but his conduct is controlled by tradition and law. When Irishmen described a good landlord they always said, 'There were no fights in our district', referring to fights between rent-collectors and tenants.

Landlords and their agents (who were often Irishmen) invented and imposed their own punishments. Rockingham was no exception. As late as the 1870s, during the last of the mass evictions, the King-Harman tenants who resisted were given a privately invented punishment which no court would have allowed. The offenders were forced to carry farmyard manure to the field in creels wearing only a shirt and trousers. The creel is woven out of hard and spiky osiers and can be fitted with shoulder-ropes like a rucksack. Manure drips all the time. After that they were brought to the big house and flogged, then locked up without food for a day before they were released.[3]

It was a dominion more lawless, if not more cruel, than that of the ancient kings of Connaught whose descendants lived nearby – the Mac Dermots and the O Conors. With their English connections and loyalties these families seemed to me no different from the rest of the gentry, but in the minds of the local people they were different. Their rights of possession were not questioned and their relationships with workmen and tenants were more intimate.

The funny thing to me was that one of them, Mac Dermot, an old friend of the Kirkwoods and the King-Harmans who came to meals frequently at Woodbrook and Rockingham, had the only real title deeds to both estates at home as he sat there talking. Not that he would have wanted either back; the remnant Cromwell had allowed his ancestors to keep had accrued enough debts already. He had a mild and humorous face and I learned years later that his name, *mac Diarmuda*, means 'son of the man without envy'. His proper title was The Mac Dermot, Prince of Coolavin. He lived at Coolavin, a mountainous place by Lough Gara, to which his family had retreated when their richer lands were confiscated in the seventeenth century. His other title, Mac Dermot of the Rock, derived from Rockingham – a principal part of the lost rich lands. The Rock was an island on the lake a few hundred yards from the house where we used to picnic in the ruins of a castle built by Timothy Mac Dermot in 1204.

Both The Mac Dermot and The O Conor Don (brown [haired] O Conor) were descendants of Hermon who was elected King of Ireland in A.D. 74. The O Conors, chosen kings of Connaught since the second century, were the grander of the two families, and The O Conor Don I knew let everyone know it. He had some reason for his pride, for as late as 1779, when Arthur Young visited his forebears, people were still paying tribute in money and kind as though he was still their king.

Very few old Irish Catholic families had been able to hold on to any land at all. I am not implying that those who did treated their people well, merely that the people's attitude towards them was one of natural acceptance. They found it easier to manage their estates than the kindest, most progressive of the

Anglo-Irish landlords. The newer landowners were treated with politeness, often with affection, but no one forgot that they were parvenus who had usurped the master's seat. The Chief Irish are taken for granted.

Most of them left the country at the time of the Penal Code. Dispossessed and barred from all professions, they had no hope. There was nowhere for the education of their children. The reward for the discovery of a Catholic schoolmaster or private tutor was £10;[4] they were forbidden to send their children to schools on the continent or to any university. If a Catholic father died, his children were placed in the custody of the State which either appointed a Protestant guardian, often a stranger to the family, or removed them from their mother's care. Two English gentlemen whose *Tour through Ireland* was published in 1748 called on the Cavanaghs of Borris soon after the death of the master of the house. They wrote of his son, 'The minor of a Roman Catholic, left so by the death of his father, is accounted the heir of the Crown and the Lord Chancellor for the time being is appointed his guardian, in order to bring him up a Protestant; and this young gentleman is now in Westminster School for that purpose.'[5] Unhappiness in families was increased by encouraging children to inform upon their parents and on teachers and priests who carried on working in secret, and most of all by the law which enabled the eldest son to become heir-at-law to the whole of his father's estate simply by declaring himself a Protestant convert. He could reduce his father to the position of life-tenant and deny his brothers any part in the inheritance.

The dispossessed landowners who remained in Ireland became powerful outlaws. Some lived just outside their old estates or in the mountains above looking like beggars but keeping a kingly authority over the people, especially in Connaught where the clan feeling survived. Of course, they would not work. They led bands of smugglers and wreckers and continually raided their successors' cattle. The Sheriff of Galway, in 1709, did not dare leave the city towards the west, and in 1747 its governor wrote of Robert Martin, 'a most dangerous murdering Jacobite', that he could bring in twenty-four hours to the gate of Galway eight hundred villains as desperate and as absolutely at his devotion as the Camerons of Lochiel.[6] Co. Sligo, where the Mac Dermots lived, and Roscommon, our county, both bordered on Galway and were said at that time to be almost as dangerous to the civil authorities.

Chapter Ten

Harvest and haymaking are the happiest times on a farm. The work is urgent, and the result of a whole year's labour, some of it boring, is visible in one exciting piece. The weather is beautiful in most years and a rainy day a holiday which gives stiff muscles a rest. When we were bringing home the hay from the meadows, Phoebe and I gave up lessons and spent days together from morning to dusk on the shifters. In her linen sunhat and old breeches, leaning back into a load of hay as though it was a cushioned chair, she could drive through the narrowest gate as neatly as any of the men, but loading the shifter was too heavy for her, which was why we kept together. In Ireland, as in the wetter parts of Great Britain, hay cannot be brought in from the ground and stacked. It is left for some time to dry in the field in cocks. The hay-shifter was a low cart with small wheels covered by a platform edged at the back with zinc as sharp as a knife. You had to tip the platform by pulling a lever, back the horse until the zinc edge, scraping over the ground, inserted itself beneath the edge of the haycock, clasp two steel cables round the cock and winch it up on to the platform by winding a heavy iron handle. When she was young, Phoebe used to try to wind the handle, then get cross and crosser still when I came to help her. Then, without a word, she would drive back to the stack-yard as fast as she could make her horse walk and return trotting, making me pull up with my load on the narrow roadway to let her pass. And then, in the meadow, she would have to wait for me to help her with her next load. But mostly it was gay and loving. If ever I am in grass country now at haytime, especially when there is an evening mist, I remember my love for Phoebe with intensity.

Her father worked at the hay too. I was with him by the

stacks one afternoon when a messenger came from Ardcarne vicarage, the Protestant one, and said that the parson wanted him. 'What about?'

'It is a matter of Colonel Kirkwood's grave, Major. Parson MacCormack and Father Martin are above in the graveyard now.'

Charlie knew what it was about. He asked James to get the car out and went into the house for a bottle of whiskey. His uncle's foot was sticking out into the Catholic part of the grave-yard. The bother of digging him up had been a threat for years. When he reached Ardcarne, he found the parson and the priest seated gloomily on the grave. They discussed 'the matter' there for some hours, all three, with the whiskey, and agreed by nightfall that old Uncle Tom's foot should remain where it was.

The parson and priest consulted each other frequently. The Government of the Irish Free State had decreed religious tol-eration in 1921 and it seems to have succeeded. Even the Prot-estant shopkeepers had long since given up excluding Catholics from their staff. Of course they could not have found enough Protestants, which must have helped. But when I left England I was told to be careful not to mention politics or religion. I tried this at first, but conversations on those subjects were so popular and funny that only a mute could have kept out of them. No one warned me about the dangers of speaking about the pos-session of land.

One morning, in my first August at Woodbrook, I was lean-ing against a wall in the cow-yard waiting with Tom Maxwell and others for the dew to leave the oats. It was often ten or eleven before the fields were dry enough to harvest and we gathered in the cow-yard and talked and messed about. Tommy said that the English were damned and taking that in a secular sense I did not care whether they were damned or not and told him so and that I was Scottish anyway. But I was damned too, he said. All Protestants were. However well they behaved on earth, they could not get to heaven, only to purgatory at the best and most of them to hell for the terrible crimes they con-tinued to commit of which he mentioned some that had been reported lately in the papers.

It astonished me to hear him talk as if serious crime did not exist in Ireland. He believed there had been in Ireland no rape, no murder, no abuse of children in his or his father's time. Of course, he did not count as murder the killing of landlords, so common in the nineteenth century – that seemed to him the only way people had of getting justice done – nor deaths in rebellion and war, but even so I denied what he said and we became angry and had an argument which we resumed at rest times in the harvest field all day. We were about the same age, eighteen, and neither of us knew much. I would admit no link between religion and lack of crime, swore that in proportion to the population there were as many murders in Ireland and that if there were fewer it was only because there were fewer provocations in a mainly rural community. I have since discovered that what he said was true with few exceptions. In Co. Leitrim, across the lake from Woodbrook, where there are coal, iron and slate industries, there has not been a murder since 1903. Co. Roscommon had long been free from murder too. But on 3 September, about a week after our argument, a man was found shot dead by the gate of his farm only twenty miles away. I felt inclined to speak smugly to Tom. It was as though I had caused it to prove my point. But I did not speak. Like everybody else he was deeply affected. The most terrible cirumstance was that, although the body was found before midnight perhaps with some life in it, no one sent for a priest until four in the morning. They did not send for a doctor either, but I cannot remember anyone mentioning that. Everyone in the county, including the Civic Guards, knew who had shot the man. They also knew why, and reading of the lengthy court proceedings week by week in the *Roscommon Herald* they laughed at the lawyers' struggles to find a motive for the crime.

John McDermott, who was killed at close range by two shots from a double-barrelled gun, had lived with his younger brother, Patrick, and his sister, Kate, on a forty acre farm which his father had left to him. Both parents were dead. His father had made a proviso in the will requiring him to pay the brother and sister £100 each, which would have been enough to set Patrick up on a farm of his own and to give Kate a dowry. The farm did not do well and from the day of his father's death

John knew that his only hope of raising the £200 was to get married and pay them out of his bride's dowry. But he had asthma. No girl's parents would consider him, and to marry without the parents' consent would be to forgo any form of marriage portion. The asthma made him often unfit for heavy work. He relied more and more on Patrick's labour.

Patrick shared one of the two bedrooms in their house with his sister. He lived like a slave, with no pocket money even, and no chance of changing his life, no hope of getting married; without land that could not be. There was nothing but to wait until his brother's old age and death. The saddest parts of his long sad trial are about tobacco. An hour before he shot his brother he asked him for some, and got it. In the early morning, after shooting him, he asked a neighbour for a cigarette and got what was left of a whole packet. He had never had any money of his own to spend.

It was time to cut the oats – a Saturday. John said they would make a start on Monday. There was one more day's cutting to be done on their uncle's farm, then their uncle would be free to help them. John went to the uncle's for the day and Patrick stayed at home to gather potatoes that lay exposed on the ridges, unearthed by crows. The oats depressed them both. It had been battered by rain and parts were lying on the ground, another easy feeding place for crows. There were only two families that Patrick might approach for the loan of a gun, but as everybody knew he had never handled one before he had to wait till the man of the house was out. He went first to the schoolmaster's wife and she said 'no', severely. Then to his cousin's wife. He told her how he had just picked up a hundredweight of potatoes the crows had exposed and that there would be nothing left of the oats by Monday. She lent him the gun and three cartridges, but said, 'Be careful, Paddy, there's something wrong in that gun.' He answered, 'I'll be careful.'

He had one practice shot in the oatfield which puzzled his cousin who heard it far away on the bog where he was working. The next two shots that anybody heard that day came just before midnight, and Jack's body was found soon afterwards at the gateway of their farm.

Patrick's conduct after the murder was naïve. He woke his cousin up in the early hours of the morning to return the gun, told some of the neighbours that he had done this and others that he had taken it back early in the evening, immediately after shooting at crows. When the Civic Guard asked him, 'Why did you bring back the gun to your cousin and waken him so early on a Sunday morning?', he answered honestly, 'I was afraid if it was found in our house, someone might think I shot my brother.' He went with the Guard to search the field for the three cartridge cases. They only found one, his practice shot, and he said boys must have picked them up and that he had seen strangers walking by. But what boys could go unquestioned in that tiny scattered group of houses, and what stranger pass unnoticed by the other people?

The coroner's inquest was held by candlelight in the McDermott's kitchen. Witnesses were called in one by one and not allowed to hear what the other said. Patrick had muddled things up, as most people innocent or guilty do, by telling his cousin that he was on a chair by the fire when he heard the shots at midnight, and telling the Guards that he was sitting outside on the windowsill.

The funeral procession left their house next day accompanied by many Guards, who overheard quiet talk. At about a mile from the cemetery, Patrick Muldoon overtook Patrick McDermott and said he had heard his sister Kate make her statement at the inquest.

'Did she say that I was at the window?'

'She did.' It was a long way to the cemetery and Muldoon said, 'It is a wonder you did not bring your bicycle with you.'

'I didn't because the Guards are following me up.'

After the funeral, Kate said to her brother, 'You didn't cry at all, Paddy.' And as the crowd began to disperse he was arrested. He was taken to Galway Jail, one of the most dismal of Ireland's ancient buildings, as sordid perhaps as our nearest hospital, the one in Boyle, and there he waited for his trial at the Central Criminal Court in Dublin.

Just as prosecuting lawyers describe every murder they deal with as the most brutal that ever happened, policemen try to show that the accused man is heartless. This affects juries and cannot be proved. The Guard who first examined the body said that Patrick stood by a little way off, smoking a cigarette – as though that was an unusual thing to do when worried. He asked Patrick whether he could think of a reason why his brother should be shot, and Patrick said, 'It might be done for robbery; he was known to carry money.' This turned against him too, for the Guard searched the dead man's pockets and found two pound notes, a shilling and a sixpence, which was in those days a large sum for anyone to carry about with him. The motive was not robbery.

The prosecution, gleaning gossip from the local Gardaí, spent a lot of time suggesting that the murdered man and his young brother were jealous of each other about a girl. This too struck everyone who knew the ways of the country people as absurd.

In those days, I used to believe the verdicts given in murder trials. I was not aware, as we all are now, of the many cases after which the wrong person was hanged, nor of the fact that only an eye-witness can know the truth, and that he may not say it. There was no witness. Patrick McDermott protested his innocence from the start and jumped to his feet in the dock at the end, crying out, 'I never did the crime. I am innocent!' Yet many of his neighbours, including his cousin, believed he did it, and believed they knew why.

I read about the case on and off for months and thought his family situation unique. The motive for murder, if he did it – hunger for land or at least for the £100 which could have brought him to America – was unheard of by me, and it was years until I knew how common a cause of quarrel it was, how often men worked at home for their father or elder brother until they were fifty or sixty, how often a bitter dispute arose about rights of possession. At the Boyle Circuit Court that same September there was another case that struck me as extraordinary. A man was sent to prison for breaking into his brother's house and turning him out by force. He had been convicted four times during the past few years for the same thing. As soon as he was released he did it again and he could not understand why the law was on his brother's side.

Patrick McDermott was hanged in Dublin on 29 December. It was the first execution since the end of English rule so they had to send to England for a hangman. In the early morning a crowd of about a hundred gathered outside Mountjoy prison and prayed in the rain, and some displayed a curious mixture of humanitarian feeling and national pride. They held banners with the inscriptions, 'Pierpoint, a British hangman, hangs Irishman. Is this freedom?' and 'British hangman destroys Irishman. Abolish the system and abolish crime.'

Chapter Eleven

During the oat harvest which, if the weather was good, came after the last of the hay had been brought home, I worked with Phoebe too. I remember her bright cotton shirts, a red one and a blue one, against the stubble and her lightness and long legs and our intense enjoyment, the papery sound of grain on straw, its brittle dusty smell, the sweaty horses, blue carts with orange painted shafts and wheels, but I cannot now distinguish the ways in which we did our work from year to year during the ten years we were near each other. I think she used to lead the horse when she was eleven or twelve and stand on the cart building the load when she grew older. I usually 'pitched' – that is pitched the sheaves up on to the cart with a two-pronged fork. The straw, tightly bound, worked like emery-paper on the prongs making them shine after months of rust and the long ash handle had been polished smooth by many hands. But at its top, against the grain, there was a rough place which made blisters on the palm of my unworkmanlike hand. There was a skill which I had learned in boyhood of placing the sheaves in the handiest position for the man who was building the load, the grain heads towards the centre, row by row as if building a house. If you did this properly, he had only to move them a little and press them down, building up the heart of the load now and then in a criss-cross pattern which he stood on. But when I was young in Scotland I used to lead the horse, as Phoebe did at first and Tony after she had been promoted.

Before the days of combine harvesters, stooks of corn were set across the fields in even rows to dry in the wind and sun. When they were ready a boy or girl led the horse from stook to stook and kept it still while the cart was being loaded. In Scotland this last stage of harvest was called 'leading'. 'We'll start leading on Monday, God willing,' people said. Older horses would move and stand at a word of command. Carnaby, the Woodbrook bay, was willing to do this, perhaps because he had splints which made him a little bit lame, but Jim a gigantic grey horse, mild but impatient, had to be led because he snatched a mouthful of oats whenever he could, shaking the sheaf apart, and greedily moved on towards the next stook before we were ready. Phoebe led him. He sometimes rested his chin on top of her head and often knocked her over by nuzzling her with his nose.

The man on the cart needed more skill than us. If he built the load lopsided, it would fall off on the bumpy journey over hillocks and ruts to the stackyard. I have only once seen this happen and that was when I had built it myself. It is my misfortune to remember distinctly only the shameful moments in my life. The long happy periods survive diffused. And so it is that when I think of bringing home the oats, every detail of that incident is clear. I was riding on top of the load, of course, and fell with it to the ground, twisting my shoulder, hearing laughter, jeering but pretending to be friendly. Tom, who had pitched that load to me, got up on the cart, and I pitched the same sheaves back to him, but now they were entangled in a muddle on the grass. It took three times as long and my shoulder hurt.

I wish I could remember as distinctly one happy incident in bringing home the oats. Almost all was happiness. I remember that much in a general way. Every load we brought into the stackyard was like the end of an act of creation and the last load, the end of the harvest, conquest of weather, redemption of accidents, the consummation of all. Elated and set free we began at once to make ready for the Harvest Dance.

It was really Phoebe's birthday dance. The first one held at Woodbrook probably had nothing to do with the harvest, but as her birthday was on 12 September the day had to be changed from year to year to fit in with the end of the year's work, or very few guests would have been able to come. So it soon became known as the Harvest Dance, known in the four counties of Leitrim, Roscommon, Sligo and Galway. I knew one man who walked thirty-three miles to get to it in one day and thirty-three miles home when it was over. Some came in traps or on sidecars, a few on horses or sharing a motor-car or ass-cart – old people that is – but mostly they were young and had bicycles. The assembly of bicycles, traps and tethered horses, jennets, asses made it seem like a fair held at night.

The ballroom was the grain loft, a long low room that stretched the whole width of the yard above the stables and coach-house. Two casement and two beautiful circular windows looked out from it across the yard to the back of the house and kitchen door, and from the windows on the far side you could see the grass of Shanwelliagh among trees and the Hill of Usna beyond. The ballroom was whitewashed inside and out, its window frames and door pale green like all the paint-work of the stable yard. Its floorboards were wide and even, unpolished except by grain and marred at the corners, or where a knot had fallen out, by ragged holes gnawn by rats. The grain that was spread there after threshing, and turned over again and again till it dried, had nearly all been moved by September and put into bins in the storehouse. Before the dance we shovelled what was left into bags and carried it down on our shoulders, but however carefully we swept the floor there were always a few scattered grains on which the dancers skidded. We sprinkled soapflakes on the boards and arranged planks on boxes along the walls for people to sit on, with a few kitchen chairs for the old ones, whose only difficulty and fear was the steep wooden staircase outside – two flights of creaking steps, some of them rotten, that were the only way into the ballroom. The stairs were a terror to Ivy too, because on those warm nights, when the loft was thick with hundreds of people and the smoke of cut flake from dozens of pipes, as many as could would crowd on to the staircase for air, talking and laughing and pushing each other about in fun, and she thought the whole ancient structure would collapse and throw them in a heap on to the cobbles. We laughed at that and Charlie said from year to year that he would get Nolan, the carpenter, to make a new one next year, until one year it really did collapse. No one was much hurt and Jimmy and I built a concrete staircase in its place. It does not look so pleasant, but when I last saw it two years ago it was still firm.

The weather sometimes stopped us from fixing the date ahead. We would decide in the morning to have the dance that night. Tom, who was a good accordionist and leader of the band, would then be out most of the day on his bicycle gathering the players. One of the fiddlers lived at Ballyfarnan, seven miles to the north; and the best man on the squeeze-box, the old type of melodeon, at Croghan, five miles to the south. Drums and tin whistles were nearer. We would stop the Dublin–Sligo bus which passed Woodbrook gates at about two o'clock and tell the driver to spread the word along the Sligo road. The news would pass from farm to farm at dinner time. No private invitations were needed.

For Phoebe celebrations began with a children's party at about three o'clock. The outhouses and the wooded garden, sheltered from the north by a high but climbable stone wall, its shrubs, long grass and broken greenhouse were perfectly laid out for hide-and-seek. There was tennis, and swimming from the boat on the lake, and an immense tea, with ham, eggs, bread with thick butter and jam, small sticky cakes made by Winnie, and a birthday cake as wide as the wheel of a barrow into which for days beforehand she had put her energy and pride. The bread, both white and brown, was made by Winnie too, also the butter and jam. Only tea and sugar came from the shop. With both spare leaves inserted, the dining-room table extended from the lakeside window almost to the fireplace. Three double blankets were laid on it and covered by two of the largest white linen tablecloths, patterned with a glazed tracery of leaves and smelling of new starch, which like the highly polished silver teapots and hot water jugs showed Winnie's loving skill again, not a crease to be seen in her ironing, not a faded stain of old spilt tea. Aunt Nina's room was noisy with children and their parents, and Ivy, who believed in life after death, in the survival of the spirit of a person in the place where he or she had lived, once said to me that Nina must be pleased to find her room so filled that had been quiet and lonely for many years.

Meanwhile, one of the Maxwell brothers had taken a farm cart in to Carrick-on-Shannon to fetch a barrel or two of porter. Even with Jim, who walked faster than the other cart-horse, the three miles there and three miles back would take him five hours including of course one hour or more for loading. Its purchase and slow noticeable journey home to Woodbrook made another form of invitation to men working in roadside fields, and was also an inevitable invitation to the Civic Guards. I do not know whether the dance itself was illegal. Perhaps the Kirkwoods should have had a licence for one that welcomed many unknown guests.

It aroused the suspicious attention of the parish priest and the superintendent of the Gardaí. The priest, who never came, but fulminated in chapel the next Sunday, which was sometimes the next morning, against all dances and this one in particular, was impossible to coax. But the superintendent who sent two or three of his men could be set at ease next morning by their reports, because Charlie with the help of the Maxwells always invited them to sit in the coach-house where the barrels were concealed. Except for their uniforms, which inhibited them from dancing in the thundering loft above their heads, they were just like any other countrymen and would spend all night talking about hurling and cattle and racing. Once or twice they would walk out, attracted by an argument, and then sit down again. No arrest was ever made that I remember.

The Harvest Dance was a sensuous meeting between men and women, the more to be feared by the Gardaí and priest because in Ireland even linking arms was usually done in private. Men and women separated after each dance, the men gathering at one end of the loft and the women ranging themselves on the planks we had placed against the walls. But the closeness of so many bodies, the smells of soap, tobacco, snuff and all the best scents from the chemists of Boyle and Carrick, made everybody warm. To me, and I daresay to many, the smell of the refreshing ground mist rising from the meadows and the lake, and the perpetual rhythmic croaking of the corncrakes, was romantic and sad.

I never could dance very well. I was happy with Phoebe against me in my arms; she was so flexible, leading and giving; but most of the time she was dancing with strangers from far away or with Woodbrook tenants or workmen who, because it was her birthday and they liked her, sought her out. Often I found a pretty girl, much older than Phoebe, and nubile, and danced with her, but when the band stopped she would run from me, as the custom was, and sit down amongst the women. My dances with Phoebe are distinct in memory and so are those with Winnie, who smelt beautifully of her Sunday bath and glowed with excitement. Perhaps it was because of my hesitant way of dancing, annoying to all girls, that she gripped the thumb of my right hand in her left palm and drove me by a sometimes painful pressure round the ballroom.

About midnight the women began to carry trays of bread and butter and gallon pots of tea across the yard from the kitchen and place them on a makeshift sideboard – two doors laid flat on boxes – at one end of the loft. They brought out buckets of hot water for washing cups and saucers and handed the tea round in relays. The band went down to the coach-house and for an hour the floor was visible, dust settled and flickering shadows cast by paraffin lamps and candles moved about on the white walls. This was the first chance Ivy had of persuading Phoebe to go to bed, the second struggle of wills, for Tony had usually after much argument already been carried off. When Phoebe had said good night, we sprinkled the floor with new soapflakes and the dance began again.

It was clear to me now that I assumed a different character as soon as Phoebe had gone, or perhaps I should say that her absence from the ballroom dissolved that concentration of emotion upon her which held back the rest of me while she was there. Anyway, I know I behaved like a different person, not from a sense of relief that I was now unobserved by her or her parents who usually went to bed soon after her, but because I felt different.

Not only her being taken off to bed but her birthday dance itself was decisive for me, like rites of burial. I buried Phoebe every autumn. She became my Persephone. I revived her in London for a few weeks during the Christmas vacation, but only had ghostly encounters with her then – in London she had many interests that I could not share – and after a Twelfth Night party I buried her again until the spring. Her birthday dance was for me like an Irish wake, where gaiety with free tobacco, food and drink and many kinds of entertainment, including nuptial games, alleviate the agony of mourners.

Soon after it we took the boat out of the water and laid it upside down on logs above the flood line, and every year it seemed to me the last time I would help to lay it there. Then one morning, usually cold and bright, in the first week of October, we rode over the Hill of Usna, trying to pretend it was an ordinary ride, but we knew that the trunks were on their way to Carrick Station on one of the farm carts. We came home into the stable yard, dismounted and unsaddled, the children smelling their ponies' necks and kissing them, which secretly I did too, and went into the house for lunch. The hall was strewn with the small luggage which Ivy had packed while we were out. The dogs whined anxiously and lay down on suitcases, got up and barked and lay down again. The postman came, as he always did at lunchtime, with letters and yesterday's *Irish Times* in an oblong canvas bag. Each house had its own bag in those days with a little brass padlock and clasp, but the Woodbrook key had been lost long ago and ours was never locked. On the last day there were no letters to send and he took the bag away empty.

Departures and arrivals were made at the front door. Any other expedition in the Fiat, for shopping or visiting friends, began and ended in the stable yard outside the coach-house which now housed nothing except the car, the trap and Nina's old bathchair. And so on this occasion which happened as the leaves were fading only once a year James Currid, like an undertaker, shaved, put on the jacket of his going-to-Mass suit, and drove the Fiat, noisily crashing the gears, up the slope to the front door, turning it carefully, with awful melancholy lines beside his mouth until he had it facing the descent towards the Carrick road. Of course he always looked melancholy and was often anxious about a slight mishap, but when he was cleanshaven every expression of his face was exposed, and he never was cleanshaven on a weekday, except on this day of our departure. There were no Sunday trains.

When the suitcases and dogs were in the car, we got in and Charlie drove us to the station, Phoebe, Tony, Ivy and me. In some years he travelled with us, but usually stayed at Wood-brook and came to London only for Christmas. Outside the station we saw Jim, harnessed to his empty cart and tethered by rope reins to a telegraph pole. The children ran from the car to kiss him good-bye. The porter came and took the suitcases, and we climbed a high stone stairway to the platform, the dogs dragging this way or that, on leads for the first time for three months. Tommy Maxwell was on the platform smoking cigarettes beside the pile of trunks. The walls of the station were built of grey limestone blocks. There were no posters: only the name of the station Cora Droma Rúisc in Irish, and in smaller letters Carrick-on-Shannon – the Weir of the Back of the Marsh.

We heard the train approaching. It passed through a mile or two of the Woodbrook land before it suddenly whistled, hidden by a bend, and then appeared, braking sharply, its huge black engine emitting clouds of steam, its yellow carriages sliding past the platform as though they could not stop in time to pick us up. We were usually the only passengers to get on at Carrick and always the only ones for Dublin which with our piles of luggage and dogs delayed the train and inspired the guard, and stationmaster, both of whom knew Charlie well, with rather a self-conscious air of ceremony.

Charlie, in those early years, would often buy first-class tickets for us, saying they cost him nothing because the Great Western Railway was his only tenant to pay rent on the proper day, and the guard would unlock the first-class coach, a Victorian drawing-room on wheels, with moveable armchairs, upholstered upright chairs, a writing table, with a pewter vase of flowers screwed on to it, a Turkish carpet and a brass-handled door leading to a private lavatory. Then, when the family had said good-bye to Charlie – sometimes Phoebe cried and he took long to comfort her – we were locked in and remained locked in, as first-class passengers always were, until the train reached Broadstone Station, Dublin. But if the dogs showed signs of need we could call the guard through the window at Mullingar, the only long stop, and be let out for a minute or two to walk them on the platform.

For about five miles after Carrick, the railway runs near to the right bank of the Shannon, then at Drumsna it crosses the river and leaves the Province of Connaught, the old Irish Kingdom of the O Conors, the smallest and poorest of the four provinces, which Cromwell had tried to make into a native reservation, driving as many of the Irish as he could into its swamps and mountains. In those days, not knowing any other part of the country, I felt I had left Ireland when we crossed the Shannon. I had left Phoebe, although she was sitting beside me. My mind did not look towards London or Oxford. I was at a standstill while the train moved on.

Part Two

Chapter One

The Modern History course at Oxford began with the year 1495 and ended, I think, at 1914, the year of my birth. Between those years you could choose a special subject to study in detail and this was like an independent voyage of discovery after having been led this way and that at school by the conflicting opinions of teachers and writers of text-books. Historians are supposed to be impartial, but no one can be. In history a mere list of facts has no meaning. It is feeling and interpretation that count and if you try to understand the feelings of people of the past your sympathies and antipathies are engaged. That is what made Anglo-Irish history so interesting to me. No one can write about it unemotionally.

I chose as my special subject the Commonwealth of 1649–60. You cannot stay in Ireland even for a week without hearing Cromwell's name and naturally I sought out everything I could about his exploits there. He is as ubiquitous in legend as Queen Elizabeth's bed, burning down every Irish town, and torturing and killing the inhabitants. In fact he and his officers spread destruction widely but many violent acts attributed to him were done before he was born or while he was two or three years old. 'The curse of Cromwell on you!' was still a common form of vituperation in the early years of this century. I have never heard it myself but am told it is used even now in parts of the country.

People often say the Irish are peculiar in cherishing hatreds hundreds of years old. The truth is that nations who forget old injuries forget because industrialism has broken the traditional life of families and groups of farming families, and scattered their members singly in tenements, flats or solitary lodgings where no one can hear any more what his grandfather heard from his. Industrialized nations forget their old songs and music in the same way, the anecdotes of happy times, the stories told not written. Famine and near famine long ago are remembered even in England by miners, fishermen, farm workers – communities who keep to hereditary occupations – but the civil wars of the seventeenth and eighteenth centuries and the terrible injuries done to the factory workers of the nineteenth century are forgotten. Also, since nations took the place of baronies in the making of war the English have suffered less from the hands of an enemy than any of the peoples of Europe. The Irish have suffered as much or more than most. To understand the deep impression Cromwell made on their minds, one has to know a bit about what went on before. The story was glossed over or distorted in my schooldays, as were other disreputable aspects of English colonial policy.

The result of my ignorance was that when I first heard the Maxwells speak bitterly of England I was shocked and thought them unjust. The most that I could remember was that Ireland had always been a 'thorn in England's side', and I only remembered that because in my prep school days I wondered how a thorn could get into one's side. The only books I had then seen implied that Irish acts of violence were unique in savagery and that the series of rebellions from the sixteenth century onwards, and all the individual agrarian crimes that ended in a sort of guerrilla warfare in Victorian times, were committed without provocation by a despicable race. My father, who had fought alongside thousands of Irishmen during the Great War, as we then called it, never forgave their countrymen for 'stabbing England in the back' in 1916. He did not speak of the long story that led to the Easter Rising.

It was Lecky's *History of Ireland in the Eighteenth Century* that guided me towards the truth and I did not read that until after I knew Phoebe and the Maxwells. In its first few pages, I came across a memorable contrast to the image of the 'thorn'. He says of the Pale – Dublin and some seventeen square miles around it which until Elizabeth's reign was the only part of the country secured by English rule – that 'like a spearpoint in a living body it inflamed all around it and deranged every vital function.'[1] He shows how until the end of her reign English rule was confined as a reality to the narrow limits of the Pale, how it proved itself incapable of founding a central government and at the same time stopped anyone else from doing so. The Romans and the Normans had imposed their laws upon the English, their customs and cultures had been gradually absorbed, but the English lived in Ireland as a hostile separate nation for centuries, effectually preventing any of the native princes from uniting the tribes as Clovis had united Gaul.

There is evidence that the Irish would have accepted English rule and, in the more turbulent parts of the country, even welcomed it, but for the first four hundred years there was none and by the time Elizabeth imposed it it was too late, too sudden, and unjustly done. Pope Adrian gave Ireland to England at a much more opportune moment. He was angered by the independence of the Church there, which had always kept aloof from the rest of Europe, and told Henry II to conquer the island and keep it. The conquest was made at a time when reverence for rank had almost the strength of religion. National emotions did not exist and the presence of a supreme king who had won his authority by war was enough to make the lesser kings and almost all the princes, temporal and spiritual, submit. When King Henry went over to Ireland in 1172, they came long distances to do homage to him. He introduced the laws of England at a public assembly and allowed them the freedom of parliaments which were to be held in Ireland in the English manner, and before he returned to England a few months later he 'received letters from them with their seals pendant in the manner of charters, testifying they had ordained him and his heirs their king'.[2] But he never went back, nor did his heirs, except one or two of them on brief visits, and in those days royal authority depended on the physical presence of the king. Sworn fealty was sacred if sworn to the person from time to time and sealed by tribute exacted by his officers. But Henry II did not even appoint a viceroy, nor any single overlord. His only representatives were Anglo-Norman barons who made war on each other and on the Irish, just as the Irish chieftains had made war among themselves. Two hundred years later the English had not even begun to rule the country, and a series of desperate measures known as the Statutes of Kilkenny were enacted whose object was to separate the natives from the colonists once for all.

The Norman settlers had mixed with the Irish, adopted their customs and learned to speak their language. The Old English, as the other medieval colonists came to be called, mingled to such a degree that they were accused of becoming 'more Irish than the Irish'. The English of England feared them and attempted to enforce a policy of segregation as severe as the apartheid of present day South Africa. By the Statutes of Kilkenny, enacted in 1366, it was 'ordained and established that no alliance by marriage, gossipred, fostering of children, concubinage or by amour, or in any other manner, be henceforth made between the English and the Irish on the one side or on the other.'[3] ('Gossipred' means the relation of godparents.) Also, any Irishman found speaking to an Englishman could be indicted as a spy and found guilty even if the conversation was proved to be innocent. All these offences were classed with regicide as High Treason.

Irish people living among the English – that is to say within the Pale – whose status was something like that of the 'coloureds' of South Africa were forbidden to speak their own language or keep their Irish names.[4] The penalty for these offences was forfeiture of property or, if the offender had none, imprisonment until security was found, which might well be for life. There was even a law against the favourite Irish games of hurley and quoits, which the colonists had learned.

A strong government would have had difficulty in enforcing rules that interfered with everybody's habits. The Anglo-Irish government was weak, and the harm came not so much from the enforcement of the law as from the ill feeling created. The whole policy was inspired by fear and hatred.

'In Ireland there are three kinds of people,' wrote Richard II; 'wild Irish, our enemies; Irish rebels, the English who have thrown off their allegiance to the crown; and obedient English.'[5] The obedient English who ruled six of the counties of Ulster from 1921 to 1972 would say the same.

Though the Statutes of Kilkenny were slackly enforced, it

was possible centuries later for anyone possessed with spite against a neighbour to invoke a clause long left in abeyance and have his way. The most tempting clause was that which dealt with murder, a crime which by the old Irish law was punished by fines payable to the relatives of the murdered person and assessed in much the same way as damages are now. Under the Statutes of Kilkenny, the murderer of an Irishman was fined, but the murderer of an Englishman was put to death, and the actual outcome was that Englishmen murdering Irishmen were often not prosecuted at all. Donal O'Neil, King of Ulster, complained to the Pope that the English of Ireland 'differ so widely in their principles of morality from those of England and all the other nations that they may be called a nation of the most extreme degree of perfidy, lay and cleric they assert that it is no more sin to kill an Irishman than it is to kill a dog.'[6] A brother of the Bishop of Coventry – Brother Simon of the Order of Friars Minor in Ireland – declared 'that it is not a sin to slay an Irishman and that if he himself committed such a deed he would not on account of it refrain from celebrating Mass.'

When I was reading about Cromwell at Oxford I knew little of this heritage from the Middle Ages. Most books overstressed the religious aspect of his and Elizabeth's policies, and the Irish people I spoke to during the long vacations thought mainly of that, just as the unfortunate inhabitants of the Six Counties think of it now. But the Statutes of Kilkenny were re-enacted before the Reformation, by Henry VII, and again after it by Henry VIII. By that time their archaic provisions had begun to harm colonists and natives alike.

Intellectually, an incurable and permanent injury was done to the English colony long before religious distinctions began. The statutes excluded Irishmen from all seats of learning – from the English monastic houses and from the universities of Oxford and Cambridge – and so all hope was lost of establishing a class of natives who could have helped to administer English law or spread English culture. Materially, too, the colonial policy was negative. Even commerce between the two nations was stopped. The Irish could not buy or sell within the English settlements, nor establish fairs or markets of their own.

'Whereby it is manifest,' wrote Davies, referring to the whole of the segregation policy, 'that such as had the government of Ireland under the Crown of England did intend to make a perpetual separation and enmity between the English and the Irish, pretending no doubt that the English should in the end root out the Irish; which the English, not being able to do, did cause a perpetual war between the nations, which continued four hundred and odd years . . .'[7]

Davies was writing nearly fifty years before Cromwell came to power. In 1603, during a time of peace, it seemed to him that this perpetual war had come to an end; and in a sense he was right, for Queen Elizabeth was the first to conquer Ireland. After 1603 the English were able to regard the country as a unit and abolish Irish law. The wars of the next three hundred and twenty years can justly be called rebellions or wars of independence, there being at last a government to rebel against.

And Elizabeth did succeed in 'rooting out the Irish' from some districts for a time. The declared policy during her reign was to exterminate them. It failed for lack of money, but the inhabitants of the large provinces of Ulster and Munster were thinned out so successfully that one of her ministers was able to tell the queen that she had little left to reign over but ashes and carcasses.[8] In 1582, one of her officials reckoned that apart from deaths in battle or by hanging thirty thousand people had died from want of food in Munster within six months.

It is surprising to know that soldiers working by hand with steel and fire could devastate a country and starve civilians to death as efficiently as they do nowadays by spraying defoliants from the air. Of course, they could not deform unborn babies as we can now with herbicides such as 2, 4, 5T, but some manual techniques used nowadays are like the ones used then. The much publicized photographs of 1969 showing American soldiers burning Vietnam villages or throwing the villagers' stores of grain on to a fire show clearly the methods used in the depopulation of Munster. Year after year, unripe corn was cut down and ripe corn burnt, such cattle as the army did not need were killed or maimed, and long after resistance had ceased, men, women and children were hunted to death.

The ruin of Irish society came from the timing of the conquest, which coincided with a peak of Philistinism in Europe, a desire to get rich quickly by any means that had not had an outlet in the Middle Ages but was encouraged notably by the governments of England, Portugal and Spain. This was an aspect of the Renascence, a concomitant of the flowering of art which we remember better. It led the English to piracy at sea on an unprecedented scale and to the grabbing of Irish land. Elizabeth fostered both.

Early in her reign an attempt to settle Englishmen in Ulster had failed because each had to fight for the land he was offered, but in Munster the terrain was so throughly prepared that the settlers found themselves in a desert that needed years of reclamation. Between Dingle and Cashel, a stretch of about 125 miles, 'not the lowing of a cow nor the voice of the ploughman was that year to be heard.'⁹ Spenser, who took over an enormous confiscated estate, described how he saw the people who survived. 'Out of every corner of the woods and glens they came creeping forth upon their hands, for their legs could not bear them; they looked like anatomies of death; they spake like ghosts crying out of their graves; they did eat the dead carrions, happy where they could find them; and if they found a plot of watercresses or shamrocks, there they flocked as to a feast for the time, yet not able long to continue there withal; that in a short space there were none almost left.'¹⁰ Spenser says that 'any stony heart would have rued' such wretchedness, but he thought the queen's authority could not have been established by any other means and he recommended a detailed scheme of even greater severity for the starvation of the people of Ulster.

It was in 1586 that new colonists were invited to move in to this mortuary of men and animals and vegetation, this new waste land. Some of it was potentially rich and the daring who had money to invest succeeded in making large profits by restoring it, but it does seem surprising that men who were accustomed to English upper-class life, in which at that time literature, music, the theatre and all kinds of lively social intercourse were flourishing, could have chosen to live in isolation surrounded by such dreadful sights. During Spenser's youth in

Ireland cannibalism was not rare: people waited by the gallows till the executioners had gone, then cut down the corpses and cooked and ate them.

Some of the colonists never went to their estates it is true, but Spenser lived on his for years, several days' journey from London or weeks if the weather for sailing was bad. His friend, Sir Walter Raleigh, had large grants of land and went to live at Youghal for a time. Their conduct becomes understandable only if one remembers the versatility of such men then, their dislike of routine, their tolerance of hardship, their love for trying new things out and their commercial greed. Spenser was at work on *The Faerie Queene* when he decided to settle in Munster. We think of him as a poet but while he lived he was esteemed also for his skill in military and civil affairs, and for his clever dealing in abbeys, castles and manor houses which he bought and sold at a profit, always in Ireland.

The men who received confiscated land were called undertakers, which seems appropriate now, but of course the word had not acquired its present use. For some reason the government did not simply transfer property to the undertaker by edict. A legal reason for forfeiture had to be found in each case. This made the situation even worse for the old owners. Not one knew where he stood and all were helpless against a newly formed group of professional 'discoverers' – lawyers and informers who for a fee would trump up any case and ensure dispossession. In Munster nearly 900 square miles were confiscated, dozens of great land holders were executed on the flimsiest of pretexts and hundreds banished to the continent or driven into the mountains where they lived as outlaws bringing with them such followers and cattle as they could save. The permanent ill-feeling engendered in this way took root not only among the great, but in the minds of thousands of poverty-stricken people who had survived for generations on meagre patches of land. The poor had always been oppressed but had always had fixed rights, the most important of which was security of tenure. They were not tenants, in the English sense, who paid rent to a landlord. They were subject often to monstrous exactions imposed on them by their chiefs but the chief was not hereditary. He was elected by a system known as tanistry,[11] and they could never be evicted, because by Irish law they owned the patch of land they lived on. They were the humblest members of a co-operative system that dated in written and oral law from pre-Christian times. The English were not ignorant of this. They dismissed it as they dismissed and despised the Irish culture which also was never the possession of one class, but shared by the poorest of the poor. And in this they did their colonists the same irrevocable harm as they did to the Irish people. The evil lasted more than three hundred years and in the six counties of Ulster which remain attached to England it has not yet been undone. Sir George Campbell, one of the great administrators of the so much better managed British Empire in India, who died in 1892, said of the system of land tenure imposed on Ireland: 'This introduction of English law and of purely English courts was a cardinal mistake ... the law must constantly have run counter to the customs and practices of the country ... The legal rights of the Irish were extinguished and their lands confiscated.'[12]

The undertakers were required as a condition of their grants to settle a fixed number of English families per square mile on the land. They were forbidden to give tenancies to natives. The intention was to drive the survivors out altogether. But the plan did not attract sufficient numbers of the poorer English, and those who went refused to pay high rents. The Irish were used to a lower standard of living and were naturally anxious to keep their homesteads at any price. It was more profitable to let them stay and the government did nothing to enforce the rule against it.

The policy of segregation and forfeiture led, of course, to a renewal of the wars. But after the subjection of Ulster, by means as cruel and unstatesmanlike as those I have described, the whole of Ireland was subdued. There was less danger there from a successful rising of subjected people than there is in South Africa now, for they had not a continent of sympathizers behind them. But the colonists, even in peacetime, could never live at ease.

James VI of Scotland succeeded to the English throne as

James I in the very year of Ireland's subjugation – 1603. He was specially interested in Ulster, the north-eastern tip of which had been absorbing Scottish immigrants since the fifteenth century. Francis Bacon drew up a scheme for its plantation and under Sir John Davies' administration, as Attorney General, six of its nine counties became from a materialistic point of view the most successful part of the whole colony. Davies went north, accompanied by the Lord Deputy with an army, 'to persuade the natives that they had no right to their lands'.[13] But no war was necessary this time. The Ulster leaders had fled to Spain and, in the richer districts which the Scottish farmers took, the depopulation policy had succeeded. The western part of the province remained well populated with natives but for the first time in the history of confiscation some provision was made for them and those influential enough to be dangerous were for a time appeased. They were promised one-fifth of the whole province, and although they were to share this portion with the 'servitors' – the lower military and civil servants of the English Crown – at twice the price paid by ordinary Scottish and English settlers, they seemed for a time to accept their lot. Except for minor risings in 1608 and 1615, and the perpetual raids of the woodkernes – the outlaws and dispossessed who had taken to mountains and woods – Ireland was at peace for nearly forty years, from 1603 until the great rebellion of 1641. After the plantation of Ulster, Bacon wrote complacently, 'Ireland is the last of the daughters of Europe which hath come in, and been reclaimed from desolation to population and plantation, and from savage and barbarous customs to humanity and civilitie.'[14]

Chapter Two

It was in this time of peace, or at the latest during the rebellion of 1641, that the Kirkwoods came to Ireland. I may not have traced the first of them but in Charles I's reign one who bore the family Christian name 'Thomas'[1] married the daughter of a Scottish Presbyterian who had settled in Ireland. She was one of six children, the eldest of three girls all of whom were married before 1650, when their father died; which means that Thomas must have obtained a suitable place to bring her to during or before the most recent hand-out, in 1642, when officers were rewarded with houses and land for their part in quelling the rebellion. This Thomas Kirkwood probably lived near Sligo or across the county border near Killala, Mayo, where his in-laws, the Knoxs, who were rich to start with, soon became very grand indeed. Also there is an Andrew Kirkwood among Cromwell's 'Forty-nine Officers' or 'Forty-nine Lots'.[2]

Several Protestant families who became linked by marriage with the Kirkwoods were established near Boyle and Carrick-on-Shannon by that time. The English upper-class custom of adding matronymics to the surname helps one to trace old connections – Thomas Yaden Lloyd Kirkwood was Uncle Tom's full name, and Charlie's was Charles Home Kingston Kirkwood (the Earls of Kingston owned Rockingham at one time and are the ancestors of the King-Harmans).

The Lloyds acquired 1,200 acres at Croghan in about 1620, and their descendants were still there in Charlie's time. During the rebellion, John and Thomas Yeedon, or Yaden, took 200 acres on the shores of Woodbrook's lake, Lough Eidin, and the Hon. Chidley Coote[3] was presented, by his brother I guess, with the largest estate of all which included Woodbrook, Usna and the nearby village of Uachtar-Tire which he renamed Coote-

111

hall. These names are written in the Books of Survey and Distribution[4] beside the names of the Irish landowners who were turned out.

I think of all these Scottish, Welsh and English people sloshing about on their horses in the rain and sleeping miles apart from each other, knowing they were hated, under leaking roofs. But it is easy to see why they stayed. Some left accounts extolling the beauties of Ireland and even the hospitality of the Irish. Land and labour was cheap; in many places both could be had for nothing; and, as Bacon and Blenerhasset both pointed out, Great Britain was overcrowded and infested with unemployed, who were in those days called paupers.

In spite of the long distances that separated their houses, the colonists soon formed a closed-in community whose members intermarried in successive generations. I think – but of course it is an unproved thought – that they were even more closely tied together than the English in India in my father's or Charlie's time. One thing is certain – the marriages the Kirkwoods and their neighbours made were limited not only to the Protestants of Ireland, but to those of Connaught, their own province.

All these Connaught colonists obtained their land in circumstances peculiarly unhappy, even for Ireland. For the Irish of Connaught, unlike those of the other three provinces, had once been given hope.

In Connaught only, a fair land settlement had been planned in Elizabeth's reign, under the exceptionally wise rule of Sir John Perrott.[5] By what was known as the 'Composition of Connaught' he persuaded the Irish chiefs and Norman lords to surrender their estates to the Crown and receive them back under royal patent in return for rent and certain military duties. The peasants were also placed directly under the Crown either as freeholders or tenants. The object was to establish English rule without uprooting the people. James I renewed the patents thirty years later, exacting fees for the renewal, but soon afterwards, under pressure from would-be planters, the government sought and found a legal flaw and declared that the Connaught proprietors had no rights to their land after all.

A plantation similar to the plantation of Ulster was devised.

112

Hoping to escape that fate, the Connaught gentry offered to pay the Crown the purchase money it would have received from the planters. Then James I died and the scheme was abandoned, but still they had no legal title to their land. They offered Charles I twelve times the amount, if he would allow them certain 'graces' (favours) in return. These he agreed to. Arrangements were made to pay the money in three annual instalments; the royal promise was given, together with an undertaking that the next parliament held in Ireland would confirm the Connaught proprietors and their heirs in the secure possession of their estates.

'The sequel,' wrote Lecky,[6] 'forms one of the most shameful passages in the history of English government of Ireland. In distinct violation of the King's solemn promise, after the subsidies that were made on the faith of that promise had been duly obtained, without provocation or pretext or excuse, Wentworth, who now presided with stern despotism over the government of Ireland, announced the withdrawal of the two principal articles of the graces, the limitation of Crown claims by a possession of sixty years and the legalization of the Connaught titles.'

It was only the fear of rebellion that stopped Wentworth, better known now as the Earl of Strafford, from enforcing a plantation of Connaught on the Ulster plan, and yet his treacherous action there was one of the principal causes of the Irish rebellion in 1641. He had made it evident all over the country that a desire to root out the Irish still prevailed. English law, which had been quietly accepted for a generation, was proved in this and other cases to be a legal form of fraud. Religious toleration decreased. The army of occupation increased. No one – noble or peasant – felt secure. Strafford put paid to the dying hope that a successful colony could ever be established. Without knowing what he was doing he came near to making Ireland into a nation.

Queen Elizabeth had conquered an island of warring principalities, so divided amongst themselves that some of them fought on her side. The O Conors of Sligo, whose descendants the Kirkwoods of my day knew so well, became Elizabeth's most powerful Irish allies – and have never forgotten it if we are to believe a report in the *Irish Press* of 1939,[7] in which they claimed kinship to George VI. Grene O'Mulloy, of Uachtar-Tíre which we called Cootehall, fought for the English under Bingham in 1584 and is described as 'fiercer' than Bingham in killing prisoners of war. In 1599 at the Battle of the Curlews, the last great Irish victory, which happened six miles west of Wood-brook, the English troops stationed in Boyle under the command of Sir Conyers Clifford were supported by the Norman-Irish earls of Clanricarde, Thomond and Inchiquin, with thousands of Irish soldiers under their command. As for the O Conor Don, it was not until Clifford's head was sent to him by hand that he agreed to surrender his castle to his fellow country-men.[8]

Yet by 1641 all these powerful families had joined the rest of the Irish. Even the Old English of the Pale, even the O'Mulloys of Cootehall, joined the rebels. Strafford had watered the faltering seed of a united nation.

I have described so many horrors that I'll miss out details of the rebellion, except to say that the much written-of massacre of the English by the Irish never took place. The rebellion was fought out with unusual brutality on both sides and put down with the usual indiscriminate slaughter; crops, cattle, fishing-boats were again systematically destroyed and famine followed in many parts of the country as before; and during the uneasy peace between the truce of 1643 and Cromwell's invasion of 1649 enormous areas were plundered and terrorized by an un-disciplined army of occupation. Cromwell immediately checked such abuses. The success of his army in the English civil war was partly due to Puritanical discipline and when he became C.-in-C. of the army in Ireland one of his first acts was to prohibit looting.[9]

The real cause of his expensive and disastrous Irish war is hard to find. It is true that the Irish nobles acknowledged Charles II as King – Ormonde invited him to head the Irish forces – and that between them they were supposed to have at least 18,000 men. But this collection of small private armies was no real threat to the Commonwealth. It could never have remained under one command for long enough to attempt a successful invasion of England, and in Ireland it would have had little chance against the army of occupation which could have been augmented at short notice. Perhaps the cause was hidden in that dangerous mixture of war motives we now know so well – fear and greed strengthened by ideology. As a commercial enterprise backed by religious zeal it resembled the crusades and in the long run it was the zeal that did most harm. The immediate result – the reduction of the population by one third – would certainly be remembered to this day, but Cromwell was the first English leader to declare that his work was done in the name of the Protestants' God, and by that he founded a deep, lasting enmity. The piety of his description of the Drogheda (Tredah) massacre is typical:

'It hath pleased God to bless our endeavours at Tredah ... The enemy were about 3,000 strong in the town ... I do not think thirty of the whole number escaped with their lives. Those that did are safe in custody for the Barbadoes ... I wish that all honest hearts may give the glory of this to God alone, to whom indeed the praise of this mercy belongs ...'[10]

Military sentiments have not changed. 'O Liberty! Liberty! how many crimes are committed in thy name!' 'O Communism, O "Free" World ...!' Of the Cromwellian party, an American historian[11] wrote in 1939, 'In the midst of the fervid declarations of its members in favor of freedom of speech and faith and worship they had done their best to suppress all save their own, and in consequence they were hated by the great majority of those whom they professed to deliver from the tyranny of church and crown ...'

Cromwell's export of captives to the West Indies was no novelty. A trade in European slaves had flourished during the Thirty Years' War and was not confined to prisoners of war. After resistance in Ireland was quelled, the Bristol merchants developed so keen an interest in Irish civilians that Parliament tried to stop them.[12] They lured adults on to their ships with promises or took them by force in the press-gang manner and even the English settlers were unsafe; but their most profitable trade was in vagrant children, especially young girls who were much in demand among the celibate planters of the West Indies. Private capitalists resident in Ireland seem to have made good profits too. The Governor of Galway, Colonel Stubbers, who was probably the executioner of Charles I, is said to have sold more than a thousand Galway people and exported them.[13]

But the war was not as profitable as the Commonwealth or the would-be planters hoped. Cromwell had had great difficulty in inducing officers and men to go there in the first place, and, though he began by paying them regularly and well, arrears were so large by the end of the war that he had to give much of the confiscated land to his troops. Adventurers who had invested money in the war were also paid with grants of land.

Very few were settled in Connaught, for Cromwell planned to make that province into a native reserve. There was not much room. It was the rockiest, most swampy of the four provinces and the small areas where the soil was good, such as the Plains of Boyle and the land near the Shannon where Woodbrook is, had already been taken by adventurers, or soldiers, such as the Cootes of Cootehall. By the Act of Settlement of 1652, all the evicted landowners from the three larger and more productive provinces, except for those condemned to banishment or death, were promised land in Connaught. Their portions were limited to one third of the value of their confiscated estates.[14]

And so began the proverbial saying, 'To Hell or Connaught'.

Chapter Three

After Phoebe had read *The Wind in the Willows* with its Toad
of Toad Hall, the name Coote of Cootehall seemed funny to us.
As soon as we heard it for the first time – from Joe Fryer, I
think, while he was shoeing horses – we heard it again and again
from everyone. Joe's brother, Jack, who worked on the farm,
had one gruesome story, the Ardcarne gravedigger another,
Tom Clancy a publican-farmer a mile away, who became one
of my best friends, the four Maxwell brothers and even the
children at Woodbrook National School each loved to tell of
the dreadful deeds of the Cootes. Cromwell's were remembered
in a vague and general way, the Cootes' in detail, but I have
never discovered which Coote it was that did which deed. I
believe the stories to be true. When Phoebe and I heard them
our joke about the name died out.

The first Sir Charles Coote and his young brother Chidley are
both described in the *D.N.B.* as having 'fought vigorously
against the Irish rebels in 1641'. In fact the old man had terrorized the whole of Connaught for the previous twenty years,
and his brother's descendants reigned as tyrants over the
Cootehall–Woodbrook district for many generations. As
J.P.s of the court which was held at Cootehall they had power
over life and death. They are known to have hanged servants
for disobedience and to have exacted tribute from their tenants
in the forms of forced labour and forced sexual intercourse.
The Cootehall people used to show some dead and ragged
beams of wood to Phoebe and me that were supposed to be
remnants of the gallows.

Cootehall is a typically Irish village; it straggles and has no
architectural design; and it is dominated by a police barracks
and a large grey, ugly Catholic chapel. The old churches that

adorn most English villages were taken over in Ireland by the Protestants and often stand alone in places where a village has died out – such as Ardcarne, the Church of Ireland church which we went to, which used long ago to serve Catholics from many miles about, including the people of Cootehall. Except for the ruin of the bawn of Cootehall – where the Cootes and the O'Mulloys before them and the Mac Dermots before them lived – the most beautiful building in the village is the long low pub whose doors face the chapel doors and which is packed with the devout every Sunday morning after mass. There is no pub opposite Ardcarne church – only a gate into Rockingham and one into the lonely vicarage at which Miss MacDonald used to shout.

It is pleasant to lean on the river bridge at Cootehall and watch the dark Boyle Water flowing from Lough Key down to Woodbrook, where it goes into Lough Eidin, shrouded all the way up and down from the bridge by overhanging trees that are reflected green and massive in the summer, bent and stripy in winter. The Boyle Water moves fast but is deep enough to appear to be still, and usually it shines black. We used sometimes to row up it from Woodbrook to the bridge of Cootehall and drift home again with the stream, Phoebe and I alone together, shut away from the fields and scattered houses by high river banks as we wound our way along the sunken lane of water. But in spite of the beauty of the river, the bawn and the pub, no stranger could easily believe that this sad village is to me one of the most romantic places in the world.

The way there from the Hill of Usna was so old and little trampled that only a few people who lived nearby could follow it. Most went a long way round by the new road that was made in the 1840s. The old road from Usna was now unmarked except here and there where cattle use a stretch of it and from the top of the hill, looking towards the dense, high 'mearing', I thought there could be no way out in that direction. But when Phoebe and I first explored it we saw it was the best route by land, the shortest and most lovely.

The horses knew the way and took us to the gap, an opening closed with cut bushes, which had been there since before the

invention of gates. Most hedged fields in Ireland have 'gaps',
invisible in winter when the growing hedge is leafless, detectable
in summer to a practised eye, but not to mine then, by the
blackness of the thorny branches that lie crosswise between the
standing leafy green.

I had by then been promoted to a younger horse called
Smuggler, a muscular, adventurous animal who got his name
from a habit he had of nuzzling everyone who came near him.
When you were sitting on his back he would turn his head
whenever he could and bite your toes. He did this at the gap that
day.

I dismounted and gave his reins to Phoebe while I pulled out
the huge thorny bushes, then, after she had ridden through it, I
led Smuggler through, gave him to her again and went back to
pull the bushes after me and fill the gap. I always had thorns in
my hands at Woodbrook.

Phoebe had been promoted too to one of her beloved long-
tails – Castor or Pollux, I forget which – and I remember how
the sun came out between clouds as I re-mounted and made her
hair a new colour and her chestnut pony gold. She was beautifully lithe and so was it. It was, I discovered, no longer a 'long-
tail'. At the age of three, the ragged ends of hair had been
trimmed straight and its long tail was about an inch shorter than
before.

The descent from the gap was steep. We zig-zagged down it
at a stumbling walk and at the bottom turned into a narrow
lane between high banks which led us past a row of little single-
storeyed houses known as Newtown. The Conlon brothers,
whose grandparents had been evicted from Usna, lived in one.
Newtown was new at the time of the Famine when people were
hounded out of Woodbrook and elsewhere.

Phoebe asked one of the Conlons how to rejoin the old way to
Cootehall. 'Keep above the flash,' he said, 'I doubt but the gap
is made up. I'll go before ye and pass ye through the wall.' I said
not to bother, I'd open it.

Stone wall gaps take longer to get through than hedge gaps,
but can be found more easily because the stones are usually
jumbled, not carefully built. You have to take the wall down

stone by stone and build it up again after you. We passed through and soon there was the 'flash' – a long shallow pond – in a valley to our left, called a flash because it only appears after wet weather and disappears suddenly. There were several in the neighbourhood and they all seemed to us enchanted, magically quick in changing a landscape that anyway was always changing with tricks of light. One day there would be a shining lake and the next a dark green valley. As we rode past that morning the Cooladye flash was still and blue with clouds reflected on it. We cantered up the next hill – the Hill of Cooladye.

I am writing the name phonetically, as nearly as I can, for the older people in this part of Ireland had forgotten how to speak their language and only used a few Irish words and place names which they could not spell, but we heard not long afterwards that the name means, 'where the head came off'. An ancient bush with a crooked trunk bent by the west wind towards Usna grew near the top of the hill, and it was called the Bush of Cooladye.

Willie Maxwell, who is getting on for eighty now, heard the story from his grandmother, his mother's mother, who died at the age of eighty-four in 1914. It is about one of the Coote family and I think its date of origin must be in the eighteenth century because the circumstances of this Coote's death, confirmed as they are by many other people, show that he died when the Penal Laws were in force.

Willie said, 'Coote was a tyrant. Every girl that'd go to get married in that time had to spend the first night with him. And there was one girl, she refused to go and the father came and told him she wouldn't come and he said to him:

' "Come, come! First bring her to me," says he, "and I won't molest her in any way."

'And she went on them conditions. And she had a long head of hair down into two plaits and he plaited each plait – he had two wild clib [young, untrained horses] inside in the stables – and he got her, he pulled her in and he tied her heads of hairs to the two clibs, and he let them off. And the road was different than what you go down to Cootehall now. It wheeled to the right and it went over. They galloped over to Oakport, to the

120

demesne of Oakport, and going up the side of the hill the head separated from the body and a bush has grown up in it, and is there yet.

'And then he [Coote] was a priest-hunter. And there was a little friar living on the Hill of Usna. He used to live there. And Coote and his retinue was out hunting the priests. So they were in pursuit of this friar. And this friar and his servant left. They seen him coming. And at that time the river wasn't made; it were only in pools; but in heavy weather there was stepping stones across. And they went across it (the friar and his servant) and they crossed over to a place called Brackloon [where Willie's father was born]. And there's a "fort" there. And the friar and his servant went into the fort there, and the servant seen Coote, heard him coming on round, and he said to the friar,

' "We'd better be moving out of here, for if we don't Coote will be on top of us in very quick time."

'He says, "Where is he now?"

' "He's coming on the turn of the road on to the ford."

' "Well," says the friar, "he won't go much further." And with that, the horse reared up on his hind legs, up straight and fell back and killed Coote.'

Many priests who carried on their ministry in secret during the penal times survived through narrow escapes and were often credited with magical powers. Some people say that this friar was invisible to Coote's evil eye but that the horse saw him in the bushes of the fort, and shied. Horses often are aware of hidden objects long before their riders, and we used to say of our most nervous ones that they were apt to see ghosts.

When Phoebe and I had passed the Bush of Colladye we saw below us the round tower of the bawn where the Cootes used to live. (The Irish word *bábhún* means the courtyard of a castle where cattle used to be sheltered against enemies, and so became used for the castle itself and, more often nowadays, for the yard of a big farm.) The ground-floor rooms were occupied by a farming family in our time, but no one had entered the upper part for two hundred years. The ghost of this most devilish Coote was said to live there alone. It had been a military barracks, living on the country, and such was its fame for riches that when he broke his neck at the ford and the garrison fled in dismay, setting fire to the bawn behind them, 'molten silver ran down the castle courtyard and on to the road for a distance of one hundred yards.'

In claiming his right to the first night he was following an old and generally accepted custom. Until the end of the eighteenth century, at least, most people accepted it and wanted it as an honour. According to John Dunton[1] some leases granted by the Earl of Cavan contained clauses asserting this right, and the usual penalty for refusal, where there was a penalty at all, was eviction or an increase in rent imposed on the girl's parents.

Even in late Victorian times a child got by the landlord had a privileged place in the community, but by then the custom itself had fallen into disrepute among most landlords and tenants, and had become secretive, the girls being summoned to the big house ostensibly as servants. And when I was tempted to ask why they went against their will, I remembered the trouble Ivy took every year to find out whether the maids she found in the house had come there of their own accord. Knowing they were needed, James Currid could command them. They and their parents had inherited the old attitude to forced labour.

'My sons will not come to you to work,' said a tenant humbly to one of the Cootes, 'for one is wild and the other lazy, God forgive them.'

'Bring them. I'll talk them out of it.'

Joe Fryer used to like to tell this story at the forge, and embellished it with images that I have forgotten.

The man forced his sons to go with him to the bawn next morning and left them there, but as they did not come home that night he went back to Coote to ask after them.

'They left off their wicked ways,' said Coote. 'You'll have ease from them now.'

'But where are they?'

'Outside. You'll find them outside.'

Their father found them hanging on the gallows – the same gallows, so Joe said, that Phoebe and I examined that morning.

Chapter Four

I used to think frequently of death. I suppose most young men do. The thought is romantic. It goes with love. At twenty you think stuffiness begins at thirty. You don't want it to happen to you or your friends and you hate to think of a girl you love chatting in grocers' shops and going for walks in the park with a pram. I fixed on the age of twenty-nine for my own death and thought about it so often that I believed it would come true; but that conviction was not morbid, as my thoughts of torture were. Awake and asleep, my mind would sometimes fill with pictures of horrors I had read about, Goya-like impressions of the distant past or photographs of mutilations suffered by soldiers during the 1914–18 war. There was a book of these published by an anti-war society which I only saw for ten minutes in someone else's room, but which occurs in my nightmares even now – photographs of broken faces of men of my father's generation who were living hidden in hospitals while I was at Woodbrook. I thought often of scenes in Prescott's *Conquest of Peru* and of the abominable behaviour of Alva in the Netherlands.

There was nothing alarming in the thought of my own death – for one thing the age of twenty-nine was far away – but the death of anyone I loved seemed near and terrifying. At Woodbrook, whenever Phoebe went riding without me I imagined a fatal accident, and if she was in bed with a cold I turned it into pneumonia at once. So that when she did become dangerously ill in the early spring of her thirteenth year it was as if my premonitions were about to be fulfilled.

She had one of the most painful diseases – a mastoid abcess in the ear. It began before the end of the Hilary term and I did not hear of it until it had reached its worst stage. We never wrote to each other in those days, but as soon as I got back to London I would telephone to fix a time for lessons to begin. On that day in March there was no reply. In the afternoon I called at their house in St John's Wood and as I approached the front steps I saw that the curtains of her mother's bedroom window were drawn. I rang the bell and waited. The house was silent. I looked through the letter-box and the hall that was usually bright from a huge window half-way up the stairs was in twilight. Dark shapes of overcoats hung in it. I knew not to ring again and was about to leave when the door opened silently and there was Ivy, thinner in the face than I had ever seen her and quite pale. She was in a black dress without her silver brooch or any ornament. I could not greet her normally and she did not smile or speak. She opened the door wide enough to let me in and closed it without so much as a click by holding the Yale lock back and releasing it slowly into its socket. It seemed endless to me, this shutting of the door, and as she walked upstairs before me, soundless in slippers with cloth soles, I tiptoed after her holding on to the banister to make my tread light. I wanted to shout. I was afraid I would burst out laughing, as once I had in a crematorium chapel during the unbearable tension of a funeral service. On the first landing, beside the curtained window, she stood to listen for a sound from Phoebe's room which was only a short flight above us, five stairs or so. Then she turned into the studio, opening the door in the same cautious manner and leaving it ajar behind us. The studio was filled with daylight. It was always a lovely room, but seemed even more so now as we came into it out of silent darkness and because she now spoke, though very quietly. It was a long room the whole depth of the house. The grand piano seemed small in it and the floor, made of polished woodblocks, pale beech, reflected the light from two large windows, one at either end. Through the front window I saw the black branches of a sycamore swaying, their narrow tips upturned. We sat down by the fire. The chairs were green, but faded. Ivy told me what had happened to Phoebe. I could hardly hear her. It was as though she was talking in her sleep. Charlie was in Paris where sometimes he went to an art school for a few weeks in the winter. Tony had been asked out to tea by friends who would look after her until the doctor had been and gone on his second visit to the house that day. Ivy had not slept for three days and nights. She used the word streptococci several times. I had never heard it before. I could not speak.

We heard the doctor's car draw up and she was downstairs and had opened the door before he reached the front steps. They went up to Phoebe's room and I heard his voice, normally loud and confident. He was not afraid of waking her. I saw a latch key on the mantelpiece, took it and went out.

The Prince Albert pub, six houses away on the corner of their street and Ordnance Road, had a little front garden in those days with benches and a table underneath a walnut tree. It was shielded from the road by a high privet hedge which was twiggy low down with gaps you could look through. I found a gap through which I could see the doctor's car outside the Kirkwoods' house – no one left their cars by the pavement then, except on a visit – and I drank two pints of old and mild before I saw it move away. Then I walked quickly back.

The telephone was ringing as I let myself in. It was in the hall and as I had heard it from outside while I was fumbling in my pockets for the key, I shut the door with a louder click than I need have, in my hurry to lift the receiver. I heard the voice of a French girl first asking if she had the right number, and then I heard Charlie interrupted by crackles and squeaks. He kept on saying, 'This is Major Kirkwood speaking from Paris', and did not understand me when I said, 'I'll fetch Ivy', which I did several times between my fruitless and speechless attempts to find her. When at last she came, I heard as I walked upstairs her voice repeating, first in a whisper and then in a hoarse shout, 'Get the boat tonight if you can. Come soon.'

I sat down by the fire. It seemed certain now, the death I had foreseen. She would never have summoned him back if the doctor had left her hope. But when she came in, she was smiling a bit.

'We'll have to send a telegram,' she said. 'He couldn't hear me. He kept on saying. "This is Major Kirkwood speaking from Paris", until we were cut off.'

When Benvenuto Cellini was five years old, his father saw a salamander in the fire, called him to look at it and gave him a great box on the ears to make sure he would remember what he had seen. All vivid memories are attached to shocks of pain or pleasure. You can sit beside a clock all afternoon and not hear it tick until a telegram announcing death arrives; then you remember the clock's rhythm all your life. That is what makes it impossible for me to give a truthful picture of my relationship with Phoebe. I remember only the intensities.

She recovered perfectly from the illness without even a defect in hearing, but as I did not see her for another four months, which made six months altogether, since the Christmas holidays, my imagination set to work to alter her and she grew gaunt and yellow like the middle-aged woman who stood selling matches at Carfax or white and frail, unable to ride or swim. I said to myself that I would love her however she looked, but I was never put to the test. Her renascence that summer took place not in my imagination but in herself.

She returned to Woodbrook with her mother and sister two or three weeks before me that year, and on my lonely railway journey from Dublin at the end of June, with a third-class carriage to myself and the window open, I was conscious for the first time of the smell of the air of Ireland, of the lowlands that is, the moist, lush, grassy smell that pervades everything with freshness in the morning and evening. I think it is unique to the climate of Ireland, and in its strongest concentration it was wafted in through the windows of all Great Southern Railway carriages from the moment they left the suburbs of Dublin behind them until they reached Mullingar in the Midlands fifty miles to the west. The old canal runs beside the railway for the whole of that fifty miles and the thick vegetation on its banks and the fine mist drawn off it by the warmth of the sun, together with the rich air rising from the fields to either side, were to me as though the scents of Woodbrook had been bottled and spilled out too strong to bear. All the idyllic feelings of the previous summer came back into my mind. I longed to revive them but knew that no experience can be repeated, and looked forward to the end of my journey with dreadful suspense.

It seems to me now that I forgot she was a child. Why else was I surprised to find she had grown taller in six months at the age of twelve? She was more mature too in her attitude to work and other people, and began to do her painting and music and even her lessons with me in quite a different way – an adolescent way, inquiring and excited, often in gloomy moods and often hopeful. Like everyone who has suffered the shock and exile of a painful illness, she had returned to the world with sharpened senses. She understood perfectly now the symbolism of Saint Lasair's healing well and how it could help invalids who believed in it to be 'reborn'.

The sun was blazing on the day of my arrival. There was only just enough breeze to move small pillowy white clouds across the sky. The lower leaves of all the trees were still, and the lake for once was without a ripple, except near its centre where the river ran. As we set out in the boat from the mouth of the 'canal', we could see a mass of tall bulrushes perfectly reflected on either side of us and I remember Phoebe asking me to steer the boat straight out into the lake so as not to break their image.

'It would form again quickly,' I said.

'It would not be the same.'

Standing near the stern I punted the boat with the blade of the oar between the rows of bulrushes and between their reflection till I could no longer reach the bottom. Then rowed far out into the lake. The oars left dimples in the water and the boat a rippling wake. I stopped before we reached the current of the river and soon the boat was almost still, its white reflection gleaming, rippling slightly as we moved and showing our faces distorted when we looked over the side. The wooded shore to the east of us in the parish of Tumna threw its reflected greenery far out into the water; the high banks of Drumharlow towards the south were in the water too; but what made us both cry out with surprise was a large clump of fir-trees by a part of the shore where we knew there were none. We rowed towards them and they disappeared. They were a mirage.

We swam all afternoon, plunging in from the boat and climbing back again or taking it in turns to row while the other swam from one beautiful stretch of water to another. We went up the Boyle River past the Salmon Hole, along a narrow winding stretch of water, and this time the leaves above us made it liquid green.

I should have explained to people who have never tried it that it is impossible to hoist oneself into an ordinary lake rowing boat from the water without help. If you try to get in at the side you must have a friend putting all his weight on the opposite side, or the boat will turn over. The safest place is the stern, by the back seat, but it was higher than the sides and from the water it looked very high. I could reach it with the palms of my hands and had learned a knack of hoisting myself up on to it by the strength of my arms alone and tumbling forwards into the boat. But Phoebe could only reach its rim with her finger-tips. I had to grasp her arms and lift her in. My hands must sometimes have been warm by then from resting on the sun-blistered paintwork of the boat, for I can remember distinctly how cold and wet her skin was at my first touch and how in a second or two the warmth of her body came through. Even on hot days some parts of the lake were like iced water from the mountain streams that fed Lough Gara and Lough Key and the River Boyle. Now almost forty years later I find that my clearest memories are those of touch.

I can see Phoebe too of course, as we tethered the boat to its post among the rushes and as we climbed the fence into the paddock, and raced across it to vault the iron railing that divided it from the garden. We walked slowly up the garden, trying to discover flowers among the weeds. Under a rhododendron she found a new hen's nest with almost twenty eggs in it. Most of them looked rotten, but we made a bag out of my shirt, which I was carrying, and took them all, except two to tempt the hen to lay there again. Phoebe was in a light blue bathing dress. I should like to describe her, but cannot. The impression she made on me that day is indelible, intensely vivid, but her beauty depended so much on movement that even a good portrait can only hint at it.

For instance, I know that her arms and legs were shapely – her legs long, her arms strong and rounded, but light – and that her body was slim and graceful. But many girls have graceful bodies, arms and legs. It is Phoebe's own grace of movement that I cannot find words for – her individual way – and this is true too of her face, because without her quick humour, her eagerness and the transparency of her emotions it was merely an attractive, simple face. Like clear water, it showed many changing lights that cannot hold.

When we had collected the eggs, we crossed the lawn to the north side of the garden which was separated from the cowshed and the cowyard by a high stone ivy-covered wall. At the lower end by the paddock there was a little greenhouse. Its white woodwork was speckled with green fungus, and there were many broken panes. We walked cautiously up to it in our bare feet, avoiding nettles and splinters of glass. Wild woodbine and long strands of bindweed with large white flowers twined in and out of the open frames. We sucked the honey out of honeysuckle and I began to pick some bindweed flowers, but she said, 'Don't. They just die in the house. Let's get some syringa if it's still flowering.'

One of the marvels of a neglected garden in a mild damp climate is the wild profusion of shrubs that were once tidy. The syringa had spread to the top of the cowshed wall, and parts of it were entangled in the leafy branches of a tree whose name I forget – a stranger to Ireland, imported and planted by one of the Kirkwoods who travelled so much. Its branches spread out almost horizontally. It gave the best shade of any tree. Its leaves were large and dark. Yet it was not a fig tree. I have often stood under it since that day. It is the first thing I look for whenever I visit Woodbrook to make sure it has not been cut down.

The syringa was still flowering entangled in the branches of this tree and hanging from the cowshed wall, some eight feet high. I put the eggs down in the grass at the foot of the tree and reached and plucked a few sprays of the rich sweet-smelling flowers. They are like orange blossom. Then, as Phoebe looked up at them, her cheeks and the rounded ends of her shoulders that had been coloured by the sun seemed almost edible to me

129

like peaches. As she took the flowers from me she looked at my eyes, then pressed the flowers to her face. I kissed her shoulder and drew her against my naked chest, slightly and only for a second. She looked at me again for only a second when I took my grasping arm away and her eyes had changed. They were like open windows. She could never draw the blinds.

'I am going in to get my shoes,' I said.

My bedroom was separated from hers by an archway closed only with matchboarding. We could talk to each other through the partition without raising our voices and one could always hear the other leaving or entering the room, and also every other movement – the sound of a drawer, the scrape of a chair, the creaking of a bed. Both rooms looked westward to the copper beech and down the drive until it turned away and left a wide view of the water-meadow, by the canal. The corncrake had begun its evening croaking hidden in the long grass there – 'crake-crake-crake-crake, crake-crake' – a monotonous and seemingly endless rhythm on one note which I have never heard anywhere but Woodbrook. It fills me with nostalgia now for the seething life of that house and farm and it reminds me of the evening of syringa.

I was slow in getting dressed. I was wearing my swimming trunks under my trousers, so I had to take everything off and search for clean clothes. All this involved many more movements than you would think and a degree of concentration of which my mind was then incapable.

I went to the window with a shirt in my hand and only discovered that I was standing there naked when I saw the familiar hunched back of the tall old woman who called at the kitchen every day with her black bag. I drew back at once, found clean trousers in the suitcase and put them on. My mind was dazed one minute and turmoiled the next by that light-seeming kiss which I knew would be serious and deep in its consequences.

I heard Phoebe go into her room, open a drawer and sit down. She was changing from her swimming things. I put on my sand-shoes. Then she called me. 'Are you dressed?'

'Yes.' I put my shirt on last.

She brought flowers in a vase and put them on my dressing-table in the arch..y. I must have put my hand on her shoulder, for I know she tu..ed at once to me and kissed me on the lips. It was a light sponta..eous kiss, a touch so quick that my lips had no time to respond, but it seemed like a pledge in answer to me by her warm lips, the fresh smell of the lake on her skin.

We went into the garden again. It was difficult to measure the frames for the high-up panes of glass we needed. The wood of the greenhouse was rotting and would only bear the weight of a ladder here and there. But we did it somehow and bought the glass, cut more or less to size, in Carrick next day. I fixed the panes in with nails and putty and Phoebe painted all the wood-work white. Later on she weeded the flowerbeds, often with my help, sowed nasturtiums and planted marigolds and common flowers like that. It seemed to me like a new beginning.

Chapter Five

It is difficult for me to distinguish the years; I no longer have
my old diaries. But I used to give each year a name when it was
over and I remember some of those, though perhaps not in the
right order – 'Syringa year', 'the year of the skull and bones',
'the year of the bees' and so on. The 'year of the bees' was the
happiest, I think, in spite of the bees. It probably came next to
'Syringa' which was the year of our first kiss.

My painful shyness among adults of my own class extended
at that time even to her parents whom I knew well. I was ill at
ease for years too with the Maxwells, much as I liked them. I
felt unacceptable in both groups and grew closer and closer to
Phoebe. And then in the year of the bees I was free from the
long periods of depression which usually subdued me. Life
never for a moment seemed purposeless. It turned into no blind
alleys. Phoebe was my purpose and I was young enough to see
the years before us stretching to infinity in a halcyon calm. Her
happiness strengthened mine.

Phoebe even at her age believed in the power of fate, or
rather in a balance between the fates of joy and sorrow. She
said joy was always followed by sorrow or physical pain. Bicycle crashes or tosses from a horse came only while riding at a
joyful speed. She said I was too happy on the day when the bees
attacked me.

There had always been two neglected bee-hives among the
trees by the garden and now that the flowers under her care had
defeated the weeds we knew they must be loaded with honey.
We got hold of a bee-keeping book and decided to take its
advice and settle the bees down with sugar to feed on in the
winter according to the rules. The rules advised 'the handler' to
wear light gloves and a veil and to move quietly. Phoebe was

not allowed that role. So she found gloves for me, and an ancient voluminous veil – perhaps Aunt Nina's. She pressed a large straw hat on to my head and wound the veil over it, covering my face and neck. Then she sat on the windowsill of Aunt Nina's room to watch.

I crept up to the first hive and tried to lift its roof cautiously but, not having been moved for years, it was stuck and came off with a wrench which shook the hive to its foundations. There was a furious buzzing, a noise like an overstrained engine, a low tone and a high-pitched whine, and in a second I could see nothing but the cloud of bees about my hands and head. They began to sting my wrists and neck, and some reached my face through a gap where the veil had come loose. It is not so much the pain that makes one want to run away from bees. It is the fearful sound and their endlessly increasing numbers. My first thought was to put back the roof, as though that would shut them in. This I did clumsily, making matters worse in my haste. Then I ran. But running away from bees is like running away from sorrows. You bring them with you.

I ran blindly past the front of the house, thinking I would plunge into the lake, yet running in the opposite direction until a field gate with a difficult latch stopped me. By now there were as many bees inside the veil as outside and I was using both hands in a futile attempt to drive them away. There were bees up my sleeves and inside my shirt, but the biggest concentration was round my head. How do they know to attack the face and leave the thickly clothed bottom alone?

I climbed up the high stone stile beside the gate, hoping I suppose that the breeze would help. I tore off the worse than useless veil and hat and threw them as far as I could into Shanwelliagh with many bees trapped inside. I tore off my shirt and threw that after them, full of bees, and it seemed to me that I had deceived the angry horde for a moment into following their dead or entangled kindred. I wonder whether they thought I was now at a safe distance from their hive. Perhaps they were merely tired or perhaps their driving impulse towards work made them feel they were wasting their time. Whatever the cause I was able to jump back off the stile with only a few of them about me and to plunge my head and arms into a rainwater butt.

This frenzied mishap introduced me to the only beekeeper in the parish. Like blacksmiths they are known for miles around for their peculiar knowledge and their eccentricities. Willie Morony was not an exception. We bicycled to his house, a mile or two away, to ask him to come and help. He was a distant relative of the Kirkwoods and used at one time to manage their estate, a misfit like me in rural society, a Protestant, landless and eccentric, just barely middle-class, who would not fit into society above or below him but had enough status to own a two-storeyed house which kept him apart from the majority of people. That day when I first met him he had not been upstairs since the night his wife died, nor, according to the Kirkwoods, had he changed his clothes. You could smell him at some distance even in the open air. He called to us to come in when I knocked on the open front door. Phoebe retreated for air as soon as she had announced me from the door of his room, but I went in out of curiosity and spoke to him there about the bees. He said I was wrong to wear gloves or a veil. The bees were like horses, he said, in their keen sense of smell. They could smell fear. Fear comes from glands you cannot control and is especially noticeable on hot days when it exudes along with your sweat. It was not pure sweat that made them sting. He said he sweated in hot weather and was never stung.

He was not tall, but large and dressed in a loose grey tweed suit. He had ample long white hair and a grey beard that hid the front of his neck and chest so that no one could tell whether he wore a stock, a tie, a collarless shirt, or no shirt at all. But his waistcoat, trousers, and the lapels of his coat were exposed, showing several mixed stains from food and drink. I took to him at once but cannot tell whether he liked me because he had that open and kind nature that makes men tolerate anyone. He said he would need my help when he came to see to the bees.

I looked at his room with intense interest too. It had originally been the dining room. An oval dining-room table and chairs were there, of Victorian mahogany – the chairs with black horsehair seats that needed darning, the table covered with dusty objects that had lain on it for years, not only books and papers, but things which he or his son Andy had happened to place on it from time to time, absentmindedly finding space to deposit whatever it was they held in their hand. When the old man Willie had a cup of tea, or tea and bread, which was almost all he ever had, he would push the books or dirty plates and cups away and clear just enough space for new ones. When all the clean crockery had been used his son would wash up and they would start again. Having lived in much the same way myself from time to time I wondered whether the dirt and chaos oppressed him as mine oppressed me. In London I used to go out when the mess got too bad, crawl into bed in the dark late at night and dash out to breakfast early in the morning, never even shaving in the house. But now, looking back, I doubt whether Willie Morony hated the mess. It certainly did not drive him from the house, but then the nearest shelter or drink or food would have been in the pubs of Boyle, five miles to walk. And usually it was raining.

Charlie fetched him in the car on the appointed day and I went barefaced and barehanded with him to the hives. He lifted the roof off one of them and laid it on the ground. Then he took from a large tin a cloth soaked in Jeyes Fluid and laid it over the frame to quieten the bees, he said, and send them down to the bottom of the hive. And it was true that there was only a little angry buzzing. He gave me the frame to hold and started to take out the honey below it. His face and hands were soon covered with bees. I could see them stinging but he appeared to feel no pain. Generations of bees had inoculated him, I suppose. But I had sixteen on one hand and fourteen on the other. I had plenty of time to count them while he worked. Afraid of his scorn and of another mass attack I held the tray till he had finished. I stood absolutely still, holding the frame while the bees stung me and as I went through the same ordeal at the second hive I wished Phoebe was near enough to see that *tableau vivant* of unflinching courage, though I knew well that it was fear not courage that kept me at my post.

I removed several bees from my clothes and their stings from my hands as we walked back to the house, but he remained

135

imperturbable. He sat in the drawing-room afterwards, drinking tea and talking with bees in his beard. Two or three were crawling on his face, but when Phoebe, alarmed for him, called his attention to them, he said, 'There's no harm in them, nothing but good. Look at St Ambrose and at Plato, the Athenian Bee – the good and the wise.'

'Was Plato called that?'

'He was indeed, because his words glowed with the sweetness of honey. Did Master David never teach you that?'

'I didn't know it,' I said.

'Oh yes. And when they were in their cradles the both of them, didn't a swarm of bees alight on their mouths? And for that we often hear St Ambrose called the beehive. And then again in Ireland in the old times the bees were supposed to be creatures of the other world.'

'They swarmed on poor David's mouth,' said Ivy, and she laughed.

'They did, he tells me. But when they stung him, they brought no gift.'

The whole family was now in the drawing-room, Phoebe and her mother sunk in the deep sofa facing the fire which had just been lit for the evening, her father and Willie Morony in the large armchairs on either side, Tony at the windowsill playing and me on the arm of the sofa, unwilling to admit that I would stay for more than a minute but held from minute to minute by what Willie said.

The kindling sticks were damp and after its first blaze of paper the fire had sunk to a smoking heap. Charlie reached for the sugar bowl, emptied it over the sticks to make them blaze, then called to the kitchen for more. But as soon as the fire was going well, Willie stood up and summoned me. There was something else to be done to the bees. They were quiet by then. It was late when Charlie drove him home.

The Kirkwoods never paid him for his work with the bees. I thought at first that this was because he was a relative. But no one paid him. No one paid old Michael Maxwell either for his ointments and cures. After a polite interval, butter, eggs, or a

136

bottle of whiskey, according to what the person could afford, would be brought as a present.

And it happened that the bee-stings came at harvest time – a late harvest, delayed by rain. I remember that because of the stiffness of my swollen hands, lifting sheaves, and the spiky sores made by straw ends and thistles. I remember how none of the extra labourers – about six who came daily – received any wages at all. All they got was a good dinner and tea. But in return the Maxwell brothers and all other employees of the Kirkwoods went to their farms as each crop was ready. It was an efficient way of getting the work done, and friendly. It was one of many traditions that kept people on isolated farms together. I sometimes went with the Maxwells to work away from home. We were always hopeful and excited. The dinner on each farm was lovely.

Woodbrook had an extraordinary advantage in this cooperative practice by owning the most up-to-date harvesting machine in the district – something called a 'reaping attachment' that was fixed to the ordinary horse-drawn mower. It seems very old-fashioned now that combine harvesters are almost everywhere used, and compared to eastern Ireland, where most farmers had had the 'reaper and binder' for years, it was old-fashioned then. But to us it was modern. Most of our neighbours still reaped their crops by scythe. Some had a mower which they used for hay as well. But whichever way they cut it the men who followed, binding the corn into sheaves with straw bands, had to divide each swathe into bundles of the right size. Our contraption did that for them, dropping each unbound sheaf on to a canvas platform. There was an extra seat beside the driver of the horses and all you had to do if that was your job, which it often was mine, was to push the sheaves off with a rake as the whole clumsy thing moved along. This left a path clear for the horses on their next round, whereas the mower laid the cut crop where it fell, which was all right for hay, but not for grain which gets pressed out if trampled. For such reasons our 'reaping attachment' was a marvel.

Ladders, ploughs, harrows and so on were lent to neighbours

137

too. The only machine in the countryside for which a charge was made was the thresher, a long apparatus on four iron wheels driven by a steam traction engine which also drew it along the roads from farm to farm. Its owner and his mate brought it to Woodbrook every spring to thresh the oats and stayed several days. The extra labourers needed at that time also worked without pay.

Chapter Six

In Uncle Tom's youth, the postman walked all the way from Carrick, carrying his bag of letters and a post-horn – a long bugle – which he sounded as he approached each of the scattered houses. People used to spare him some miles by setting out to meet him when they heard it. His arrival was announced to us by the crunch of bicycle wheels on the gravel that started near the copper beech. No one else, unless a stranger, would ride up to the front door. I looked forward to the frequent letters from my mother, Charlie to yesterday's *Irish Times*, but personal letters were rare to the family and I think the excitement of running out to meet the postman came from our isolation. He was the only regular visitor. He came between half past twelve and one, unless he was delayed, and was in no hurry. If a letter needed an urgent reply, he would wait while you wrote it. He took outgoing letters away in the same flat canvas bag.

But usually there would be at the most a dozen bills, which Charlie, standing in the open doorway, would throw behind him on to the hall table and glancing at the headlines of the newspaper say good-bye to the postman. When the headlines were dull he would sometimes open one or two of the bills with his thumb, while waiting for lunch, throw them down again and light his pipe.

'No post,' he would say if anyone was near, but Ivy one day caught a glance of a cheque and picked it up – £200 odd.

'Look, Charlie, this is wonderful. The rates are just due.'

It was from the grocer, which puzzled them both until she discovered he had paid the bill twice, a year late the first time and six months after that, an old 'account rendered'. Paying bills was an occupation for the dark winter evenings, not disagreeable.

He was quite unworried by events that drive many people into mental hospitals, and worried by successes that would have made other horse-breeders euphoric. He sold an excellent horse one morning, at a time when he had too many to cope with, to a man who lived twenty miles away, and bicycled to buy it back in the evening at a higher price because he could not bear to part with it. Another escaped from its new owner and came home. The new owner arrived to reclaim it and was bought off in the same way. And all this time his creditors were pressing him for money he had to borrow. There were also emotional troubles at one time which I did not understand.

I envied his extraordinary composure and put it down to Yoga, but now I think he must have had a passive form of strength before he found that frame for it in India. In the early morning occasionally, when I had something to tell him, I would go to his bedroom – his door was always open – and if I looked in while he was doing his Yoga exercises he would not know I was there. The movements of his body were such as I had never seen before; his eyes were open but unseeing outwardly; the expression of his face was reserved. An old Greek icon, in its intelligent calm, is the nearest image I have since seen.

Then sometimes, at two or three in the morning, or even four if I was reading or writing downstairs, I would hear him cough on my way to bed, see his light and go in to say good night. And there he was sitting up in bed in his pyjamas, their top unbuttoned however cold the night, reading or looking at the sky through the front window before him, with an open book in one hand resting on the blanket and a huge back pipe in his mouth. His head would be in a wispy, moving cloud of smoke, lit by the paraffin lamp on his bedside chamber-pot cabinet, marble-topped, and in summer there were always dozens of moths about the lamp, for he liked to keep both windows open, the one to the right of his pillow, which looked out on to the avenue and the copper beech, and the one before him through which from the bed he could only see the sky. He always went to bed with two thermoses of tea, which he drank at his frequent wakings through the night. In winter he liked to have a stone hot-water bottle at his feet and some teaspoonsful of dry tea. When the thermoses were finished he would make a last cup from the hot-water bottle. At night he seemed supernatural to me.

Once or twice he seemed supernatural in the daytime too. I remember when he ruptured himself acutely, schooling a violent young horse. He rode it home, looking deathly pale, dismounted with difficulty and was helped upstairs to bed. He hated doctors, but one was sent for who, following the medical rules of those days, told him to lie in bed for six weeks. Next morning he was up, walking out somewhat painfully and stiffly to ride the same horse. Of course, now that I have had ruptures myself I am not quite so impressed by his feat. The intense pain only lasts a day or so, and nowadays one is not told to stay in bed. But none of us knew anything about it then and most people would have been afraid to disobey a doctor's solemn warning.

Much to my embarrassment, I often caught myself calling him 'Daddy' as though he was my own father. Sometimes I could smother the word in time, sometimes he must have heard it, but when he did he took no notice, which gave me a little relief. I thought he was an ideal father of the non-authoritarian kind, always interested in what the children said or did but seldom showing disapproval. In his greatest expertise – horse management and riding – he was a natural teacher, never finding fault but correcting faults he appeared not to see by a light remark that made one laugh. And his example, the perfect ease and good humour with which he managed difficulties, his wholehearted enjoyment, was always part of the lesson which was never called a lesson but a morning ride. Phoebe and Tony became perfect riders and I was able in the end to sit on young horses that had never been ridden before and get bucked off on a marshy place specially chosen for its softness.

My suppressed instinct to call him 'Daddy' made me secretly afraid of him too. Each time I stifled the word I remembered that he was Phoebe's father, not mine, and in all the love stories I had ever read it was the father, not the mother, who tried to protect the daughter from a lover. It never occurred to me at first that he or Ivy might be worried when they saw I was deeply in love with her. I was only afraid they might listen to friends and ask me to leave, for it was, I discovered, usual for girls to have a governess. Private tutors, especially young ones, usually got dreary jobs with boys. So I thought they might be persuaded to adopt that convention after all – for there had been several occasions both in England and Ireland when people showed surprise, and a friend at Oxford laughed when I told him, in describing life at Woodbrook, that both my pupils had their lessons sitting on my lap.

I do not think it is chance that brings love stories to people in love, but when it happens you think it is chance. When I was happy with Phoebe I came across for the first time the stories of Tristan and Iseult, Deirdre and Naoise, and Abélard and Héloïse. Together we read *Romeo and Juliet* and heard from country people the tragedy of Úna Bhán. In each of these stories there is a jealous parent, usually the father of the girl.

Úna Bhán – that is the fair-haired Úna – was born and brought up on Rock or Castle Island, a daughter of one of the Mac Dermots of the Rock whose power and grandeur was much to be feared. Lough Key, where she was born, that large and beautiful lake which we used to explore by boat, has more than thirty islands in it. Her birthplace and the island where her grave is are nearest to the southern shore, and are much written of in Irish literature. Her story is the subject of poems in both languages. But we did not know that then. You could not stay long in the district without hearing several versions, and at Woodbrook old Michael Maxwell liked to tell it again and again.

Tomás Costello was the son of a poor woman who lived in one of the gate houses of French Park, which was the Costello's demesne at that time, and looked after the gentleman's fowl. One day when he was twelve years of age, the poor woman asked the gentleman for as much straw as would thatch her little house and he told her to send up the gossoon for a back-load. Tomás brought up a rope to the stackyard and placed it under a stack of straw and brought that home to his mother, and when the gentleman saw his great strength he adopted him as his own son and from that day he went under the name of

142

Costello. Soon after that, the boy was walking by Lough Gara when he saw eight of Costello's men trying to pull a boatload of sand up on the shore. When he saw the boat was grounded and they could not move it, he told them to stand aside and he pulled it up himself, and when old Costello heard of this he sent for him, and when he was speaking to him he knew that he was starved. He ordered twelve men's feed to be brought to the gossoon and watched him eat it, and he ate twelve men's feed every day for a week and the second week he ate six men's feed. And, from then, old Costello kept him in his house and fed him on the best and gave him a good education.

When the old gentleman was dying he left all he was worth to him.

The way young Costello got acquainted with Úna Bhán Mac Dermot was this. There was a horse that was the best her father had and it fell in the Boyle River in a place where the bank was steep. Six men could not lift it out. And Costello came by. He went down and he landed Mac Dermot's horse on the bank. But when he was at this, he caught his boot and legging on a stone and split them. The Mac Dermot asked him to the castle, and although the Costellos and the Mac Dermots were enemies he was invited again for saving the horse, and he was in love with Úna.

He was invited to a feast where all the sons of the great lords of Connaught were feasted and The Mac Dermot was drinking with them and choosing in his mind the best man for his daughter and he told her to drink to the man she loved best and she raised her glass to Costello. And when she was taking the first sip, her father took the glass from her and dashed the wine in her face. She took snuff from the snuff box, pretending that that brought tears to her eyes, and went away to her room.

'It was strong snuff,' said Costello and commanded The Mac Dermot to apologize. The Mac Dermot threw him out of the castle. He went away to the mainland, swearing to come back.

Úna Bhán was locked up and Costello was banished from The Mac Dermot's country.

Soon she fell ill and when she was nearly dying the doctors said that the only man who could save her was Costello. So The

Mac Dermot sent for him and let him sit by her bedside. When she fell asleep again, he asked to marry her but still her father refused. So he said, 'I will go to the mainland and I will ride as far as the ford of the river. Send word within an hour that you have changed your mind, or I will cross the ford and never return.'

So he rode with his companion and they stood their horses in the middle of the ford and his companion was feeling cold and said had he no pride. So they shoved their horses across and when they stood on the far bank they heard The Mac Dermot coming after them, shouting to come back, that he would give his daughter. But Costello said he would not break his word and rode on.

Úna Bhán died and was buried on Trinity Island in the grounds of the old abbey and Costello with grief came one night every week to pray and sleep on her grave. When they knew this they took the boat from him and he swam. But one night there was a storm that drowned him. The Mac Dermot was sorry at last and buried him beside Úna. And two trees grew up, one from each grave, and twined into one another.

I once rowed out to Trinity Island. I was by myself on a still cloudy day. The water was black. The island was an impenetrable thicket of briars and brambles; whitethorn and blackthorn blocked the way between larger twisted trees. It was hard to see the ruins of the abbey, impossible to identify a grave. And anyway I was melancholy. But Willie told me I would not have found the original twining trees. He says there was a Scottish steward in Rockingham 'who used to wonder what used to be bringing the people across to Trinity Island in the summer time o' the year, and he was told it was to see Úna Mac Dermot's grave and Costello's, to look at the two trees that twined up.

' "Well," he said, "they'll come no more!"

'He sent out his woodsmen and they cut the two trees down. And when Lord Lorton heard what he had done he sacked him there on the minute. He said he'd rather see all Rockingham gone than them two trees cut.'

144

Chapter Seven

The life of young people in Ireland in the 1930s appeared to be sexless, almost loveless. Even students in Dublin would not dare to be seen holding hands and in the country to make love before marriage was to risk banishment. Any mention of it would send old bachelors of forty into fits of embarrassed schoolboy laughter, and if a girl became pregnant by mistake, they were all ready to revile and spit on her, however much they had liked her before her disgrace. She would, as a matter of course, be separated from her baby as soon as it was born and imprisoned for life in a convent. It would not have surprised Tom Maxwell but it now surprises me to remember how openly the Protestant community near Woodbrook allowed their feelings to be known. Tom would have said that Protestants parade their sins with pride, or, which is worse, that they do not know the difference between good and evil.

Not that he ever mentioned those sins to me. There were only two examples that I knew of and those he must have known of too. One concerned the son of an Anglo-Irish landlord who had a short affair with a young Catholic girl who worked as a servant in his parents' house. The girl's angry father was calmed with money. One hundred pounds saw to that. The girl was sent to a convent and the baby to an orphanage. The other concerned the Protestant parson's eldest daughter who was exiled in England with her illegitimate child and never written to. In both cases the sinners seemed to me to be the grandparents. In both, the unhappy protagonists were hidden away. Yet all through those hot summers, even during long weeks of warm rain, young Protestants would bicycle or ride their horses up and down the country in search of their beloved girls for everyone to see. They all seemed forlorn and frustrated. There were not

145

many eligible Protestant girls. The Catholic boys who spent their spare time playing pitch and toss or football, in celibate groups by the crossroads, or in visiting each other's houses, where there might be an unmarried sister, seemed carefree by comparison. I never heard them mention love except as a joke. Perhaps that was because I was a stranger. Perhaps in my presence they were inhibited by what they knew about my love for Phoebe. They may have been ashamed to speak of anything touching on that delicate subject.

For I was completely innocent at first – to use the word in the Irish colloquial sense which is something between guileless and ignorant. I was so innocent in the year of the bees that I laid my happiness open for all to see – Phoebe on my lap at lessons, laughing by the open window of Aunt Nina's room, reciting Latin chants I had invented. 'Feles Felix, Felix Feles', cat happy, happy cat – Phoebe with her cheek resting on the open pages of *Heath's French Grammar* in the long grass by the tennis court and my arm about her and my wandering caress – Phoebe and me in the boat on the lake or walking home hand in hand, or bicycling with my arm round her shoulder pretending to help her up a hill. Her affectionate familiarity was unhidden too. When guests of the stiffer sort were expected, Ivy used to entreat her not to speak to me as though I was her favourite dog.

I judge my innocence by the spontaneous response I made a year later to Ivy's first expression of worry, so delicately put to me one rainy afternoon when she found me alone in the drawing-room.

'Phoebe's too taken up with you,' she said, and I answered at once, 'It's all right. You needn't worry, because I feel the same about her. But more so.'

I was startled and downhearted when I saw this did not re-assure her. I meant that I would not suddenly leave Phoebe heartbroken, which was the only bad result I could foresee in the affair, which had inevitably, as Ivy must have known, developed into a state of passion too strong to be fulfilled by a light and loving kiss. It was fulfilled, though not in an adult way, and Ivy never spoiled it for Phoebe by inspiring her with guilt, although, when at last she grew frightened, she did find a way of separating us.

This 'innocence', or ignorance of the judgement of the world, allowed us into an exclusive state of grace that shut out guilt, from which I fell by stages. I remember for example a sense of relief when she became fourteen, because, although the law said sixteen, fourteen was I knew a normal age for marriage in some countries. No such thought would have entered my head in the state of grace. It was inspired by other people's anxiety. And when at last an open accusation came it fell like a blot of ink on a poem.

The blot was spilled by a girl of my own age, whom I rather liked – one of the summer guests who were often invited to Woodbrook. I think she was genuinely shocked by observing through an open window my conduct of Phoebe's algebra lesson. It was algebra that day. I remember the day, as I remember all days marked by shocks of unwelcome surprise. But I don't think she would have mentioned it to anyone, except perhaps to me, had it not been for the chance that late that night, as I was searching for a book after I thought everybody else had gone to bed, I went into the drawing-room and found her and Charlie kissing. I felt shy but not surprised, pretended I was looking for my paraffin lamp – there were three alight in the room – took one and went upstairs without my book. Next day she spoke to Ivy and Ivy I now guess tried to persuade Charlie to lecture me. But of course he would not, and poor Ivy could not. The most she could do, after a long silence whose cause I did not guess at, was to quote.

'She says she doesn't like the way you mess about with Phoebe.' I hated the words, and so I think did she. In the anger of my surprise I said, 'She said that?' and for a second I wanted to have my revenge which came to my mind ready-made from the night before. We looked at each other. We were in Aunt Nina's room, the only place, I suppose, where she knew she would find me alone. Neither of us spoke after those small strong words. And she never mentioned the subject again. I cannot remember how we parted. I know I looked out at the mountains and the lake, which were dark. Perhaps she left the room while I was gazing there. I know I remained alone in the room for some time. I remember sitting down by the bare polished dining-room table and rolling a cigarette, searching my pockets for matches in vain, and finding some at last in a candlestick on the sideboard – 'Friendly Matches', the usual Irish brand. I could hear Phoebe practising the violin upstairs.

The honeymoon is said to have been the month in which hydromel, the wine of honey, was drunk after a wedding. Atilla the Hun drank so much after his that he died. There ought to be a ceremonial form of disengagement too, a specially chosen drink could be part of it, to be taken during the last month and used among other forms of diversion, as marriage games and whiskey were till recently used at wakes to dissipate some of the sorrows of death and construct a new life upon each grave.

My disengagement was gradual. It seems to me now that it took about a month – from her Harvest Dance until the Ballinasloe Horse Fair, which is held in the first week of October – an autumn month that has distilled itself in my memory into one eventful day, the day of the journey to the horse fair of Ballinasloe. I say my disengagement, not ours, because I feel sure that that month was not specially memorable to Phoebe. I do not think it caused her any distress. She confided in her mother and made a promise and one day confided the promise to me. She kept the promise. I had to keep it. But I was not taken from her in the sense that she was taken from me. I continued to teach her, but from now on we had a chair each. We went on riding, and reading, and swimming and walking together, and joined in the same enterprises, such as climbing to the top of the highest chimney of the house, building a raft for the lake, a concrete hen-house, with the help of Jimmy Maxwell, and with him and Tom to help a low dome-like cabin, made out of sods of grass, like an igloo in shape, in exactly the same style as the dwellings of the eighteenth-century poor. The cabin was a plaything for Phoebe and Tony, like the raft, but only two miles from Woodbrook we knew one that was lived in by an American who had come home with plenty of money but quarrelled with his relatives and chose to live in the woods. In a sentimental way, that month, I foresaw some such future for myself, thinking that the Kirkwoods might retire to London in the end and that even without them I would remain in Ireland.

The two days that I remember with glaring clarity that sometimes makes me wince and sometimes laugh began early with a ride to Carrick-on-Shannon station by the old grass-covered road. These were the days distilled. The first was more like March than October, blustery, showery, the sky dark and bright by turns giving sudden windy showers that frightened our horses. We started early for the station with three horses, Phoebe and me riding six-year-olds and Charlie riding a very nervous young one. We took the old road to Carrick-on-Shannon station, a road that had been covered with grass for almost a hundred years, and it was secret and beautiful.

We passed the remains of an imposing gateway that seemed to lead straight into a bog. The roadsides of Ireland are dotted with these attempts at grandeur, grey square pillars usually of limestone, far too heavy for the gates between them, and now that so many of the gates have been replaced by bedsteads they look heavier still. They were symbols of power I suppose, for they never had any practical purpose, the fences on each side of them being low. The great demesnes had walls to match their gateposts, eight or ten feet high, but small landowners like the Kirkwoods or the richer tradesmen, such as butchers who reared their own cattle, put these marks by the roadside during their lifetime, just as they raised headstones after death a little way off from the flat graves of the common people.

There seemed to be no place for a house inside this gateway, nothing but the bog and an old plantation of trees that must have been grown as a windbreak.

'That's Clongoonagh,' said Charlie, aware of my curiosity as we passed it at a walk. 'When Billy and I were boys, you could see the foundations of the gate lodge here and you could trace the line of the old avenue up to the house. It curved round to the right, through those trees.'

Clongoonagh House, where Phoebe's cousins still lived, had not changed much in a hundred years except that many more trees and shrubs had grown up to darken it. But when the old road from Boyle to Carrick was closed they had to alter the main entrance. I discovered later that the old gateway had been the scene of a scandal that was brought before the House of Lords.

The station was deserted when we reached it. The horsebox we had ordered stood all by itself on the one siding. It looked large and strong enough to hold an elephant, Phoebe said. It was made for three horses. They stood side by side facing the engine in a padded windowless truck, but could put their heads out into their groom's compartment, a narrow space, but light and airy, fitted with a wooden bench across the van from side to side. Our horsebox that day looked old and weather-beaten, but the porter said it was a new type which even he had not seen before.

We dismounted, led our horses up the paved slope of the siding and waited on the platform, allowing them to nibble the grass and weeds that grew between the stones.

'Dash my buttons,' said Charlie, putting his monocle into his eye to look around. 'What's happened to Tom?' He is the only man I have ever heard use expressions like that. Tom Maxwell had promised to be at the station to help us.

'He's probably had a puncture,' Phoebe said. But in spite of our delays we were early.

Tom arrived on time on his bicycle, but by then we had five or six willing helpers – the sound of horses' hoofs in any unusual place used to draw men away from whatever they happened to be doing. But still we had to wait for the porter who was delayed on the telephone by something that had gone wrong farther down the line. The young horse began to fidget and upset the other two. We were anxious to get all three into their padded cells well before the train to which we were to be attached came smoking and clattering into the station.

The porter came. He pulled a lever and the whole side of the railway truck, except for the groom's compartment, opened like a mouth, the lower jaw falling on the platform as a ramp for the horses to walk up. It was this that was the almost fatal new device. The old type of horsebox had half-doors, like a stable except that the lower half was hinged to the floor. You opened and shut it by letting it down on to the platform or lifting it up by hand, one man each side. The new type could in theory be worked by one man. It was controlled by the lever and it opened and shut with tremendous force. Its jaws were edged with iron flanges. We covered the ramp, its lower jaw, with straw.

Phoebe's horse and mine allowed Tom to lead them in quietly. Both had travelled in a railway horsebox before. He changed their bitted bridles for halters and tied them loosely, each head to its looking-out place. There were partitions on hinges between each horse, long padded boards about three feet deep and two feet up from the floor, yellowy white, firm but soft, to keep them from bumping into each other or getting bruised by the rocking of the train. These he closed. We hoped the two-year-old would go in quietly after them, seeing her stable companions calmly standing there. But she was afraid to step up on to the ramp. After three tries, Tom coaxed her in with one hand on the bridle and the other on her neck. It was his talent to give horses confidence but as soon as he tied her by the head and left she swung her hindquarters out again on to the ramp. The uninvited helpers, now feeling sure of her character, that she would not kick, leant all their weight against her and pushed her back, then retreated quickly to the platform. But Nolan, the carpenter, a very tall man, seeing that her halter had slipped over one ear in the struggle, leant into the box to put it straight, and just in that second the porter pulled the lever which worked the sprung doors. The carpenter's head was within them. We all cried out, and he drew back just in time. The jaws clanged shut, missing his head by less than an inch. There was an awful silence. I, who was standing next to him, was dumb, almost sick. Then all the others were shocked into loud laughter, a ghastly fit of laughter such as I have only heard since at moments of disaster in Japanese films.

When the train arrived, Phoebe and I climbed into the groom's compartment and said good-bye. We were shunted up and down, then attached to the back of the passenger train.

The journey took nearly all day and has stayed in my memory like one of those vivid dreams that recur throughout one's life about places that one never visits when awake. We were in a railway carriage of a surrealist kind, sitting on a hard narrow bench with a very straight back that was punctured here and there by hurtful bolts and nuts, facing a wall that had three wooden openings through which hung three horses' heads, like the stags' heads you see mounted on boards in some people's houses. Our bench was high, Phoebe's feet were dangling, and when we sat on it our eyes were level with the horses' eyes, and their mouths were near enough to us for them to bite all the buttons off my coat as the day slid on. With the drowsy rhythm of the wheels, as the day grew warmer towards noon, we seemed to slide suspended in this unlikely container, quite alone with our horses in a private world. Looking out from the unglazed window space on either side, we could see neither wheels below us, nor anything behind us except a long view of the single track between green banks, and though clouds of smoke floated past us, we could never see the engine or carriages by leaning out; the projecting windows of the guard's van to which we were hooked were in the way. We felt suspended in space and time. So strong was that feeling that whenever the train stopped in the open country, the world outside with its cattle, sheep and horses and only once a man seemed utterly removed from us and unnaturally quiet. Our voices were suddenly hushed when the train stood still and the horses were as startled by the silence as they were by the clanking it made when it ran over points or its clattering in tunnels or its letting off steam at the stations. All such disturbances happened when we least expected them and we would jump up to hold our charges by the head.

Phoebe and I, who till then had seized every chance to clasp hold of each other when we found ourselves alone, did not even touch hands for the whole of the journey. And yet we were literally locked in alone, ignored.

The train stopped at every station. Our horsebox never even reached the platform, except at junctions which had longer ones. All human activity took place beyond our reach and even beyond earshot of our cries. 'Ve shouted at two stations for water for the horses, and at the third where we were heard I could not get out to fetch it. The door had jammed. The guard brought three buckets, one by one, and handed them through the window. At the two junctions all the other passengers who had to change trains were able to walk about or have drinks in the bar while they waited, while we were shunted helplessly up and down, abandoned in sidings, dragged out again on to the main line and propelled with violent jolts into the back of our next train. Twice, when the horses had sneezing fits, our clothes were drenched. We could not get out of the way. We spent some parts of the journey laughing helplessly. But all the incidents were spaced between long periods of happy calm suspension during which we seldom spoke and had no thoughts, unless sensations count as thoughts – the rhythmic rocking and its soporific sound, the sweet wet smell of the October country air that came wafting through the box to mingle with the smell of horses that was so homely and ordinary to us.

Charlie and Tom, who had gone ahead in the Fiat, were at Ballinasloe station to meet us and we were released by a railwayman with a heavy hammer and cold chisel. The horses came out quietly, but from that moment on we entered with them into a tumultuous assembly. We emerged from our dream with a plunge into physical life, into streets filled with men and horses, boys running, women wandering in and out, voices screaming, cajoling, shouting, neighing. A drunk man and a sober one were hitting each other, without success because both were kept on their feet by the press of people. While we were stuck in a jam at a corner, holding our horses, someone pushed a bottle to my lips, a blue one such as chemists use for poison but it smelt of whiskey and I took a sip. There was a jumble of music everywhere, tin whistles, melodeons and fiddles all playing different tunes for money. Tinker women with babies in their shawls and little children clinging to their skirts held out their arms to us and said rapid prayers for money.

With relief we emerged from the street into a dusty open space where the main part of the fair was held. It was now the end of the first day and only a few horses were being trotted up and down. There were dozens of empty carts and traps, some with horses tethered to their wheels eating bundles of cut grass. Donkeys stood sleepily here and there, and groups of blue-

153

suited men, each carrying a stick, bowed their heads together talking in low voices. There were a few parked cars. The space and the quietness made it like a backwater compared to the streaming streets. The business of the fair is almost silent, the pleasure clamorous.

When Thackeray visited Ballinasloe in 1842, he wrote, 'As it was not fairtime the town did not seem particularly busy, nor was there much to remark in it, except a church, and a magnificent lunatic asylum, that lies outside the town on the Dublin road, and is as handsome and stately as a palace.'[1] It was to this building that we led our horses. The town had spread beyond it since his time. Charlie called it the workhouse but I am sure it was the building Thackeray saw. There are only three kinds of buildings that dominate provincial towns like palaces – workhouses, lunatic asylums, and barracks for English soldiers – and many of these have been used for all three purposes at different times. Police barracks and churches are smaller and easily distinguished from each other.

When Charlie said the only stables he could get were in the workhouse, I thought he meant the old workhouse stables and was not surprised, knowing that every bit of stabling in the town would be made available, but we were directed to lead our horses not to the outbuildings of Thackeray's palace but through its magnificently arched double front doors. They stood trembling and snorting in the stone paved vestibule while we tried to find out which of three long corridors led to their cells. Three warders in shirtsleeves and breeches were obliging to us but disagreed with each other, and while they searched the building and came back with contradictory messages, night fell. At last they brought paraffin lamps and walked before us down one narrow, high-ceilinged cave, casting frightening black shadows on pale walls. The horses were also scared by the enclosed echo of their own hoofs and by the smell of mildew. We coaxed the two older ones along hoping that the two-year-old which was with Tom would look for safety in company and follow them. But she would not. She struggled and turned and the more she struggled the louder the noise of her hoofs. At last Charlie had a plan that succeeded. He brought her and one of

154

the six-year-olds down the corridor side by side, though there was scarcely room for two abreast.

A grey painted door, like a bedroom door, with a brass knob handle was opened for each and each was locked into a little square room, about ten foot square and fifteen high, a small barred window well above reach of their heads. The walls were not padded – perhaps it had all worn away – but they found comfort in the oat-straw that thickly covered the floor and deadened the sound of their hoofs, and in their bags of hay and grocery boxes with a feed of oats in each. Tom put the keys of the three cells in his pocket, and we came out feeling like cheats.

Charlie always hated selling horses, anyway, although that was the only way he knew of keeping Woodbrook. He said with a laugh that was meant to be cheerful, as we walked to the hotel, that things had come to a pretty pass when a creature reared at Woodbrook had to go to the workhouse before it found a new life.

'I think it's the lunatic asylum,' I said.

'Is that any better, do you think?'

For a reason I cannot explain, I thought it was a bit better. But I did not say so.

All three horses were sold next day.

Chapter Eight

Carrick-on-Shannon is shaped like a T. We thought it ugly compared to Boyle, but at least it had the same eighteenth-century look, its colour-washed shops and houses being more or less uniform in height, most of them two storeys and the highest three. It had once been a busy inland port. The quays curved gracefully with the bend of the river and low warehouses of dark limestone, detached from each other, made a pleasant skirting to the lower part of the town.

Approaching Carrick from Boyle on the Sligo–Dublin road, you pass Woodbrook on your left, then two miles farther on Clongoonagh where the other branch of the Kirkwood family had lived for several generations. Then the road slopes down. You cross the Shannon by an old stone bridge, pleasantly narrow and long, with low parapets that give a view of the wide river that shines like gun-metal in cloudy weather and on clear days is blue like a calm sea bay. To the right as you cross you catch a glimpse of green fields between the warehouses, for the town is narrow, and to your left the remains of a mass of old buildings which used to be one of the larger workhouses of Ireland. Its remains still cover several acres. Those parts of it which have not fallen down or been demolished purposely are now used as offices by the Leitrim County Council and have kept the beauty of their architect's design – arched gateways, shallow slated roofs, wide gables, windows much lovelier than those of the mansions in Merrion Square, Dublin, where Oscar Wilde was brought up. The only reminder of its workhouse days lies covered in dust on the floor of an upstairs room of a block to the left of the main entrance where the Board of Guardians held their meetings in the years succeeding the Irish Poor Law of 1838 – I mean the large piles of huge leather-bound volumes of their minutes written in various hands. At one time I sat there reading them, day after day.

To reach this workhouse you have to go up the hill from the bridge, the Main Street or stem of the T, a hill lined with small bars and shops, till you reach a crossways at the top where a clock with four faces used to stand on its pedestal. There the right-hand stroke of the T leads to Dublin and is lined by shops and bars of the usual size but is interrupted in a startling way by a hotel four storeys high and green. Only the spire of the chapel opposite is higher. The military barracks of the British Army, an enormous thing which once diminished both hotel and chapel, was pulled down to the cheers of a jubilant crowd in the 1930s.

The left-hand stroke of the T is a blind alley leading to the workhouse, a real blind alley stopped by the Shannon and the Boyle Water which form a bay at the edge of its grounds. It suited the English Poor Law Act, which was adapted to Ireland's needs in 1838; it had all the prison-like security the law required. The street leading to it from the town was cut off by its strong entrance gates. It was bounded by a high stone wall that had only one other opening in it – a side door for the use of the staff leading into the Main Street and always locked. This door fell off its hinges during the famine and allowed a crowd of women paupers out just at the moment when Mr James Kirkwood, J.P., on his way home to Woodbrook, was walking down the Main Street towards the stables where he had left his horse. They mobbed him, entreating him to come to the workhouse to see for himself the sort of food they were given. He went with the women and was shocked by what he saw. Three years later he was obliged to go to London and give a description of the kitchens and dining-room to a select committee of the House of Lords, for in 1850 this magnificently built deadend of Carrick, and particularly its side door, became a *cause célèbre* in England.

It was James Kirkwood's brother, Thomas of Clongoonagh, who disturbed the Lords, never dreaming how far his one angry letter would go. He had written to the Poor Law Commissioners in Dublin not out of concern for the welfare of the paupers but because his son saw, or imagined he saw, one of their paid employees, the workhouse inspector, seducing a pauper woman among the trees that lined the avenue to his house.

'Sirs,' wrote Mr Kirkwood on 29 June 1848,

> Both as a payer of rates to a large amount and as a magistrate, I beg to call your attention to the Carrick-on-Shannon Poorhouse which I understand is turned into a den of infamy, particularly so, by the Inspector, Captain Wynne; and not content with that, he brings these bad characters to my gate, and which I have positive proof of. I would not be surprised if the Union rebelled against the rates, when they are turned to such use.
>
> I am etc.
>
> Thomas Kirkwood.[1]

When the commissioners sent this letter to Captain Wynne, he defended the conduct of the workhouse and enclosed with his reply supporting letters from the Protestant and Roman Catholic chaplains. About himself he said, 'with regard to that portion of the letter which refers to my conduct as a private individual, I need not trouble the Commissioners further than to be permitted to state that it is a malicious falsehood; but that my indignation was in some measure appeased when, upon calling on the gentleman, I found him perfectly mad.'

The letters by themselves seem to be inspired by private animosity but really they were a symptom of the hatred and suspicion with which almost every landowner regarded the Poor Law. Irish landowners and Poor Law officials were at that time beset by a disaster unique in Europe – the Great Famine of 1845 to 1849. As famine developed the poor rate rose from year to year, administration became deadlocked and corruption uncontrollable. Landlords, unlike their English fellows, had never had to pay poor rates before and their one safeguard, effective in England – the harsh conditions imposed on workhouse inmates to keep all but the desperately poor away – collapsed, as hunger brought millions crowding at the gates like uninvited guests to a feast. After three years of that, by 1848, Ireland's first Poor Law, only ten years old, was crumbling to bits. It was Captain Wynne's job to try to save it in the enormous Unions of Boyle and Carrick of which he was temporary inspector.

The Act had formed groups of parishes into unions for the relief of the poor, each governed by a board of elected guardians who worked part-time and were not paid. Some of these boards were cumbersome – the Carrick Union had thirty-six members – and it was often difficult to get even a quorum to meet regularly. It was one of the temporary inspectors' thankless tasks to insist on proper meetings being held, and often their authority was challenged. Because they were paid and usually younger than the elected guardians they were scorned as upstarts.

Captain Wynne was particularly exposed to animosity, for although he was forty-five and could be called a gentleman, his forebears only one generation back, though they kept up no house in the county and were free from local responsibilities, had spent their time grubbing in the Leitrim Mountains for copper ore, leaving huge pits everywhere. He himself lived as a lodger in a house a short ride from Boyle and did not know what it was to pay rates. Yet the commissioners in Dublin encouraged him to decide how the rates should be spent and supported him whenever he wrote to them wishing to overrule the guardians who, being with two or three exceptions large and responsible landowners, either paid or owed enormous sums in rates.

He was appointed in November 1847, at a time when deaths by starvation, disease and exposure greatly exceeded the numbers to which the guardians had become accustomed. The Poor Rate was at its highest, most of it uncollected or uncollectable, there being few cattle or movable goods left to distrain upon; two of the principal rate-collectors had absconded with the money; the books were in confusion; and corruption among tradesmen who supplied the workhouse and some of the badly paid officials responsible for buying supplies was an accepted evil.

Wynne tried energetically to correct all this and to arouse the guardians from lethargy. In his reports, the first December after his arrival, he wrote of Carrick, 'I have met a greater amount of urgent and pressing destitution in this Union than in any other part of Ireland I have visited, as in addition to want of food which exists to as great an extent as in any other part of Ireland, want of shelter from the inclemency of the seasons exists to a far greater extent ... vast numbers of families have been unhoused and their houses destroyed. You cannot admit them to the workhouse, there is no room; you cannot give them outdoor relief, they have no houses ... Their cries may be heard all night in the streets of this town [Carrick]; and since my arrival here I have constantly been obliged to procure shelter in the stables in the neighbourhood for persons I have found perishing in the streets at 12 o'clock at night.'

Every landed member of the Board of Guardians added, even in the hardest winter weather, to the number of claimants for the Poor Relief they so much hated paying out. It was not enough to lock a tenant's door. If the roof was on rates had to be paid. Hence the number of ghastly scenes that remain in literature and painting showing little 'cabins' being tumbled down while families sit watching huddled together in their rags. James Kirkwood of Woodbrook, High Sheriff of County Roscommon and one of the more attentive members of the Board of Guardians, evicted eighteen families from Usna alone, the smallest part of his estate, nearest the house.

The Poor Law Commissioners were moved by Captain Wynne's report. In their reply on 28 December they referred to his statement that 'the cries of the destitute may be heard in the streets of Carrick-on-Shannon all night' and issued an order 'authorizing out-door relief to the ablebodied', which could be permitted under a seldom used amendment to the Act. This meant that porridge, soup or bread could be given to the starving even if they had no houses. But it was impossible to implement the order without the help of the guardians. For one thing the workhouse master and several other members of the staff were ill in bed, suffering from one or other of the epidemics that were raging everywhere, and for another the distribution of a vast amount of food required supervision not only in Carrick but at appointed places many miles apart throughout the Union. Wynne persuaded the guardians to pass a resolution by which they agreed to meet daily 'so long as the necessity for doing so continue'. Relying on this he had notices posted in numerous villages telling those entitled to outdoor relief to collect their weekly rations next Monday. But not one of the guardians turned up for any of the daily meetings at which detailed plans were to be made and on the Monday he found himself alone as the only person with authority to carry out this complex and unprecedented scheme. 'With considerable difficulty and the exertions of persons unconnected with the Poor Law, I succeeded in preventing any more serious consequences than a few hours' delay.'

The guardians continued to ignore him and on 19 January 1848 he wrote, 'I have the honour to state for the information of the Commissioners, that I can no longer hope to get on with the present Board of Guardians, who appear to have completely deserted their post.'

The commissioners immediately sacked all thirty-six of them, including of course the two Kirkwood brothers, and put in their place two paid officials called vice-guardians who were to administer the whole Union of Carrick-on-Shannon under the direction of Captain Wynne.

Everything steadily improved, except the collection of rates. Among the smaller rate-payers there was a genuine shortage of money; pigs and poultry, which depended upon the potato crop, could no longer be reared. But most of the large proprietors, who should have been the union's main source of income, simply refused to pay. 'They are at present sending to market as fast as possible.' The only movable property they could hide was money and, surprising as it now seems, they succeeded in that without being taken to court. Hugh Barton, the rich Dublin wine merchant who had bought the whole of the Cootehall estate and a vast area of land in County Kildare, had paid no rates for many years and did not intend to. On his arrival as the Kirkwoods' neighbour, he had made himself notorious by the most savage, sudden and numerous evictions yet known in the county,[2] and one of the discoveries made by Captain Wynne was that the rate-collector whose task it was to confront him was one of the few tenants who had been allowed to stay. Naturally this man had not dared to ask Barton for a penny.

Wynne advised the appointment of strangers and engaged

one collector from as far away as Wales. The new policy made him even more unpopular with the ex-guardians.

With the frosts of February 1848, and the cold wind and rain of March, more and more money was needed to provide shelter. Many sheds were built and a large disused mill acquired as an auxiliary workhouse. This again was a form of expenditure that had not existed under the rule of the board. Its ex-members complained that 'immoderate expenditure' was 'an encouragement to the vice of idleness'. They blamed outdoor relief for the difficulty they had in obtaining labourers.

Captain Wynne inquired about the wages offered and found that most employers offered work to be paid 'by the bit', that is one daily meal; many withheld payment of any kind from working tenants whose rent was in arrears. Eightpence to tenpence a day was a good wage for the time. The only man who paid it, and in cash, was Mr Lloyd of Croghan. Lloyd, who was related to the Kirkwoods, had been described about twenty years before as a rare example of a fair employer and a good farmer. He was unique in that enormous union.

The employers knew that a system of money wages was inevitable, yet refused to commit themselves to it. The labourers, having no confidence that they would be paid at all, refused unless starving to go to work. And so most of the land remained untilled. In country such as this where no ploughs were used and every field was dug by spade, employment would have saved thousands of people and at the same time restored the farmers' fortunes.

This was an especially tragic situation in the spring of 1848 when the land was beginning to recover from three years' famine; supplies of seed oats were available and for the first time stocks of blight-free seed potatoes had been imported. Gentlemen of the Kirkwoods' rank who had never handled a farming implement before were 'now struggling to till their land with their own hands. Such is the scarcity of money and the anxiety of those who have it to hold it.'

A month after describing this new practice in his report, Captain Wynne met with that instance of it that was to bring him before the House of Lords, for no labourer seeing him and a woman on the Clongoonagh avenue would have done more than gossip locally. It was young Andrew Kirkwood, handling a loy for the first time in his life, who saw them. He left work at once bringing with him a workman who lived in his father's house, and they stalked the pair of them approaching from different sides of the wood into which they guessed she had gone. That he and his father's man were together cutting turf on the bog was a circumstance till then unknown, but turf-cutting was something that had to be done whatever happened to the crops, for on it depended the whole household fuel for a year, and it had to be done quickly in snatches of good weather. Andrew told his father what they saw, or thought they saw, and old Thomas Kirkwood clutched the golden straws of moral righteousness. Although he was surrounded like everybody else by corpses in his ditches, by the barely living, sick and starving, and by land gone to waste for want of paid labour, he used the salacious spying of his son to inaugurate a negative inquiry into the past. He did this at a time when a positive plan to effect and encourage reforms in the workhouse could have saved many lives in the winter to come.

The Lords began to take evidence two years later, on 6 May 1850. By then the Board of Guardians had been reconstituted and the Kirkwood brothers were back in office.

Captain Wynne's most powerful opponent was the Marquis of Westmeath who had been made chairman of the new Board of Guardians. Had he not been shown Thomas Kirkwood's letter the case would never have reached the House of Lords. His all-important signature was at the head of the thirty-five others who signed the petition that led to the inquiry. Thomas was not called as a witness, but his brother James of Woodbrook answered many questions. He was asked about the incident which became known as the 'breakfast riot'.

'I saw a very large crowd of women armed with different sorts of sticks and things; to the best of my opinion there were about 300 altogether . . . I proceeded to their eating-room. This, to the best of my recollection, happened between two and three o'clock in the day, and their breakfast was on the table.'

163

'At two or three o'clock in the day their breakfast was on the table?'

'Yes, and a very wretched breakfast, very wretched indeed. The Assistant Apothecary came down with me, and he drew my attention to the food, as to the milk, which could not be called milk; it appeared to me half water.'

'Worse than London milk?'

'It was very bad. The gruel or sort of thing they were getting was wretchedly bad ... After I had looked over that I proceeded to the kitchens, and really I regretted having gone, for the stench was very bad in them, the smell from the boilers; there was some of this wretched porridge at the bottom of one of the boilers which I recollect, and really it was offensive to go near it, it was in such a state ... I then proceeded to the Board Room and in the Board Room I met the Inspecting Officer [Captain Wynne] and one of the Vice-Guardians. I was a little excited, certainly. I was a little annoyed at finding the state that parts of the house I visited were in, after such a quantity of money being extracted from the pockets of the people ... and I might, perhaps, have said more than was altogether right; however I forget now exactly what I said, I was so annoyed ...'

'Did [they] in reply give you any explanation?'

'I cannot charge my memory with that.'

Mr Kirkwood kept repeating himself, rushing on in a torrent of words until stumped by a question when he invariably said 'I cannot charge my memory with that.' He said that almost everything in the workhouse had been sold through the side-door that had fallen off its hinges – porridge for pig food, bread, soap, paupers' clothes. Peculation, he said, was carried on by members of the staff and by the paupers themselves. He must have struck their Lordships as an excitable and nervous man and as an honest, if forgetful, witness. He may have seemed wild and uncouth to them too. He probably spoke with a North Roscommon accent much more marked than Charlie's. The Roscommon manner of speech is rapid and suits voluble natures; the first words burst out in an explosion and the rest stream like water through a hole in a dam.

Other witnesses eagerly described both filth and peculations, but no such evils could be precisely dated. 'We went into the laundry yard,' said one of the members of the new Board of Guardians, who like James Kirkwood could not say when, 'and we caused the store to be opened; we got a portion of paupers to take out an immense quantity of clothes and they were in a most awful state ... They were perfectly rotten, and when they were carried out they were in a smoking condition, as if the most of them would take fire ...'

The rot and smoke were caused by lime which had been sprinkled on the unwashed clothes and then become damp. As in my time at Woodbrook, lime, either dry or as whitewash, was the only kind of disinfectant used. It had been put on to the dirty clothes because the workhouse pump had failed and no washing could be done, and at the same time the lower floor, where the laundry was, had been flooded by rain, the drains and rainpipes being blocked. The cess-pools also needed clearing, and when Dr Denis Phelan came to inspect the workhouse on 16 December 1849 he reported that 'The male probationary Ward was in the most discreditable state, the room and stairs being so filthy with faeces, urine, etc., that the matron and porter cautioned him against going into the ward.'

'But,' said the Lords' Committee, remembering that the re-constituted Board of Guardians came to office six weeks earlier, 'had no means been taken between the 1st of November and the 16th of December to remove the filth?' and in fact another visiting physician had commended the sanitary state of the house in a special report only three days after the vice-guardians had been removed.

The inquiry was supposed to be confined to the period of the vice-guardians' rule – from January 1848 until 31 October 1849 – but it was impossible to discover the dates at which various evils had begun. Some had been inherited from the old Board of Guardians, and much of the evidence hostile to Wynne and the vice-guardians was based on inspections made long after their departure. Straw – the paupers' bedding – which was supposed to be renewed every two months had remained unchanged for four months the guardians said, but their Visiting Committee, of which Thomas Kirkwood was a member, did not discover

165

that until Christmas eve. The vice-guardians had renewed it six weeks before their departure. No one could tell when the illicit trade in soap began through that side door, but the result of the action the new board took against it – a drastic cut in its supply – was clear; the laundry had not been made use of from the date of their appointment until 21 December. They had economized on water too; when the pump broke down, the vice-guardians had paid for water to be carted from the Shannon. The new board stopped that, to save money. But neither they, nor Captain Wynne and his vice-guardians, could stop the enormous frauds committed by contractors. So great was the demand for food and fuel all over the country that any successful attempt to do so would have cut supplies off altogether. Captain Wynne and the vice-guardians admitted conniving at the contractors' frauds. 'I cannot swear that it [the milk] was paid for,' said the workhouse clerk, 'because the contractors could not all be paid from the low state of the funds.' The contractors always had the upper hand. At one time bailiffs were planted in the house, though there was little to distrain upon. The paupers had no beds and even plates were so scarce that meals were taken in relays; hence the breakfast at 2 p.m. Dinner, which was supposed to be at 2, was often delayed till 10 at night.

Captain Wynne and his colleagues were also found to have kept the books improperly, and, though none at all had been kept by the old Board of Guardians for three years, that made no excuse for them. The tally of inmates, births and deaths, was a hopeless muddle. No roll-call system was practicable with such a huge unwonted crowd of paupers; large numbers absconded through the gate with the broken hinges and rations were frequently drawn for them and for the dead.

Working as he was for long hours every day among the dead and dying, debt and fraud must have seemed to Wynne the least of evils. He was evidently a man of unusual energy and compassion, but the task he was given was worse than the Augean stables, for at every successful step he took to clean up Carrick's workhouse, more mess than ever swamped him in the shape of barely living human beings crowding at the gates. Even two

166

years after the beginning of the famine, when he was first appointed in November 1847, there were only 350 paupers in the workhouse. Seeing the distress around him, he got permission to raise the number first to 900, and then with some help from the sheds and auxiliary houses to 1,900 – the number the vice-guardians estimated to the Lords to have been under their care. With scant money, worn equipment and a tiny, ill-paid inefficient staff, no one could have managed it.

The Lords had listened for eight days to revolting details of how the paupers lived and died, and now for another nine weeks they heard about Captain Wynne's private life. This and the publicity attached to it was the nastiest part for him, but it was fairly conducted and not ruinous to his career because accusations against him for immoral behaviour were only relevant if it could be proved that he gave female paupers privileges in return for sexual intercourse.

Between Carrick and Boyle Captain Wynne had to ride past the gates of the two Kirkwood brothers – Clongoonagh about two miles from Carrick, and Woodbrook on the other side of the road a mile and a bit farther on towards Boyle. He often called at Woodbrook and knew James Kirkwood well, but he never met Thomas except at board meetings nor had been inside his gates until the shameful day that led to the inquiry.

In June 1848 he had been asked to suggest alterations in the boundary between the two unions under his charge. It was this, he said, that made him enter Mr Thomas Kirkwood's grounds. He left his horse at the gate-lodge and walked with his paper, pencil and map up the drive and into a plantation of fir-trees. If he had ridden there he might have escaped attention. 'What made you remember it particularly?' said one of the peers to the gate-house keeper Ann Cresswell, and she replied, 'A gentleman takes his beast along to the house with him.'

She said she saw him follow a woman up the avenue. Her brother Josie Kelly who was cutting turf with young Andrew Kirkwood watched them from the bog, then crept up close and stooped behind a tree. Kelly saw Captain Wynne 'between her legs', Andrew 'heard some groaning and saw Captain Wynne in connection with the woman there'. Kelly said young Mr Kirkwood was laughing about it, but young Mr Kirkwood cross-examined separately declared himself to have been so shocked and angered as to have gone immediately to the gate-house and turned Wynne's horse loose upon the mail-coach road.

'What was your motive in turning it out of the gate-house?' asked the Lords. 'What induced you to go and skulk behind a tree?' They were suspicious of all his motives. To turn the horse loose seemed to them a shocking and spiteful act, yet no nine-teenth-century Irishman would have wondered at it because horses everywhere in Ireland earned the homage or disdain that was their master's due. When Lord Ventry's horses were led by grooms up the long village street to the forge, every man stood still and raised his hat to them; if not, a groom or jealous neigh-bour might report disrespect which could be an excuse for evic-tion. Fortunately for Wynne and his horse a boy ran out and caught it, and held it by the roadside verge until he was ready to go. Wynne gave the boy a fourpenny piece and rode off appar-ently without suspecting that his visit had caused any trouble.

He heard nothing of that until he received Thomas Kirk-wood's letter, which had been forwarded to him from Dublin by the Poor Law Commissioners. At the House of Lords in-quiry he was asked whether this was a copy or the original letter. It was the original, he said. He had taken it at once to the house and said, 'Is this your handwriting, Mr Kirkwood, and what authority have you for making this statement?' Mr Kirk-wood had refused to answer. All he would say was, 'Captain Wynne, you are come here to quarrel with me; I cannot fight you; I am bound over; the gentleman of the country will state that I am bound over; but my son shall fight you.' 'I stated, "Mr Kirkwood, I am a public officer and have not come here for the purpose of fighting ... I have come here to ascertain ... on what grounds you have made this charge against my public and official character, as well as my private character ..." The only answer I could get from him was "I cannot fight you; I am bound over." I then stated, "your conduct is that of a madman, and I must treat you as such. I wish you good morning." Under the excitement of the moment ... I sent by that night's post my report to the Commissioners, in which I reverted to the opinion I had formed of Mr Kirkwood.'

'That he was mad?'

'Yes . . . With regard to bringing "those improper characters to his gate" . . . I was followed everywhere by women of every description and character.'

The woman in the avenue, he said, had a certificate to show that her fare would be paid from Liverpool to America, but had no means of getting to Liverpool. He promised to help her with part of the fare out of his own pocket and to ask the vice-guardians to contribute the rest if she came to see them in Carrick next day. Together next day they gave her ten or twelve shillings to bring her to Liverpool.

It was implied, though never clearly said, that he was blameless in his conduct towards that woman, but members of the old Board of Guardians had been skulking, not behind trees, but in the workhouse passages and were now able to produce witnesses who said they had seen him 'in connexion' with half a dozen women in the house or near it. Their case was strengthened by Wynne's declared approval of the permissive clauses in the Poor Law Act. Members of the Lords' Committee, discovering details for the first time, were grieved to hear that 'women whose husbands are beyond the seas, or in custody of the law or in a lunatic asylum, shall be dealt with in the same way as widows'; and most shocking of all to those who had not actually witnessed starvation was an order that allowed public funds to be spent on mothers of illegitimate children. Here before them was a public servant who had interpreted such rules in the widest possible sense with shameless approval and who now appeared to be equally shameless in his conduct towards immoral female paupers.

Day after day girls were spoken of to the committee – a new name every few days – with much circumstantial and some actual evidence of Wynne's misconduct with each. His denials were convincing.

But when the imperative question came, 'Do you know Catherine Foley?' he began to inculpate himself at once. She was an orphan twenty-five years younger than him, who had been admitted to the workhouse as a child in 1846, a year before his appointment. As soon as her name was mentioned words poured from him, showing that he knew her too well. Among all those thousands of paupers he remembered every detail of her life, never having to plead for time to refer to records, and when he was asked whether he knew anything against her character he replied, too firmly for his good, 'nothing in the world, nor ever knew anything against her'. He said he had personally chosen her as an emigrant to Australia, but when he was called before the committee again three weeks later he denied it.

Even without his self-indictment, the case against him was strong. Free emigration was a favour which only female paupers could obtain, and all over Ireland during the famine influential men were pursued with demands. To the starving emigration was often the only hope left. Mothers pleaded for their daughters to be sent. Young women sought it as an escape from the workhouse. It was clear to Captain Wynne's enemies that only one form of bribery was available to pauper women.

It seemed at first that Catherine Foley had no wish to leave the country, no need to bribe anyone. After Wynne's appointment she had suffered none of the common pauper's hardships. She had been especially favoured, first as the assistant matron's servant – a job that gave her better rations than the rest – and then, after her discharge, as maid to Mrs Phayre, the wife of the workhouse clerk, who lived in Boyle, a post which Captain Wynne had obtained for her close to his own lodgings. It therefore seemed improbable that she should wish to emigrate.

But the girl, they hinted, was pregnant. Captain Wynne succeeded in putting her on the Australian list just in time. The Lords found no proof of that, but much of the evidence, except his, seemed to show that he had had an affair with her; and all, including his, implied that he loved her.

On 16 July the last witness was 'directed to withdraw' and the Lords settled down to prepare their report which reads now as a model of fairness.

In their report they referred to these private matters and to the public conduct of the workhouse. 'In both portions of the investigations the Committee have met with conflicting evidence; nor have their difficulties been wholly removed by the voluminous reports to be found in the Appendix. Even in this documentary evidence much inconsistency prevails.' Captain Wynne was severely criticized, but not dismissed from the Poor Law service. The Kirkwood brothers and their fellow guardians were censured but remained in office. They had, the Lords said in conclusion, 'formed an inadequate idea of the proper mode of performing their important duties. Unless a strict supervision is exercised over the conduct of the officers – unless the accounts are periodically examined and controlled – unless the house is regularly inspected ... the relief of distress will be inadequately provided for. Successful fraud will lead to the demoralization of the people; unprincipled prodigality will dry up the sources of industry. These remarks, true in all countries, apply to Ireland with peculiar force. What in more fortunate countries may produce danger, cannot fail to lead to absolute ruin in Ireland, where the difficulties of administering a Poor Law are so great, and the consequences of failure are so fatal.'

Ireland was different. That was true. But when people of any nation starve they grow the same. Their stinking, bloated bodies crawl about, or lie in the streets and country ditches alive or dead, to the annoyance of anyone going about his business.

The most remarkable feature of that heart-rending report is to me that during its twenty-eight foolscap pages of documents and transcripts of cross-examination no mention is made of the famine. The omission of that dreaded word tells another truth. It is the key to government policy enacted by Lord John Russell, the Prime Minister, who in spite of plentiful evidence to the contrary stuck to the theory that Ireland should look after itself – a policy which was the cause of millions of unnecessary deaths. It was his government that refused to treat the famine as a unique emergency that could only be relieved from Treasury funds. The destitute had increased in numbers, that was all; and, incredible though it seems, even the normal financial support from Westminster was suddenly withdrawn. The Irish

Poor Law Extension Act threw the whole burden of famine relief on to local rates, and this in the summer of 1847 was at a time when many poor unions such as Carrick-on-Shannon were known to be bankrupt. It was well known too in Government circles that even if every property-owner in Ireland paid his rates to the full, relief of distress would be minimal.

Utterly inadequate imports of Indian corn were made and meanly distributed so as not to interfere with private trade in oatmeal and flour. Indian corn was known to the people as Peel's brimstone because most of it was rotten when they first tasted it during his ministry in the first and mildest year of the famine. He had chosen it because it was a foreign crop that could not be said to compete with home trade, but because half Europe was famine-stricken in 1846 the price he offered was outbidden by other countries and supplies to Ireland were allowed to fail at a critical time (autumn 1846).

It would not have saved many of the starving if all home produce had been kept in Ireland, but an order forbidding exports would certainly have done something to quell the impotent rage people felt against their rulers as wretched multitudes gathered at the seaports to watch cargoes of grain, butter, pigs and cattle being loaded under military guard for shipment to England.[3] Word of this was carried throughout the country by 'travelling men', the wandering story-tellers and beggars who in normal times were the only source of news and who now in their swollen numbers found shelter as before mainly in the crowded cabins of the very poor. Naturally no one knew how tiny this produce was, coming as it did from good land on the east coast and from some river valleys.

Queen Elizabeth and Cromwell after her had openly declared their policy to be the extinction of the Irish people. The English governments during the famine had no such conscious wish. But they acted on theories that came nearer to achieving that old policy than any of the long gone wars.

Chapter Nine

Once, at the fair of Boyle when I was buying seed potatoes with Tommy Maxwell's expert help, I saw on an ass-cart a small load of a variety I had never seen before, white ones with bluish-red markings. I wanted to try them. He said no one would buy them and that it was a poor mountainy man that was selling them who would drive his ass home in the evening with the load on the cart the same as he drove in to town. The potatoes were 'Blacksmith's' he said, the kind that everybody grew in the 'bad times' – the famine times. I persuaded him to let me buy a few, enough for a couple of ridges, but he was very upset. We planted them at the side of the field. They got the blight. The rest of our crop – about six acres – grew perfectly. His prejudice was not a superstition. Some varieties are more vulnerable than others and in a warm wet summer can succumb even after being sprayed. And I did not think then how near the famine was to him. His grandparents lived through it, but some of their first children starved to death. They had fifteen of whom Nanny, his mother, was the youngest.

All Irish countrymen are reminded of the famine every summer when the time comes to spray the potatoes. In England growers only spray after warnings from the Ministry of Agriculture – for the blight fungus *Phytophthora Infestans* can only thrive in certain weathers – but in Ireland where in my time everybody was a grower everybody sprayed his crop with Bordeaux mixture, however dry the summer, just as everybody everywhere dips sheep. The life history of the fungus was discovered in Ireland long after the famine. The remedy was first used in 1885.

Spraying the potato fields became one of my special jobs. It was lonely and monotonous walking slowly up and down all day between rows that seemed endless, especially from the bottom of the hill where the top was out of sight, but the rhythm became like a pleasure-giving drug. It reminded me of wading knee-deep in the sea; the dense leaves hid my feet, gave way and closed in again behind me, and before me stretched forever rich and dark the delicate potato blossoms wavering, purple or white according to their kind. The colour of the Bordeaux mixture was beautiful too and I even liked its smell. My clothes, face and hands would be covered with it by the evening and sometimes it stung my eyes a bit.

Early in the morning Tommy and I would load a cart with large empty Guinness barrels and lead the horse across the Bottoms to the 'canal' at a place near the gate-lodge where it was easy to dip buckets. We would leave one barrel empty for the mixture and tie sacks over the full ones to stop the water splashing out. But even so a lot was lost on the bumpy way over the fields. Phoebe would meet us by the potatoes. I think she liked measuring and stirring the stuff – white crystals of soda and clear blue translucent crystals of that brilliant chemical used in washing linen. The soda crystals were jagged, with shining irregular facets, and the blue looked like cut gems. Together, mixed in water, they were cloudy like absinthe. We stirred the barrel with long ashplants cut from a tree on the avenue. Then she filled my sprayer for me and rode home on the empty cart with Tom.

I must be remembering a new sprayer, for it shone in the sun, with streaks of bluey-green mixture on it here and there. It was made of copper and shaped to fit one's back like a knapsack, with leather shoulder straps and a belt to keep it from banging about. A copper pipe attached to a rubber tube was in my right hand. It had a fine rose nozzle. And in my left hand, I held a pump handle which I kept working up and down and up and down all day in rhythm with my step. I learned to judge the time for refills by the weight of the knapsack. It was best to refill it before it was completely empty, rather than walk back to the barrels from the far end of the field. The spray dulled the rich green of the potato plants as it dried. They looked as though they had been powdered, whitish-blue. Long after our disengagement, I liked it when Phoebe saw Bordeaux stains on my face. She would wipe them away, standing close to me and holding the lapel of my coat.

It was spraying that led me to talk about the famine to Nanny. Our potato field that year was near her house and I used to leave my can with her on the way home. I had run out of water one afternoon, too late to cart more, and came to her door at about four o'clock, at a time when she was usually sitting by the fire alone, her work done until her sons came home for tea. She dusted a chair for me – however clean it was and however dirty my clothes it had to be dusted before a guest sat on it – and fanned the fire to make the kettle boil. It was to be only a cup of tea in my hand, she said, which means without bread and butter, but she cut bread and put butter and jam on the table as I knew she would.

She said Michael could tell me more about the famine than she and I could see him when it was time for me to leave. He was by the gate with his pipe (I had climbed the wall at the side of the house). But after a little while she began to speak of it vividly and when I got home I wrote down all I remembered. It was the first of many talks of which I made notes. Some notes have survived.

Her parents were married very young, as was the custom then, and had at least one baby before 1845, more during the famine – she could not remember how many and was not very sure of her own age. She knew she was born in the 1860s, the last of fifteen, and said she knew less about the bad times than many people of her age 'on account of her brothers being all hot men that would not listen'. Her father and mother used often to be talking about the hunger and the fever and the terrible evictions, but the brothers would say 'Don't be telling us about those bad times' and walk out the door, and I along with them. I suppose it was something like listening to war reminiscences now. But soon it was evident to me that she had listened to her parents. Part of what they told her made her very unhappy and I guessed she had never repeated it to her children. She told me this part in the end, although I never pressed her. It is easier to speak of misery to someone emotionally detached.

I was full of newly read books and talked more than she did at first. For one thing, she was busy with the teapot and with shooing out the hens which came in when they heard the clink of china, hoping for crumbs; and then I think she really did not wish to talk about it. She would hear of no earthly reason for the famine and when I said that disaster could have been averted she stood still and looked at me.

'It was the hand of God,' she said. 'What else would it be but the hand of God when a white mist came down over the whole of Ireland on that day, and in the morning – imagine if you was to walk out where you was working that yoke today' (she meant the copper can by the doorway) 'and say to yourself, "There's a grand crop growing", and the stalks thick and strong and all full green with the flowers on them. And in the morning the whole country black with rotten stalks.'

I forget the name of the field I was spraying that year, but am sure she mentioned it, for it was during that conversation that I found the origin of the field names we used daily without wondering why they were called so, as in a town one uses names of streets. There were Flanagan's rock, Clancy's rock, Meehan's garden, Martin's garden, M'Lannie's, Higgin's, Cresswell's, Conlon's, Cregan's, Luggy's and five or six places with the names Feely in them, Nanny's maiden name. She knew the Christian names of everyone who had lived in the townland of Usna when the famine began. Her house was the only one standing after it, and most of the names had no landmarks now, the walls of the gardens having been pulled down with the houses to make a wide open space of the Hill of Usna, where the beasts grazed and where we roamed on our horses every day. She said there were eighteen families living there in 1845, but I think there were nearly thirty, all tenants of farms, called 'gardens', of under five acres surrounded by low stone walls. Most of them kept no animals at all, but her parents and some others had one cow, a pig, a few fowl and space enough to grow a little barley. Corn, animals and butter were not used to feed the family but to pay the rent.

She said the summer of 1845 began with the best growing weather her parents could remember and that in August, before the evening of the mist, every garden on Usna, as far as they could see from their house, 'shined with plants' and promised a big crop. Some people managed to save enough good tubers to keep them alive that year, but the crop of 1846 was a total failure. When the eldest baby died next winter, her father persuaded her mother to go to the poorhouse with the other one or two – she could not remember how many – while he prepared the land in spring. He had enough barley seed to give them hope. Hunger and dysentery had weakened them and the weather was bad, but they walked to Carrick 'without misfortune' and waited in a crowd of hundreds outside the workhouse gates, hoping to see Captain Wynne who was said to be a good man. They were admitted to the gate-lodge after a couple of hours, but it was Captain Wynne's day at the poorhouse of Boyle. Only the workhouse master was there, at a table, but at least there was a warm fire. He asked if they were still in possession of their land. They held three acres, yes, from Mr Kirkwood of Woodbrook and the rent was paid.

'Then I can do nothing,' the workhouse master said.

By a new law from Westminster they were not destitute.[1] He told them to go home to Mr Kirkwood, sign a paper giving up their land and bring it back to him. Then he would admit the whole family. When they pleaded, he reminded them that their landlord was one of the Poor Law Guardians. How could he go against the rules and Mr Kirkwood not know?

They walked home in the dark. Of course they did not give up their land. They were ill and almost starving like the rest, but they had escaped the cholera and had hope. Without their land they would have had stirabout and no hope.

In January or February 1848 they were offered an alternative even more cruel. James Kirkwood sent for Nanny's father to the big house and told him he wanted no rent from that day on. He said he would give them enough wheat flour to make bread for the year and barley seed for spring sowing, and when the baby boy was old enough he would take him into the stable yard to work with the horses. He was buying cattle, he said, and would need Nanny's father for a herd, and a herd is a permanent position which passes from one generation to the next,

177

the house and 'garden' and the right of grazing a settled number of bullocks on the master's land being free of charges. Nanny's father knew all about that, but asked how many cattle and where would they run, the only land for them being Shanwelliagh and the Bottoms which was bad grass, being rushy, and 'the Bottoms often times flooded'.

Mr Kirkwood said he would put the cattle on the Hill of Usna which was the best limestone grass, dry and could keep sheep and horses too. Nanny's father said, 'It is, it is the best of land all right and will be again with the help of God.' But he was thinking of the people's walls and crops and houses that would stop the cattle. Nearly half of the houses were empty, their people having died or the lucky ones gone to America. Even so there were many that hoped for a crop next year.

Mr Kirkwood then flattered him, saying he was the best tenant he had and that the others all looked up to him and came to him for advice. He said all the others must give up their houses and land and go to the workhouse, or to America if they could. He said it was best for them, that they would be fed. He said he did not want the police or military to put them out, that Nanny's father was to persuade them to go quietly, showing them how it was for their own good. He was, he said, their leader.

At that meeting her father refused, saying he would leave only when the military tumbled his house down over his head along with the others. But when the day of the eviction came hunger and illness got the better of him.

'With the children and my mother sick, and another baby promised, what could he do?' said Nanny. 'He stood up on the houses and threw down the roofs of his own uncles even, many of his uncles and cousins, and he tumbled the walls down after. In the teeming sleet and snow the people were cast out to die on the road. Some few that had strength won through to America and more reached the poorhouse of Carrick, but the poorhouse was already filled and many died outside it lying against the walls.'

James Kirkwood was not exceptionally callous. He probably thought, as many of his neighbours did, that he was doing the

178

best he could not only for himself but for his tenants. Whether he threw them out or not, the people would die. If he tumbled down their houses, his rates would decrease and the land, opened out for cattle, start to pay, and the evicted would have a chance however small of being fed in the workhouse. All these considerations led him to the harsh decisions which he made.

Nanny's father had to make a similar decision, but for him it was ten times worse because he could only save his family by turning against his own people. For him it was solely a moral problem; his decision could not help or harm anyone, except his wife and children. If he refused Mr Kirkwood's demand, the 'crowbar brigade' – a gang of freelance ruffians – would be called in with soldiers and police to guard them. He would save his honour and almost certainly commit his family to death, for it was unlikely that the Master, having been crossed in so important a matter, would have found him land elsewhere as he did at Newtown for the Conlons and a few others whose rent was up to date. Feely's choice was also governed by the long established instinct of a subject people. A few individuals shot their masters and hid, but most were peaceable, even subservient. It seemed to them impossible to refuse a command from above. Even the shopping, which in my childhood in Scotland was called the 'messages', was called in Ireland the 'commands'. (Winnie used to say, as she watched me from the dairy window harnessing the pony and trap to set out for Boyle or Carrick, 'Is the major's tobacco remembered on your commands?')

Nanny's memories came bit by bit on different days and always she walked about, as she listened to me, or stood still to talk. I cannot remember ever seeing her sitting down, except during the short lull of her afternoon. At harvest time, when her sons brought me home with them for dinner at midday, she and her daughter stood to serve us as we ate, and long before they came home to tea she would be working again, baking bread or slicing great quantities of it, and getting food ready for the pig and hens. The only quick gesture I ever saw her make was at the hens. One or two would walk in, looking sideways at the floor, one eye at a time, and Nanny would flap her black apron at them. I always saw the hen first, she being occupied, and watched its jerky progress till the flapping of the big black wing sent it flapping through the open kitchen door. But there was never much to be found on the floor, for every few minutes she would take the twig from its corner and sweep out a mote invisible to me, with long easy strokes that were the very opposite of that sudden apron action.

About twenty yards from the door, in a hollow, stood the thatched house where she was born and where her sisters and eldest brother had died of starvation. It was used for animals now. And all about it lay their lovely garden – the same three acres within stone walls – large enough still to provide the family with potatoes and cabbage throughout the year and to grow enough oats and coarse potatoes – Arran Banners – for the animals. I think they usually managed some extra oats to sell. I had read that no such variety existed in the old days, that the people had forgotten how to grow anything except potatoes and therefore starved when those failed, but Nanny assured me again that in her father's youth one could see patches of barley and oats all over Usna and here and there a cow. Skimmed milk and sometimes buttermilk was eaten with potatoes, by those who owned a cow, but butter from the cream was stored salted in a firkin and sold with the corn to raise money. In the autumn before the eviction the 'driver', as she called the Kirkwoods' rent-collector, had put a cross and keepers on her father's little stack of barley to show that it belonged to his master in lieu of rent. The master had promised to take the cross and keepers off in return for those terrible deeds.

In a country where most people had never tasted bread, there were few mills and none of the poor had a notion of how to grind grain into flour at home. They were equally ignorant of meat. Some of the Usna tenants who owned pigs sold them for the price of half a stone of meal and one starving family near Cootehall allowed theirs to roam about for years, feeding on grass and rotten potatoes. It never occurred to them to kill it and in any case they would not have known how to use its body for food. Yet one pig cured by the ordinary method used by English cottagers would have fed a family for more than a year.

Nanny never uttered a word of indignation in speaking of those tragic years. She described what had happened to the people of Usna as the child of a survivor might describe a shipwreck long ago. Neither she nor her parents felt any bitterness towards the English over that. Cut off from public information, supported only by religious faith, they could not have known. But the politically informed did know and the truth soon spread urged on by a rapid growth in literacy, so much so that English policy during the famine and for seventy years after it created ill-feeling between the two countries more bitter or at least more generally felt than any that had gone before.

It is possible in English Law to commit manslaughter or murder by negligence. 'An unlawful omission (where there is a duty to act) where the accused foresees that harm may result may be manslaughter, e.g. the accused had in his care an aged, sick and helpless aunt. He gave her no food or nursing for ten days. She died. R. v Instant', or 'An unlawful omission (where there is a duty to act) if done deliberately and with intent to kill or cause grievous bodily harm may be murder.'[2]

Those who are unwilling to condemn members of the government personally on either of these grounds may blame two abstract principles which in England in the 1840s were revered like the word of God: the theory of Malthus as the motive for murder, *laissez-faire* as the cause of manslaughter.

In 1798 Malthus foretold doom as the inevitable result of increasing population everywhere and argued the necessity of 'checks' on the growth of population. 'Misery' was one of these necessities.

The theory of *laissez-faire* – let things alone – fitted in with this well. Its cruellest effect at the time was to allow what little food there was to be sold at exorbitant prices to the few who had money, but its long-term results are in some ways more disheartening to read of.

'The most serious charge against the British Government . . .' is that 'Neither during the famine nor for decades afterwards were any measures of reconstruction or agricultural improvement attempted, and this neglect condemned Ireland to decline.'[3] For at least seventy more years most people continued to depend only on potatoes, and local famines recurred. Their tenancies remained insecure; they could still be thrown out at a landlord's whim and could claim no compensation for improvements.

In their place as the Kirkwoods' herds, the Feelys and the Maxwells, after Michael married Nanny, held what in England is called a tied house, a house that goes with the job. English cowmen hated that because if they got the sack they lost their house as well. But in Ireland it remained the one security against eviction. Even so, and even though the Feelys and the Maxwells after them lived near the big house where extra pickings and occasional gifts were to be had, they continued to go hungry in high summer throughout Nanny's youth and early married life. In bad years they were almost at starvation level during the 'hungry' months, or 'meal' months as some people called them, because they had no money for oat or barley meal to bridge the gap between the old potatoes and the new.

Sometimes in England I had been fascinated by countrymen's talk of 'the good old days'. They too had had bad old days of course; it was youth that was good, that was all. In Ireland I never heard anyone speak in that way. Neither Michael nor Nanny nor anyone else of their class and age ever spoke of a happy past. Their good old days began a few years after Ireland won its independence, when the Free State gained control at the end of the civil war.

Part Three

Chapter One

When I left the university I began to spend longer and longer at Woodbrook every year. At first I was searching half-heartedly for a full-time job, but few of my friends could find one, even with a whole heart, and none found one he liked. I worked hard writing unpublishable stuff and added to the pound a week the Kirkwoods paid me by teaching private pupils in London. In London I needed more. There was nothing to spend money on at Woodbrook except tobacco. The pubs were miles away and I hated new clothes. But the Kirkwoods, getting money matters wrong as they always did, decided that I should earn more to make up for the extra time I spent with them in Ireland. They probably knew I would have refused an increase in pay, and gave me rights like the rights of a herd. I could buy bullocks (two I think at first) on credit, graze them free and keep the profit. In return for looking after the breeding sows, they allowed me one or two from each litter. They also encouraged me to invite a pupil over from London, and once when I was delayed there Phoebe wrote telling me to 'bring all my poor things over'.

The only one who came was Anthony Trevor-Roper, a boy of about her age. He spent some school holidays at Woodbrook and after September 1939 he stayed with us until he was old enough to go to war. He intended to become a farmer and, old-fashioned though our farming was, gained more by working with the Maxwells than by the hour or two he spent with me in Aunt Nina's room. He was afraid of the Maxwells at first – he arrived with the usual warning not to speak of religion or politics – but they liked him at once and remember him affectionately to this day. He was very English but overcame that barrier and his natural shyness by a quick, enthusiastic

185

grasp of what was going on around him. He soon entered into everything they did, and spoke without restraint.

I liked him too, but so did Phoebe and I became more jealous than I have ever been in my life. I never knew how much she liked him, or for how long, but he had more time to spend with her than I had. There was by then a ping-pong table in the ballroom-loft; to imagine them there out of sight and hearing was annoying and the sounds of tennis through the open windows of the house made me feel like a boy kept in after school as I sat trying to write my book. I could play neither tennis nor ping-pong, which made matters worse, in the childish mood I was in. I was a much better rider than he but would no longer seek her out and ride by her side, and as for bicycling, two is company, three is none. I forgot the deep attachment that continued between us. It seemed not to exist any more.

At the same time the first tokens of doom were delivered at Woodbrook by the Bank of Ireland and one of the big English banks, which had both allowed four-figure overdrafts to run for years. More land was sold. It was on the far side of the Sligo road, where the young horses ran wild, and it was no great loss to the farm. But it depressed us all, knowing as we did that hope of solvency lay in expansion not contraction. Ivy, with her usual resilience, began at once to knock down the wall of Phoebe's new bedroom and even employed Nolan, the professional carpenter, to make french windows that opened on to the flat roof with a view of the garden, lake and mountains. This roof, above the dining-room, had always been the leakiest and was now re-made with some newly patented stuff to make it safe to walk on and cure the leaks as well, they said – for we now had tradesmen, as builders and such were called, at the house all day for weeks. Winnie gave them their meals in the kitchen. I think they went home at night, but they increased the size of the establishment in an exciting way, climbing up and down ladders with buckets and having long-distance conversations with each other and with us. They were the wildest, gayest tradesmen I have ever seen, except in Africa, witty and possessed by enjoyment. They and this chance to spend money after dismal threats gave us all hope, and the work when it was

186

finished enhanced the beauty of the house by opening it out into the country on a level with the tree-tops, and by the grace of the french windows themselves. It was one of Ivy's instinctive acts for restoration of the spirit.

Phoebe had gone to this bedroom before our disengagement, and long before Trevor-Roper's arrival, and I had moved into her old one on the other side of the matchboard partition through which we used to talk. Both our old rooms looked out on to the avenue and copper beech, but from hers you could see the giant ashes too, that lined the approach to the stable yard. It was wider than my old one and had space for a writing-table at its window. There was a built-in cupboard on my right as I sat there, for my books and clothes, and next to it a little black fireplace with a mantelpiece, painted yellowy white like the walls and cupboard door, with pebbles on it and bits of wood that she or I had picked up somewhere.

I loved her old room. There were one and sometimes two of her paintings on the wall and other signs that made me feel she would come back from a distant country. If auras exist, it was hers that gave me there an anchorage calm enough to write in. I remember it more distinctly than my first room, where I did no writing, and it recurs in dreams as her french-windowed bedroom does but it, I am sure, recurs as it actually was, while the french-windowed one is the last of a long chain of rooms, connected by curtains or open doors, where I wander alone in my dreams so often that I don't know whether I was ever physically in them.

The dream rooms are empty except for beds and light, stripy drapery, like curtains in Greece, and yet when I wake I think I have dreamt about Woodbrook. They have some roots in a physical world, for Ivy's bedroom was certainly long and large. Its door was opposite mine, on the lake side of the corridor, and Phoebe's, also on the lake side, was at the front of the house beyond the staircase landing, as far from me as it could be. There may have been several rooms in between, to form my chain. I cannot remember where Tony slept, nor the four or five people who often came to stay at one time.

The upper floor of Woodbrook inspired most newcomers

with fear of the inexplicable kind. It may have been partly
the moving shadows of candles that accompanied one along the
corridor on the way to bed or the flickering dimness of the
paraffin bedside lamps. The downstairs lamps were shaded and
so large that they were seldom moved from place to place. And
it may have been the ghost stories with which the children furnished every visitor's arrival – the usual stories that grow in a
lonely old house, but luridly embellished. One, of a wicked
landlord who was shot in the famine times – a guest of their
ancestors, they said of course – seemed so substantial one
autumn that Charlie hid by his bedroom door to watch. The
ghost had been heard by us all, night after night, walking upstairs step by step, with long pauses between each step. Anyone
brave enough to get out of his bed saw nothing. The footsteps
ceased. There was sometimes a scuffle, then silence, and then as
soon as you were safely back in bed it all began again. During
his vigil in the moonlight that came through the landing
windows, Charlie saw a rat. It was carrying a potato from the
kitchen to its nest upstairs, dropping it on each stair and climbing after it. Guests were not allowed to hear this commonplace
end to the story unless they showed sufficient fear and one, a
new piano-tuner who refused to go to bed on the night of his
arrival from Dublin, was more scared by the truth than the
fiction.

Trevor-Roper's ghost was never explained and unless he now
knows that it lived inside him he must be terrified of it still. We
all were. It attacked him night after night till he grew pale and
bruised with sleeplessness. He too began to be afraid to go to
bed, nor would he sleep downstairs on the sofa, nor be anywhere alone when the rest of us had gone to bed. I used to stay
in the drawing-room late, trying to explain it, trying to persuade
him that it wouldn't happen again if he ate no cheese or meat
for supper – I believed in old-fashioned nonsense of the kind
and only when I was too tired to keep awake would he follow
me upstairs as the lesser of two evils. For our rooms were side
by side; he slept in my old bedroom; it was now his movements
and voice that I heard through the partition.

I have since heard men in the terror of nightmare and in the wakeful frenzies of madness but I had no such experience then and the inarticulate cries with which he woke me made me sit up in bed afraid to go to him. Then I would light my candle and cautiously open his door, the door of my old room where I had slept peacefully through so many nights. Sometimes I would find him awake lying on his back with his mouth open, his features drawn tight like a mask, sometimes crouching with his arms raised to protect his head and neck. His eyes were open and staring and he always protested strongly when I tried to explain his terror as a dream. He would be trembling, unable to speak for several minutes, or strike a match. More light was what he wanted most. I learned to light his lamp as soon as I came into his room, place my candle beside it and sit on his bed until he could speak clearly enough to tell me what had happened. It was always the same. Someone, or thing with arms, came in through the window and lay on him – an amorphous, suffocating weight on his chest made him unable to move, and then its hands gripped his throat. He could still feel its stranglehold and would hardly believe me when I saw no marks. When I stood up to go back to bed he pleaded with me to stay, and for several nights I sat by him for over an hour until he grew calm. I was infected by his fear, but pretended not to be.

At last it grew so bad that he had to bring his mattress into my room and sleep on the floor beside my bed. He was peaceful there but the next night, back in his own room, the demon was worse than ever and I decided that our only hope was to swap rooms. He entreated me not to go to his. His fear for me was passionate and touching. I was a fool to risk it, he said. He literally trembled for me and I went to bed the first night in secret trepidation, thinking our roles would be interchanged. Nothing happened. I slept peacefully and so did he next door.

So I lost Phoebe's old room until he left for England.

In this distressing way there had grown between us an intimate sympathy which tinged my jealousy with love, and I now think I might have escaped the worst of my derangement had I not been obsessed with those conflicting emotions. I never expressed either openly, and so increased their strength. There I was silently watching a parody of my first stay at Woodbrook.

The character who played my part, ineptly as I thought, without even knowing he was playing it, was beside me day and night. Ill-cast as he was, he took over Phoebe's part as well. I could hear him dressing in her room, turning over in his sleep at night, even tapping on the matchboard to ask me the time. How many times had I longed to go into Phoebe's room at night and not dared because her mother's door was opposite! I hated the convention that permitted me to sit on Trevor-Roper's bed and console him. I decided to clean the chimneys. It was I suppose my form of knocking down walls.

I knew the roof of Woodbrook better than the interior, in more detail that is. Whenever it leaked, I would climb it and search for the weak spot. I knew every chipped slate, every crack in a lead valley. I had patched them so often. Also I had a perfect sense of balance and loved heights. So at chimney-cleaning time I chose to work above, shouting down to Tommy Maxwell through the booming speaking tube of the shaft as he crouched in the fireplace two floors below me. There were no chimney pots, just wide rectangular stacks built of stone and mortar. First we went to Shanwelliagh to choose and cut a blackthorn bush. I climbed the roof with that, a long rope and a stone, tied the bush to the middle of the rope and the stone to one end, then let the weighted end drop down to the fireplace below where Tommy caught it. Then he pulled the bush into the chimney, I pulled it up a bit and he pulled again, and we worked it up and down, and up and down, till it reached him on the ground floor bringing with it the last of the soot. Pulling upwards from a precarious foothold was strenuous and made me sweat. I liked it, but on that day, for the first time, I slipped and hurt my arm.

It began to rain as we were cleaning up the mess downstairs and, sheltering in the cart-shed where we went to stow the rope and bush, Tommy said two things that shocked me. He said them lightly – first that in the old days they pulled a goose, instead of a bush, through the chimneys; the beating of its wings cleaned the soot; and then that Trevor-Roper had been boasting of his intention to marry Phoebe and become the master of Woodbrook with plans to root out certain trees and hedges from the pastures, which seemed sensible to Tommy, but destructive to me. These unconnected bits of information became welded together in my mind.

It rained for days. The hay was ready to bring in and we repaired the shifters endlessly under the roof of the empty hayshed, with Charlie to encourage us by seeing every hour a break in the clouds that no one else could see. It rained until the haycocks turned black and sank into the ground, and till some on the Bottoms were floating. It rained until there was nothing to do except saw wood for the winter.

Trevor-Roper worked one end of the cross-cut and I the other, and the rain clattered on the corrugated iron roof of the woodshed, a lean-to built outside the stable yard against the back wall of the harness room, gloomy like all woodsheds, overshadowed by the huge ash trees one of which had been felled for logs. It was beside the stile into Shanwelliagh which I and my bees had climbed, and the water-butt was overflowing, splashing into a morass of mud. Sawing with a cross-cut needs mental unison as well as physical. If that exists the rhythm and companionship are pleasant. One cannot talk, but unity or disunity appear through the blade of the saw. It was disunity that afternoon, and when we were tired of it, he left me. We had done enough for one day, anyway, and splitting the round logs into sections with the axe was a job for one person. I was skilled at that and stayed on in the woodshed alone.

I began with the unnecessary but lighter job of cutting sticks for kindling. I knew perfectly well that the end of a springy branch will fly unless it is resting flat on a chopping block when the axe falls, but I was impatient. One piece clashed on the corrugated iron above me, another struck the wall and a third, with a jagged end, struck me below the eye, less than a quarter of an inch below it as I saw when the blood and dirt were washed away. It broke one lens of my spectacles. I went into the house to fetch a spare pair and collided with Ivy who patched me up.

I was annoyed when she told me the truth, that I had done it on purpose, and I suspected her of blaming me, and not Cor-phetua, for my most dangerous fall some days before. Cor-phetua, who never ran away with anyone, ran away with me into a spinney, plunging and swerving to avoid the trees and tossing me over her head. I landed on my back on stony ground, saw the gleaming steel of her shoes near my face, but she managed to jump over me in her flight. That was humiliating, but Ivy's kindness as she dressed this cut drowned me in a deeper shame. She said little, and all she said was sympathetic, but I knew then that she knew more about my jealousy than I would admit before she spoke. I wanted to leave Woodbrook for ever, live alone for ever. And just as I was thinking that, she suggested that I should go off on my bicycle and stay away for as long as I liked. She said that if I wanted to go to the West I should look at a cottage on an island off the coast of Connemara that was to let. Charlie and she were thinking of taking the family there in September for a break. If I liked it, they would. And she reminded me that tomorrow was the day of the Sligo show. None of the Woodbrook horses was competing that year and no one but me would want to go in the rain. I could start early next morning, stay the night in Sligo and cycle on the next day. She gave me a few pounds. The rain stopped for a bit. I put my razor and a shirt in a knapsack and left that afternoon without even saying good-bye to Phoebe.

Chapter Two

I had a boil at the base of my spine, which made cycling
difficult, but I covered the thirty miles to Sligo, before dark.
The boil had the same relationship with my private woes as my
woes had with the threat of war. Boils and the threat had gone
on for years and were seldom mentioned. The small, immediate
troubles took attention away from the greater. The Sligo show
was early in August and this was the August of 1939, wet in
Ireland, terrifying for the rest of Europe.

Instead of a mountain hermitage, I found lodgings in a
dismal, small house that smelled all night of the rancid bacon
they gave me next morning for breakfast. The permanent
lodgers had obviously had it for supper as well. I did not sleep.
There was nothing to read and no one could have trimmed the
torn wick of my lamp to make it give sufficient light. I lay
listening to the ping-pang-pong-ping of a drip on a dustbin,
trying to make its irregular rhythm into music, waiting tensely
from the ping to the pang which came either sooner than I
expected it or after I had relaxed, thinking that the concert had
mercifully been broken short. It was like a nightmare, but
longer than any I have known. The room was horrible and so
were my thoughts of a future without Phoebe.

At the show next day, the rain stopped for a while but the
ground was sodden and the jumping slow.

I left the show gloomily on my bike. After an hour or so I
found I was cycling in the wrong direction. I was at the north-
western tip of Co. Leitrim where for a few miles the Atlantic
touches it. I spread my map out on a rock and saw that the
island cottage was about a hundred and fifty miles to the south
over mountain roads with long detours by lakes. Malin Head,
the most northerly point of Ireland, was much nearer and I was

tempted to reach it as one will go out of his way to get to the top of a hill, so I went on and came to Bundoran about twenty miles north of Sligo, just as its inhabitants were assembling for a dance. Bundoran is a seaside resort, famous for its cliffs and strand, but all I can remember of it is a concrete garage, a half-built pub that served drinks under a tarpaulin and a large marquee on a spacious green where the dance was held. I sat on a box in a dark corner under the tarpaulin drinking black pints, hoping no one would speak to me, which would have been impossible in any other place, but here they were used to holiday-makers and showed no curiosity. Then I went for a walk. Then it grew dark and began to rain again. I bought a ticket for the dance and sheltered in the crowded marquee. Girls laughed at me but there was nowhere else to go. I had forgotten to look for a room.

When the band stopped at 2 a.m., I left with the others, but crawled into the tent again. It was vast and eery now that I was alone in it and the rain made a fearful drumming on the canvas. I was wet and cold and the wind blew under the skirt of the marquee across its bare floorboards. I groped about to find a mat by the entrance and stumbled into the piano, which to my great pleasure had been covered with a huge soft cloth. I stripped the piano and wrapping myself up underneath it slept without waking till eight in the morning.

I had not eaten anything since I left Woodbrook except the egg that went with Sligo's rancid bacon and too much porter in the half-built pub had given me a parrot's mouth, but the pub and garage were both asleep and not equipped even with rain-water butts to drink from, so I got on my bike and found a signpost pointing to Donegal. Donegal was in Ulster, I knew, and it was a sentimental shock to learn that I had left Connaught, a reminder of crossing the Shannon in the train at Drumsna, but this time it was a symbol of renunciation. I had resolved not to return to Woodbrook, to write to Ivy when I had seen the island cottage, then hide. I don't know how I forgot about money, but I did.

I never reached Malin Head. A lorry-driver gave me a lift and again, after some time, I found I was travelling in the wrong direction. He passed me as I was pushing my bicycle up a hill and I found him waiting for me at the top. The lorry was loaded with broken rock that turned the rainwater white as it streamed out by the tail-board. He tied my bicycle on and invited me into the cab as though it was his house – 'come inside and be dry' – and I spent most of the day with him, sharing his bread and thermos of tea and going through so many hazards with him that we were at ease like old friends.

He had too much of a load on, he said, as we were crossing the mountains, and that was why we had to travel tail first for much of the way. We drove backwards up the steepest hills, his reverse gear being more powerful than the third, and several times skidded on muddy declines so severely that we came to a stop facing the way we had come, and every time he laughed so much that I thought he would let go of the wheel. He managed the skids perfectly with open enjoyment, and was only annoyed at one moment when we nearly turned over and some of the rocks fell into a ditch, my bicycle flying away beyond them on to the bog. The rope had broken. 'That will give us a chance to bring the weight forward a bitteen,' he said. 'It is what was needed.' We picked them up together and placed them in the driver's cab, leaving enough room for me to crouch on top of them. He was about my own age – twenty-five – red-haired, blue-eyed, quick-faced, and so thin that the muscles on his sun-scorched arms reminded me of an anatomy textbook. The front wheel of the bicycle was buckled. 'That's no harm,' he said as he tied the broken rope to it. 'I'll make that like new at the house with the help of God.'

His house was near a place called Kindrum, not far as the crow flies from Malin Head, but cut off from it by two sea loughs, Mulroy Bay and Lough Swilly. It was the usual long, low shape, thatched, with three rooms, the main one, the kitchen, in the middle and a small bedroom on each side. His parents, who welcomed us with bacon and eggs and tea, reminded me of Nanny and Michael Maxwell, not in looks, but their talk of the past. Their son had not asked me anything about myself, which was a sign perhaps of a new generation. My English accent made him assume that I knew Birmingham and as soon as I assured him I knew nothing of his chances of work as a mechanic there he laughed and said no more. His parents, keeping to the old convention, began with searching questions and I answered as fully as I could. It is unfriendly not to, and can be rude. So I said what occurred to me about my parents and sisters in London and about the Kirkwoods and the fairs where they bought and sold cattle in counties Roscommon and Leitrim.

It was something I said about the fair of Mohill, near Carrick, that set the whole family alight – at least seven younger editions of the lorry driver sat at the table with us – because that was the principal residence of the 3rd Earl of Leitrim, the most conspicuous landlord of Victorian times, who owned vast estates in Leitrim, Donegal and Galway and unlike most of the great landowners was never an absentee. All four grandparents of the children had been tenants of his in Donegal, the 5th Earl still stayed from time to time at the big house of Mulroy, and, so they told me, the lorry-driver and I had driven past the scene of his assassination only half an hour ago. It was in Cratlagh Wood, less than two statute miles, or as near one mile Irish as makes no difference, from the chair I sat in now.

I had never heard of Lord Leitrim then, but thirty years later when I returned to Kindrum I was shown a monument to the three men who ambushed and killed him, a Celtic cross with an inscription in Irish on its plinth, which in translation says, 'To the endearing memory of the three heroes from Fanad ... [Their names are given] ... who on the morning of April 2nd, 1878, by their heroic action at Cratlagh, put an end to the tyranny of the landlords.'

It is too great a claim. The worst years of that terrible guerilla war, the greatest cruelty and largest number of deaths on both sides, began in the 1880s, and Lord Leitrim's death, which was discussed at Westminster for days, had by then given impetus to a policy of repression.

The 3rd Earl was a lonely, hardworking man, unpopular not only among his tenants but his peers. Two attempts on his life had been made in the previous thirty years and it is a wonder that Lord Carlisle, the viceroy, did not make a third; and a

196

wonder too that Leitrim did not kill any of the few who dared disobey him, for he was violent when angered and very strong. The only man to beat him without a weapon was 'Big' John Canning, a so-called giant of the Carrick-on-Shannon district, who long outlived him and died about 1930 at the age of a hundred and one. Leitrim had given permission for a Catholic church to be built, choosing the site himself. Canning and his friends started work on another site, which they thought more convenient for their neighbours, and when Leitrim saw Canning mixing mortar there he ordered him to stop. Canning went on mixing mortar. Leitrim struck him a terrible blow on the face. Canning remained calm enough to drop his shovel and they wrestled. Leitrim was only saved from strangulation by the other men who pulled the giant off him. As Canning was not one of his tenants all Leitrim could do was to ask the neighbouring landlord, Lord Massey, to evict him. Lord Massey refused but to appease his neighbour's fury agreed in the end to punish Canning by raising his rent by ten shillings a year.[1]

Lord Leitrim was often escorted through his estates by one or more side-cars of police, and like most of his fellows carried loaded pistols everywhere he went. I think there is no truth in the rumour that he shot every goat that he saw grazing by the roadside, but he certainly hated goats and, whenever he saw one, found out who the owner was and ordered it to be killed. He devoted most of his enormous energy to the improvement of farming, knowing as Maria Edgeworth's father knew before him that the poverty of his tenants could be relieved by the use of new techniques, but unlike Edgeworth he had no understanding of his people; he tried to force his textbook farming on them with no regard for their feelings or for immediate necessities. He read a lot and certainly knew Edward Wakefield's great work on Irish rural economy in which goats are praised as essential to the country poor, but he knew goats damaged trees and recommended cows which very few of his tenants could afford to keep, for apart from their buying price or the time it took to rear a heifer calf to maturity they could not be left by the roadside without a herd to watch them; also, on a farm of three acres, which was the average size, a cow was like a rhinoceros in a market garden. Most of the common land had been appropriated by the earl for his own cattle.

The need for goats was so great that tenants in out of the way places risked keeping them. An old man, Francis Scally, evaded the injunction for years but his two strayed along the road one day as his Lordship approached. 'Kill those gourmandisers' was all he said and Scally, fearing eviction, obeyed.

His passionate care for trees, whether dead or alive, makes me believe the popular saying that 'he had not all his sense'. Bog fir or oak, which is found buried deep below the turf in a hard blackened state half-way to coal, was retrieved all over Ireland for many purposes including the carving of toys and ornaments. Lord Leitrim forbade this and forbade the cutting of ash, an essential for spade handles and carts. Even bushes for cleaning the chimney had to be cut in secret. 'How would you like to have your fingers cut off?' he used to say. 'Why would you go to bleed the poor bush?' But he gave some people free timber for roofing. James Reynolds asked for some when he was badly in arrears of rent and Leitrim said 'You'll be the last man to get it.' He asked again next year and Leitrim said 'What did I tell you last time?' 'You said I'd be the last man on the property to get timber, and now I think you have all the rest supplied.' He got it.

While many estates were wasting from neglect by absentees, Leitrim's suffered from close patronage. To plant potatoes on a plot he had not personally approved was to invite eviction, and it is said that however impoverished tillage land was he never would allow the breaking-up of lea. After noticing a newly planted field, one spring day on his way to Carrick-on-Shannon, he forced the farmer to dig up every piece of seed-potato and turn the sods back with the grass uppermost – a slow, laborious process in those days when tillage was done by spade. He rightly hated the custom of burning the land, but senselessly forbade it, knowing as he did that without animals, without even goats, there was no other form of manure. Burning, like excessive use of artificials, gives an immediate impetus to growth and long-lasting ill-effects which could, for example, be seen at Woodbrook where ploughs often turned up old burnt soil, brittle and coloured like fireclay. To encourage the autumn growth of grass he fixed a date, regardless of weather, by which every man had to clear his turf from the bog. He had one tenant jailed for bringing his home late.

The landlords' agents were the curse of absentee estates; left to themselves with impossibly high rents to collect and sometimes seeking their own profit, they were usually unjust, and tyrannical. Leitrim supervised his agents closely, built good houses for them, paid them well, and received rents in person whenever he could, listening to individual pleas. But at all times he was utterly despotic. On rent day the tenants had to wait in the courtyard at Lough Rynn with their hats off 'and if sleet or snow were falling it did not matter, and you could not smoke'. There was a forge in the yard, where the landlord's private blacksmith worked, one Jeremiah Johnstone who was known as the best smith in the Parish of Mohill, and here the people sometimes went to warm themselves at the fire. But forges are as famous as pubs as places to stand and talk in. Leitrim forbade it, accusing Jeremiah of wasting time, and one cold day, when Jeremiah allowed a few to come in, he was sacked.

Even before the Famine an image of the Irish Lord, derived from shocked travellers' reports, had become a European cliché like that of the Turkish Pasha. The illiterate poor were conscious of its effect on strangers and used it when begging whether they had a landlord good or bad, or none at all. It seemed a ludicrous convention even to Maria Edgeworth who had expressed better than any other writer her anger against bad landlords. She was travelling through Connemara with 'an Englishman born and bred', who believed in 'political economy stories exemplifying the mischief of charity', when an old woman followed them telling 'heaps of lies about her high rent and her cruel landlord'. She was amused, but gave enough money to make up for her companion's parsimonious principles.

Maria Edgeworth must have known Lord Leitrim – he lived only thirty miles from Edgeworthstown, and who could escape him? – but she died in 1849, five years before he succeeded to his title, five years before his notoriety began. Another ten years of life would have given her a real-life version of the legend close at hand. He was good-looking in a military style, agile and tall. He was successful – colonel of the Leitrim regiment, M.P. for the county and magistrate for Leitrim, Donegal and Galway – an appointment which gratified him more than any other, for he owned estates in those three counties and was able to enforce his more unconventional acts of despotism from the bench. He had a house in London, in Grosvenor Street, the centre of high society, and spent plenty of money. He was keen on women but never got married.

He was as unpopular in high society as among the poor. For years his speeches in the House of Lords had been scorned or laughed at. It was only the scandal raised in parliament about the motive of his murderers that rallied peers and commoners to defend his honour.

The scene in the House of Commons ten days after his death was extraordinary even at that time when Irish members habitually angered everybody else. O'Donnell, supported by Parnell, speaking against new repressive measures which were proposed as a result of the assassination, tried to say that the motive for the crime was not agrarian, but personal. 'Mr O'Donnell accused the deceased nobleman of using his authority and power as a landlord for the dishonour of the peasant girls on his estate.'[2] As his story advanced frantic attempts were made to call him to order, but the speaker ruled that he was in order, so everyone listened until King-Harman, alarmed by the beginning of the old local scandal about James Murphy's niece, cried 'I spy strangers!' The strangers were journalists and because they were thrown out newspapers printed for weeks dark hints more damaging than anything O'Donnell had to say.

Lord Leitrim's family had made a similar blunder some days before. They brought his body to Celbridge, an estate he owned near Dublin but seldom visited, and from there conducted an almost royal funeral to their ancestral vaults in the ancient church of St Michan in the very centre of one of Dublin's poorest districts. The people mobbed the hearse, uttering shocking execrations, and tried to pull the coffin off. The mourners were squeezed through the churchyard gates in peril, guarded by police, and after the funeral service, the new 4th Earl left, guarded, by a side door.

O'Donnell was wrong about the motive for the final crime, and probably he knew it. Lord Leitrim was ambushed and killed on his way to an eviction. His clerk, who was to conduct the business side of it, and the driver of the side-car they rode on, were killed with him. Lord Leitrim, then seventy-two years old, fought bravely until he was felled with the stock of a gun. Many people in the district knew it was going to happen and why – to forestall an eviction. The smith had purposely lamed the horse that was to pull the bodyguard's car, so that came slowly far behind. A priest whom Leitrim was suing over property was credited with uncanny powers for saying that his opponent would not appear in court. Also, the very fact that it took place in Donegal makes it probable that the motive was agrarian, for there the feud between Leitrim and his tenants was more hateful than anywhere else. Its bitterness was due to a law of property peculiar to the North of Ireland and known as Ulster Tenant Right.

Leitrim had suffered a terrible humiliation in the House of Lords, when the Land Act of 1870, granting compensation to evicted tenants, was passed in spite of his raging oratory, but in Ulster he had always had to fight a lonely battle against this older law which gave his tenants rights unheard of in the rest of Ireland, the most important of which was the right to sell their leases. From the day of his accession to his father's throne in 1854, the 3rd Earl set out to destroy these rights by endless lawsuits or quick private action. Of the Right of Sale, he said in court 'When one tenant sells his interest to another, I evict the parties.' This was the immediate cause of his assassination. Eighty-nine evictions were pending at the time.[3]

In spite of all this he had inherited, at least on his Connaught estates, some of the feudal devotion, a mixture of ridicule and reverence that amounted almost to love, which most of the despotic landlords of the eighteenth century enjoyed. It was something like the present English attitude to royalty. You may laugh or grumble privately, but not in the newspapers. So when a meeting of tenants was called at Mohill, inspired by King-

Harman and led by two principal tenants, his late lordship's doctor and solicitor, seventy farmers signed a document denying all scandalous stories and saying that 'No man did more for his tenantry than Lord Leitrim did. His chief aim was their welfare' etc.

The lorry-driver's father mentioned that at tea and said it was true that he cared better than most for the welfare of those tenants he approved of.

But the lorry-driver hated all talk, good or bad, about the past, especially his father's stories of 1916 to 1921, and after his last mouthful he escaped, beckoning me to the edge of the little roadside field where he had left his lorry. We unloaded and piled the stones. He wanted to build a small repair shop with them and get a petrol pump, which seemed to me an airy castle, for the only vehicles I had seen there were pulled by donkeys. But he said the 'tourist crowd' was growing. He took a wheel off his own bicycle and fixed it on to mine and early next morning I left.

Chapter Three

The taste of lively company in the lorry-driver's house, where I had shared a bed with three boys who talked themselves to sleep (in Irish, which I could not understand) made me feel lonelier than ever as I rode away. I knew I would never see them again and imagined I would never see the Kirkwoods. My own family – parents and three sisters – were remote and though I longed often to see them, I hoped never to live in London again. At Woodbrook I had left the almost finished manuscript of the book I was writing and had abandoned with it all the rest of the routine without which no one can live – in my case the girls' lessons, the vegetable garden, some of the cleaning of saddlery, the filling and trimming of a dozen paraffin lamps, the feeding of cart-horses and the care of two breeding sows. I was unanchored. Even my essential faith – that I would go on writing – left me for a time and I saved myself from despair only by remembering that I had set out with a purpose, to look at an empty cottage on an island in Bertraghboy Bay. I remembered that as I was cycling north towards Fanad Point – my compromise for missing Malin Head – and at the next side-road I turned right, towards the east, hoping to find some southward way without going back past the lorry-driver's house.

I went, mostly pushing my bike, over the mountains by a crinkle-crankle of stony tracks to the western shore of Lough Swilly where I turned south along a smoother road towards Letterkenny. When I think of the monument to Lord Leitrim's assassins, I now know that on that morning I passed places much more significant in Irish history, for 'The Flight of the Earls' took place from this shore in 1607 and it was here that Wolfe Tone and his fellow officers of the French Army were

203

brought ashore after their capture at sea and marched to Letter-kenny. That was in October 1798.

If he had landed there with a French army in 1796, the year he had agreed on with Carnot and General Hoche, or better still in 1797, with the added help of the Dutch Navy, the whole of Ireland would have become a united inde-pendent country, at least for a time, and even if drawn back later by English claws there would have been a workable pre-cedent to forestall the unworkable Government of Ireland Act of 1920, which partitioned the country and inevitably led to the disasters of the 1970s.

But the rebellion of 1798, which is sometimes called Wolfe Tone's, took place without him. He knew it had no chance of success without the help of a professional army, and during the years of frustration which he had spent in France working to realize the promises of the *Directoire* his constant fear was that it would happen too soon. It did. It began in the spring and was completely crushed by early August, three weeks before the French arrived. On 24 August General Humbert with a few Irish officers on his staff and about a thousand experienced French soldiers made a successful landing at Killala in County Mayo.

On my way south from Lough Swilly I had to pass through Sligo again. I cycled through it quickly and spent the night in a Dutch barn half filled with hay some miles farther on near the shore of Ballysadare Bay. Next day, going westwards towards Ballina I kept to the coast road which is beautiful but rough and slow and, though my detour through County Donegal had added four days to my journey, I determined at the risk of reaching Connemara too late to make another shorter one and see Killala. This worried me, but I did it. If someone else had taken the cottage before I got there, I would have spoiled the Kirkwoods' holiday, especially Phoebe's or so I thought; my parting from her would be tainted with carelessness. I was still resolved not to return to Woodbrook, merely to send a postcard about the cottage. And yet the carelessness, or rather my longing to explore the country near Killala, prevailed.

It was old Kirkwood country and I searched the coast road

for a demesne called Curramabla which I had first seen mentioned in the mildewed copy of *Burke's Irish Landed Gentry* which stood next to the *Racing Calendar* at Woodbrook, in which Charlie's father was listed as Colonel James Kirkwood of Woodbrook, County Roscommon and of Curramabla, County Sligo. The house was said to be more beautiful than Woodbrook; it and the land faced the sea. Ivy had often thought of moving there but it had been let for many years before Charlie inherited the estate and no one could find the lease or prove ownership. The rent remained at the original sixty pounds a year and naturally the tenant wished to stay. I never found it, though I must have passed nearby. I had crossed the border into County Mayo before I realized that I had missed it.

North Mayo was, so far as I can discover, the part of Connaught where the Kirkwoods first made their home. It was at Castlereagh, a few miles from Killala, that the Knoxs, presbyterian relatives of John Knox, had settled in Charles I's reign and there that Thomas Kirkwood had married one of their daughters in or about the year 1642. There was still, I was told, a distant relative of Charlie's living on an island in Killala Bay. I spent the night at an inn in the town and had the usual friendly questioning and talk but can remember little of the people I met or of the place. It was like a small village then, with about nine hundred inhabitants, but in 1798, when the French landed, it was still a cathedral city and a flourishing seaport. On the site of its church of St Patrick, founded in the fifth century, there had been built in the seventeenth a Protestant cathedral whose tall and beautiful spire can still be seen from miles away, but whose status has long been lowered to that of an ordinary church. Its ruined castle, said to have been partially ruined even in the eighteenth century when it was the bishop's palace, was still there in bits and there was a sombre warehouse near the sea which in 1798 belonged to Captain Kirkwood, magistrate and merchant, and during the famine had been turned into an auxiliary workhouse where thousands died.

Early in the summer of 1798 a new bishop, the Reverend Dr Joseph Stock, distinguished scholar of Trinity College, Dublin, was appointed to this remote and quiet see. On 23 August his

205

peaceful life was broken by a party of French officers who politely demanded quarters for themselves and their men in the palace. Dr Stock kept a diary and afterwards wrote 'A Narrative of what passed at Killala in the County of Mayo, and the parts adjacent, during the summer of 1798. By an eye-witness'[1] – a lucid account which shows incidentally his gentleness and wisdom. He is loyal to the Crown, and pities the insurgents who flocked to the French standard because he knew from the start how they would suffer and not win. His 'Narrative' is memorable not only for its story, but as an example of the views of one of the many Protestants in power whose tolerance helped to defeat the object of the Penal Code. The only religious prejudice he expressed concerned the aims of the Orange Society.

He wrote of himself in the third person: 'On the very day when the invasion happened, he was busy entering a protest, in his primary visitation charge, against the first sentence of the oath by which Orangemen are united together, "I am not a Roman Catholic". The words sounded in his ears too like those in the prophet: *Stand off, I am holier than thou*; and assuredly they are not calculated to conciliate.'

The invasion force was formidable in skill, not numbers. It was commanded by Humbert, a general experienced in the guerilla warfare of La Vendée. Most of his men had served under Bonaparte in Italy, and the rest in the Army of the Rhine. They were small, pale and dressed in worn-out uniforms. One officer, pointing to his leather breeches, told the bishop that he had not taken them off for a year. They quartered themselves, their thousands of pamphlets, tons of powder and plentiful arms for distribution in the bishop's palace and grounds.

General Humbert was delighted to find that the bishop spoke fluent French and evidently preferred him and his friends to the native Irish. Filled with the idealistic, now outdated, notions that had been brought to France by exiles such as Wolfe Tone, he assumed that Protestants and Catholics, rich and poor alike, would be eager to 'Throw off the English yoke', and having been commanded to set up a provisional government for the district in which he landed he offered a place in the Directory of Connaught to the bishop. When the bishop politely declined, mentioning the many oaths he had taken to the king, Humbert and his second in command replied that 'he was a man of honour and it was far from the intention of their government to force liberty on any man.'

This happened on their first evening in Ireland, but they were to meet with the same disappointment everywhere they went, for almost every man 'of ability and consequence' was a Protestant, loyal to the English King. The Penal Laws had seen to that. And then they had landed by chance and through their ignorance in the only peaceable province of the country, Connaught, which had escaped the reign of terror that brought the rebellion on too soon and remained detached throughout it.

Humbert's search for professional men was futile at first, though later on, after his victory at Castlebar, he did manage to scrape together a provisional government all of whose members were of some distinction, though none had previously held office of any kind. These were all Catholic.

In Killala, next to the bishop, the magistrate – Captain William Kirkwood – would have been an obvious choice. His authority was established not only through the law, but by his trade, for he was one of the most important merchants in the province, trafficking in oats, salt, iron, etc. with English as well as Irish ports. He was bilingual in English and Irish and would have made a perfect liaison between the people and the French command. But he was also commander of the local yeomanry and it was as prisoner of war that he first spoke to the French general, whose respect he had already won on that first day by defending himself alone against more than fifty shots, after his troops had fled leaving him standing by two of their dead, not far from the door of his own house where he might have taken refuge. Together with Sills, an English lieutenant who commanded a company of Fencibles, he was imprisoned and interrogated in the bishop's drawing-room.

'The remainder of the first evening was employed in a strict examination of Captain Kirkwood, the magistrate, as to the supplies that could be drawn from the town and neighbourhood to assist the progress of the invaders. The queries were interpreted by some Irish officers who came with the French. Mr

Kirkwood answered with such an appearance of frankness and candour, that he gained the esteem of the French general, who told him he was on his parole, and should have full permission to return to his family, and attend to his private affairs. But this good humour between them did not continue long. Kirkwood had a sickly wife, an amiable woman of whom he was doatingly fond. The terror of the invasion wrought so upon her weak nerves, that, after escaping on the first night to the castle, she crept away the day after to some hiding place in the mountains four or five miles from the town, from which she sent word to her husband that she was but just alive. Attentive only to her, he forgot his parole of honour to the French; and it was not till after he had been some time by his wife's bedside, that he recollected the circumstances of his having transgressed the bounds within which he had promised to confine himself. Not knowing what punishment he might have incurred by this breach of the laws of war, he took the desperate resolution of withdrawing himself to the wild district of Erris, about ten miles from Killala, on the sea-coast, into which a carriage cannot pass, as it is a frightful tract of bog and mountain, though tolerably well peopled. Here he remained several days ... in the constant dread of being robbed or murdered by the rebels, and forced to take up his residence at night in caves among the rocks, when he could not reach a smoky hut belonging to some peasant whom he could trust.'

Though the bishop says that 'no man was better known nor more popular in all that neighbourhood, being a good humoured man, well versed in the Irish language', his good name was no protection now that he was known to have fought against the French and it was only through the kindness of an ex-revenue officer who knew him personally that his life was saved. This was a young man named O'Donnel, the Ferdy O'Donnel whom the French soon appointed as leader of the volunteers who flocked into Killala. 'With difficulty O'Donnel was able to protect the fugitive for one night only in his farmhouse; but he incurred the hatred of the rebels so much by this act of humanity, that after sending Kirkwood away in the morning, he was fain to take the road to Killala himself the same day.' In Killala he offered his services to the French and was soon put in charge of the very same rebels, who came in thousands as volunteers.

But Kirkwood did not dare go home. In terror of the Irish and the French alike, he was hounded from one hiding place to another until through a country parson he managed to get a message to the bishop describing his plight. The bishop interceded for him with the French officers and at last he came under their protection again, without punishment, as prisoner on parole in his own house. Throughout the invasion the French gave Irish prisoners preferential treatment. Lieutenant Sills, an Englishman, had been put on board one of their ships to be taken to France. They considered Captain Kirkwood to be as Irish as any of the men who served under him in the yeomanry. I think he would have claimed that nationality, but that his men would have denied it to him.

Perhaps Humbert thought he had already been punished enough, for 'Enraged at his breach of parole, the French had taken everything they wanted out of his stores, oats and salt and iron to a considerable amount; nor had they been careful to prevent depredations by the rebels in his dwelling-house, as they would have done if he had not fled; so that when he returned, he found it almost a wreck.'

Captain Kirkwood's house was in a prominent position at the top of the Main Street near the palace at a point which took the brunt both of fighting and looting.

It is a pity that Ferdy O'Donnel or some such gifted 'rebel' left no eye-witness account, for the bishop, wise and just as he was, could not believe that the poor joined the French for anything but meat rations, shoes and gaudy uniforms. These and the chance of adventure had always been good reasons for joining the king's yeomanry too; there was also, especially in Mayo, a traditional love of fighting as a popular sport as Carleton[2] shows in his stories of 'faction' and 'party' fights. It is the strength of the abstract appeal that is difficult to assess. How could neighbours and often brothers acquire opposing loyalties and turn against each other with such savagery? The bishop takes it for granted that all but the most ignorant and easily led would be loyal to the king and his established government, and many of all classes were. The legend 'Ireland for Ever!' seemed to him a pathetic illusion: 'God save the King' seemed real.

'In war, it is said,' wrote Bishop Stock, 'the first success is everything. The maxim was at least verified here by the instant accession of many hundreds of country people to the cause of the French, which they affected to style the cause of Ireland and liberty. A green flag was mounted over the castle gate, with the inscription ERIN GO BRAGH, importing, as I am told, *Ireland for Ever!* This flag was the signal to invite as many as had the spirit to assert their freedom to join a brave people, who were come for no other purpose than to make them independent and happy ... It was a melancholy spectacle to those in the castle, to witness the eagerness with which the unfortunate rustics pressed forward to lay hold of these fatal trappings, the sure harbingers of their speedy destruction ... The uncombed, ragged peasant, who had never before known the luxury of shoes and stockings, now washed, powdered and full dressed, was metamorphosed into another being, the rather because the far greater part of these mountaineers were by no means deficient in size or person ... A still stronger temptation offered itself to people unaccustomed to animal food – the lowest allowance of beef for a day was one pound to each recruit ... Chests containing each forty fusils, and others filled with new French uniforms and gaudy helmets, being heaped together in the castle yard, the first that offered their service received complete clothing; and these, by credible report, were about a thousand in number. The next comers, who were at least as many, had everything but shoes and stockings. To the last, arms only were given. And of arms ... not less than 5,500 stand were in this place delivered out to the insurgents ... Swords and pistols, of which there was no great plenty, were referred as marks of distinction, to be distributed only to the rebel officers.'

One of those French swords was still in the Maxwells' house at Woodbrook when I first arrived, though later old Michael gave it away to someone from Carrick who kept pestering him for it. It had a beautifully decorated hilt and three generations had preserved it well. The bishop's garden in Killala was the only place where arms were distributed, so it must be that Michael's grandfather was one of the volunteers who came down from the mountains and that he was chosen as an officer by the French.

According to the family tradition, which Michael passed on, the Maxwells' history was rather like the Kirkwoods', except that, being Catholic, they married into Irish families and became indistinguishable, both in language and customs, from people of indigenous descent. Only their name showed their Scottish origin. The first of them to settle in Ireland had arrived as part of James II's army and after one of his lost battles had fled into the wild and roadless mountains of Erris, not very far from Castlereagh, the seat of the Knox family. The French invasion just over a hundred years later led them, again as part of a defeated army, to settle near another branch of the Kirkwood family in North Roscommon on the upper reaches of the Shannon, cut off from Usna and Woodbrook only by the Boyle water and the lake. Such was the series of chances that brought Michael and Nancy Feely together and made their sons believe that Woodbrook and Usna should be theirs by hereditary right, since the Feelys had been farming there long before any foreigners came.

Chapter Four

The French regarded the Irish volunteers with a mixture of amusement and contempt. They were astonished to begin with by their ignorance of the meaning of the French Revolution. Cries of welcome greeted them everywhere, thanking God that the French had come to save Ireland in the name of the Blessed Virgin. 'We have just sent Mr Pope away from Italy,' said one of the officers, 'and who knows but that we may find him in this country.'[1] Then the Irish used those muskets and carbines that had been carried overseas in peril of the English fleet, with such amateurish lack of care that the French Colonel Charost refused to supply them with any more powder and shot. They were drilled hard enough in the precincts of the bishop's palace but would not save their ammunition for their meeting with the enemy, which was still several days ahead. One of them nearly killed General Humbert. 'As he was standing at an open window in the castle, the general heard a ball whistle by his ear, discharged by an awkward recruit in the yard below, whom he instantly punished with an unmerciful caning. The ball passed into the cieling [sic] where the mark is still apparent ... It was common with them to put their cartridges in at the wrong end, and when they stuck in the passage (as they often did) the inverted barrel was set to work against the ground, till it was bent and useless ... A crowd got about Charost one day, clamouring for a supply of powder and shot. "Tell them," said the commandant in a passion, "they shall have no more, till I am sure they will not waste their charges upon ravens." ' In a footnote the bishop added, 'The raven is an object of pursuit for his quills [presumably for quill pens.] It was remarked that these birds, not common before in our fields, began to multiply, in

212

proportion as unburied bodies (a curse on war!) became a spectacle familiar to us.

' "Do you know what I'd do with those Irish devils if I had a body [corps] to form out of them?" said one old officer. "I would pick out one third of them, and, by the Lord, I would shoot the rest." '[2]

A few of the French officers were Irish émigrés, which helped understanding a little; Wolfe Tone's brother, Matthew, was one – Wolfe Tone himself was still impatiently waiting at Brest to embark with another invasion fleet – and somehow an auxiliary force was drilled in time to accompany Humbert's troops on their first advance inland to meet the enemy. Out of more than five thousand volunteers, this force numbered seven hundred or so. The rest were not shot, unless caught by the royalists, but even if one allows for the scorn and class-prejudice of those who left recorded memories, it seems true that they were more an embarrassment than a help to the French. Even if each was obedient and willing to learn, no soldier – nor any genius – could have instructed them in the use of arms and made them accept discipline within a week.

Even in Eastern Europe the chances would have been better. The mountain people of Connaught were untouched by European traditions either of peace or war. Their techniques of farming or fishing were simple and old. Even proper harness for horses, in the few places where horses were used, was unknown; ploughs and harrows were attached to the horse's tail, and pulled that way.[3] Wooden boats that could hold heavy nets and a large catch were unheard of; they fished from curraghs, a long shallow type of rowing boat made of skins on a light framework with hardly any draft, that was ideal for their wild rocky coastline but unable to supply anyone except a few local people with fish. Their music, dancing and storytelling were among the best of the traditional arts of the world but no one from outside their community took any notice of those.

In many respects these people had held on to vestiges of medieval life; some of their customs and beliefs were pre-Christian; but their old tribal warfare and the discipline and skill that

213

it entailed was only a memory recited in stories hundreds of years old, and war itself was a myth; there had been none in Ireland for over a hundred years. So their disorderly gaiety, their sudden bursts of unheard-of bravery and their more frequent collapses into panic-stricken flight, should not have astonished anyone.

Leaving two hundred of his own men, and thousands of these partisans to garrison Killala and hold the bridgehead to his ships, Humbert led his small army inland to Ballina six miles away. The enemy fled without fighting and the road was clear to the strongly garrisoned county town of Castlebar, with only one obstacle, Foxford and its easily defended bridge, in the way. In Ballina there was no civic welcome, not even one person of importance to receive him, and although the populace was friendly there was little hope of consolidating his position either from a political or military point of view. He wanted a striking victory in battle. Only that would bring republican men of influence out into the open to control and organize the partisans. Only that would satisfy his own longing for action.

In taking Ballina, a large town on the River Moy, strategically important as a junction of four coach roads, he had really done all that was necessary. His orders were to establish defensive positions and wait until the landing of General Hardy's expeditionary force of 3,000 men whose arrival from Brest was expected any day. But he could not wait. There were reported to be nearly 4,000 troops of the regular English Army, together with 1,500 yeomanry, all hurriedly concentrated at Castlebar after the news of the French landing. Not only were Humbert's men outnumbered by at least three to one, but the English artillery, which included a howitzer, was far superior to theirs. Yet he took the offensive.

There are two ways from Ballina to Castlebar – one via Foxford by the old coach road to the left of Lough Conn, one by a very bad mountainous way that takes a long circuit on the other side of the lake. This bad road, which I chose because I knew it would be more interesting, was still rough and stony in 1939, and very steep and crooked especially where it rises near the summit of Ben Nephin, high above the huge lake. In 1798 it was more like a bridle track than a road and was interrupted by gullies and huge boulders that had slipped from the mountains above. General Humbert was perhaps the first to attempt to use it for wheeled traffic. The English command did not believe that he would attempt this route. For one thing they must have known about the shortage of horses in North Mayo and then, even with good horses, the chance of drawing artillery over that rocky wilderness was faint. So General Hutchinson took up strong positions on the Foxford Road and was careful to fortify the Foxford bridge which barred the way south. This meant that on the night of the French advance a large part of the English force was eleven miles away from Castlebar. The French bypassed them.

Humbert had confirmed what seemed obvious to his enemy, first by making public his intention of attacking Foxford in the certain knowledge that spies would report his plan, then by marching out from Ballina in that direction. Near the head of Lough Conn, two or three miles from the town, he wheeled to the right along a little-used track that joined the mountain road. The lack of horses had been one of his troubles from the start. He had commandeered all of the bishop's save one, and scoured the countryside for more, but only a few well-off families possessed them and those he needed for messengers, scouts and so on. So he ordered his men to harness gangs of Irish recruits to the guns and wagons, and all that night of 25 August they dragged them over the hills, lifting and carrying them over crevices and rocks, through the precipitous pass of Barnageeragh, until about eight in the morning they saw the town of Castlebar below them and a formidable army on high ground about it.

The royalists had been warned of this astounding move in the early hours of the morning, just in time to recall some of their troops from Foxford, but too late to defend the steep and narrow pass which one historian[4] called 'a Thermopylae' considered by the commanders not to be worth the trouble of defence. Even so they remained far superior both in numbers and guns and had taken up strong positions on the low hills and ridges commanding the river valley and the town.

Before coming within range of the royalist guns, the French

grenadiers were able to advance under cover of a ridge. They climbed to the top under cover of a body of Irishmen selected by Humbert for the honour of drawing the enemy fire, from those unlucky enough to be dressed more or less completely in French uniforms. Twice they were repulsed with some casualties and both Irish and French fell back behind the ridge. At the third attempt Humbert used a medieval technique which, unless he had seen it used in the guerrilla war of La Vendée, which is unlikely, he must have learned from the Irish; they had always used it in their ancient wars and it brought them great advantage during this rebellion. They and the grenadiers drove a herd of cattle over the ridge before them.

At last they deployed. The artillery was less effective against a long line. The royalist infantry either in panic or ignorance wasted their ammunition by firing long before the French came near and, when they did come near, broke line and fled leaving their artillery without support. The French rushed the guns and captured them. This was the beginning of that famous rout, which from the speed of the thousands of royalist fugitives and the distance they covered in their flight became known as 'The Races of Castlebar'. It was one of the greatest military defeats in English history. 'In the course of twenty-four eventful years,' wrote Lord Auckland, the Viceroy's Chief Secretary, 'it has happened to me to receive many unpleasant and unexpected accounts of military defeats and disgraces. One of the hardest strokes in that way was the surrender of Burgoyne's army at Saratoga; but I do not think it either affected or surprised me so much as your Castlebar catastrophe ... If the impression of that business should have encouraged ... a general explosion, the consequences may be very serious and God send us a good deliverance.'[5] Which shows that not only the French but the English government believed that the invasion was not too late to put life into the insurrection once again. Humbert and his fellow officers believed so but their hope for a general rising dwindled fast, for apart from political reasons the weather was too good. Harvest comes late in Connaught and during those days of late August and early September everyone was busy in the fields. The mass of recruits to Killala came from country

216

too poor to grow anything except potatoes which needed no care till the end of September.

Having set up the seat of a Republic of Connaught at Castlebar, after appointing local people to a provisional government there, Humbert marched his little army northwards again, intending to reach Ulster via Sligo. He was doubly disappointed in his victory. First, he expected it to lead to widespread insurrection which had it happened two years earlier would certainly have been its instant result. Second, he knew that even without the help of insurrection he could have consolidated his victory if only the expeditionary force from Brest had arrived in time. He still had no news of it, but expected it to make its landing on the north-western coast of Ulster where local support was reputed to be strongest. Ulster, where Catholics and non-conformist Protestants were united against the British Government, had been the principle stronghold of the rebel movement.

But at Collooney, a few miles outside Sligo, the longed-for news of an uprising reached him not from Ulster but the midlands. It seemed that the victory at Castlebar had after all given courage to a mass of people who had taken no part in the rebellion until then. And he suddenly turned his army eastwards towards Dublin. The uprising had begun in County Longford, half-way between Sligo and the capital, about thirty miles east of Carrick-on-Shannon. By a series of forced marches he tried to reach the rebels. As no news had come from France, they were his only hope.

The shortest way he could have taken from Collooney was the mail coach road to Dublin, along which I had bicycled to the Sligo show. But Boyle was a strongly fortified town and Carrick, nine miles farther on, with its narrow bridge across the Shannon, would have been a formidable obstacle too, especially as the viceroy, Lord Cornwallis, was marching rapidly towards it with 20,000 men. So Humbert took a more northerly route and crossed the Shannon farther up, pursued but unopposed.

His situation grew more and more perilous. General Lake's army was chasing him from the rear and Cornwallis was making forced marches to outflank him. And, although he did not know it, the insurgents ahead of him had been crushed. In

his long rapid march (110 miles in three days) he had to aban-
don many of the captured guns, to make speed, and worst of all
had no time to destroy the bridge of Ballintra by which he had
crossed the Shannon.

After the crossing the French army and those partisans who
had remained with them were allowed their first good rest,
twelve miles farther on at Cloone, near the border of County
Longford. It was the night of 7 September. Cornwallis was
camping close to them now. He had reached Carrick the same
day and pushed on late at night to Mohill which is only five
miles from Cloone. The final battle – if such an inequal contest
can be called a battle – took place next day, five miles farther
on towards Granard, near the village of Ballinamuck. Here the
French, now reduced to fewer than 800 men, and the Irish
partisans who numbered perhaps a thousand stood to face,
without artillery, the two great armies that surrounded them.
They knew they had no chance but, for the sake of honour,
fought fiercely for half an hour before surrendering.

There followed immediately one of those great injustices that
are justified by law.

It was a law accepted I suppose by the English community in
America during their war of independence, and by revolutionaries living at home that anyone caught fighting against the
supreme government would be sentenced to death. But in Ireland the partisans had no reason to think they would be treated
worse than the soldiers of the French army.

It is true that some had been warned that no quarter would
be given, and many including Michael Maxwell's grandfather
escaped. The kindest action on the Royalist side after Ballinamuck is quoted by Thomas Pakenham. 'Captain Pakenham,
Lord Longford's uncle and Lieutenant General of the Ordnance . . . rode up to the rebel lines. "Run away boys," he is said
to have shouted, "otherwise you'll all be cut down." But his
warning came too late. All the French were taken prisoner and
treated well, the officers handsomely. Their Irish auxiliaries
were hunted for the rest of the day, mostly by soldiers on horse-
back who regarded their slaughter as an enjoyable sport. " 'Tis
incredible," said one, "the number of them, exclusive of the

French, lay on the field ... however we had a most glorious day." '6

Of those who surrendered or were discovered hiding, hundreds were hanged from the branches of trees and some were marched to Carrick where it seems that the junior English officers wished to keep them alive as ordinary prisoners of war. 'After the action, the regiment were marched to Carrick-on-Shannon – where in the court-house, there were collected a couple of hundred rebel prisoners, taken in arms. An order arrived from Lord Cornwallis directing a certain number of them to be hanged without further ceremony – and a number of bits of paper were rolled up, the word "death" being written on the number ordered; and with these in his hat, the adjutant Captain Kay (on whom devolved the management of this wretched lottery), entered the court-house, and the drawing began. As fast as a wretch drew the fatal ticket, he was handed out and hanged at the door ... it was a dreadful duty to devolve upon any regiment; but, somehow or other, men's minds had grown as hard as the nether millstone. I know it from my own feelings. I would go some miles out of my way to avoid an execution *now*, yet I well remember the indifference with which I looked upon such a spectacle in 1798.'7

Even exiles such as the officers Bartholomew Teeling and Matthew Tone who had joined the French army in France were refused the status of prisoners of war. While 'Humbert, Sarrazin and the other staff officers were lodged in the best hotel [of Dublin] the Mail Coach Hotel in Dawson Street [now the Hibernian]'8 the Irish officers awaited trial for treason and were afterwards hanged. They were even refused the military form of execution – shooting.

So this short campaign which had started with high hopes and the glorious elation of adventure, this alliance between thousands of enthusiasts and one thousand hardened troops, appears to have left behind it only bitter memories and a few souvenirs, such as the Maxwells' sword. And the bitterness was not so much between the king's men and the rebels – who knew what to expect of each other – as between the rebels and the French. After Ballinamuck, 'the French officers loaded the United Irishmen, their allies, with execrations, for having deceived and disappointed them, by inviting them to undertake a fruitless expedition. They also declared that the people of Ireland were the most treacherous and cowardly they ever knew.' And captured Irish prisoners 'gave a pitiable account of their campaign and treatment by the French, described themselves as being nearly starved, very seldom obtaining even raw potatoes, never time to cook, excessively harassed by long and rapid marches, spoke with great bitterness of the invading army, who lived extremely well on the plunder of gentlemen's houses'.[9]

While the hangings went on at Carrick and Longford, the French prisoners were brought to Tullamore, the nearest town on the Royal Canal, and embarked on barges for Dublin. The first barge 'contained the band of the Fermanagh Militia, the second the French officers and the remaining boats were occupied by the privates, amounting to near eight hundred men. Nothing could exceed the *nonchalance* and merriment with which the French bore their situation, collecting in parties ... and singing the Marseillaise.'[10]

The long procession, gliding at walking pace in beautiful September weather and pulled probably by the same barge horses that had taken Cornwallis's army to meet them, seemed more like a triumph than a defeat. But it was curiosity, not worship, that brought thousands of people out to line the banks of the canal.

For Cornwallis and his staff the campaign was over except for mopping up near Killala.

Chapter Five

All this time the Bishop of Killala, the magistrate William Kirkwood and every Protestant gentleman 'of consequence' there had lived in fear of death and robbery. Their only protectors had been their enemies, now very few in number, commanded by the three French officers whom Humbert had left in command of the town. The commandant, Lt. Col. Charost, became a close friend of the bishop and his wife and children – eleven out of their fifteen were at home. The two junior officers amused them all and were good company at meals. They did not like Ferdy O'Donnel, the young man who had befriended Kirkwood and was now town-major and commander of the rebel forces, or hordes as they would have called them. O'Donnel 'took to himself one of the bedchambers of the middle floor, from which it was not possible afterwards to dislodge him; and this apartment he was pleased to distinguish by the name of *his* room ... The bishop, disgusted with his forwardness and vulgar manners, avoided as much as he could all intercourse with him, and when he did ask him to sit down at his table (as at times he could scarcely help doing so without rudeness) it was evidently the result of constraint ... Disagreeable as an inmate, O'Donnel was not however without merit as an officer, and a guardian of the public peace.'

He went on to describe gratefully how much O'Donnel had done to check murder and plunder, acknowledging him along with the French officers as one of his protectors, but certainly did not say so to his face, for O'Donnel spoke bitterly about his, the bishop's, ingratitude. The antipathy between them was personal, arising not from class as one might guess, nor from religion, the other supposed fundament of bitterness at that time. The bishop disregarded class rules. Charost was the son of a

Paris watchmaker. Humbert, whom he respected from the moment of their first alarming meeting and gradually grew fond of, had also risen from the ranks. In religious matters the bishop was perfectly tolerant and opposed only to the Orange society because it had 'disgraced itself by an infamy new to Protestants, an actual expulsion of Roman Catholics from their homes. The name of Orangemen had but just begun to be heard of in Connaught . . .'

The mere name was enough, as the bishop went on to say, to give some Catholics cause for alarm and to stir up hostility towards Protestants in general, but, as it turned out, religious hatreds and fears played a small part in the troubles of Connaught that autumn; the sackings of houses and the thefts of cattle and stores were not accompanied by murder and torture such as had gone together with the war in Wexford and Wicklow. Class hatred and the ideas of the French revolution played a smaller part too than elsewhere. Or so it seems to us now. But at the time, and especially when the news of Ballinamuck reached them, the County Mayo Protestants lived in terror of their lives.

In Killala itself and nearby it appears that attacks on Protestants were at first inspired not so much by hatred as by boredom. The huge rebel army left behind by Humbert had camped in the bishop's meadows for weeks with nothing to do. When they became dangerously restless, the French garrison would tire them out on the forecourt which had been turned into a parade ground, or quieten them 'with beef and mutton, and a moderate share of whiskey'. The raiding of houses was the only form of active service left, and although it was forbidden by O'Donnel and sometimes effectively stopped by the French, no one could entirely control that disorderly force.

Catholics and their property were not molested but this was because the many of them who were opposed to the rebels were difficult to identify. All Protestants, so far as anyone knew, were opposed. Also, all landlords were Protestants. To attack the 'big house' was a challenge which needed great courage to meet, and to those who thought mainly of loot the reward could be great.

To all it meant justice, after the slavish humility in which they and their parents had been brought up.

It is certain that neither loot nor sectarianism was the cause of these raids. When the partisans attacked and robbed a humble Protestant community in the village of Multifarragh, the loot was not worth the danger, and the sixty prisoners taken were taken not as ordinary Protestants but as members of the Orange Society whose oath was believed to include the words, 'I will exterminate, as far as I am able, the Catholics of Ireland.'[1] The Protestants of Multifarragh were refugees from East Ulster, whence they had been driven by the 'United Irishmen' – a mainly Protestant society in that province – because of their loyalty to the king and his government. When Colonel Charost heard of their imprisonment at Ballina in the hands of the French garrison there, he went at once to question them and released them all in one day, believing that his junior officer, the commandant of Ballina, had listened to 'accusations on a religious account' which was entirely contrary to French policy. This happened on 9 September, the day after Ballinamuck. But the news of Humbert's defeat had not yet reached Mayo.

Two days later the greatest house in the county was sacked – Castlereagh, the seat of the Knox family, a few miles from Killala to the west. On the 12th the bishop wrote in his journal, 'I was groaning in bed this morning, with a sharp fit of the rheumatism, and counting up the persons now under my roof (who are seventy-eight in number), when a faithful domestic of Castlereagh came to tell me, that all endeavours to protect that house had proved ineffectual, for that yesterday, at noon, a mob broke in and demolished everything that was valuable, except the wine which he had concealed; but as there was no chance of its remaining long so, he thought it best that the commandant should take it ... my only remaining horse was dispatched to Castlereagh, with a French officer, for the wine.'

This horse pulled a car with the officer, the bishop's butler and some other servants who rode on it, and 'No expedient for saving the wine and spirits from the unworthy mouths that were preparing to swallow them appeared to the messengers to be so ready and effectual, as that of using the liquor instantly themselves. In consequence the bishop's butler returned from the expedition pot-valiant, quarrelled with the gardener and carter, presented a blunderbuss at the former, and provoked the bishop himself so much by saucy language, that he lost his temper, and almost knocked the fellow down by a box on the ear. The commandant interposing, locked him up in his own pantry, and left him to sleep there till morning.'

The bishop and his family, although shocked at first by the pleasure they got from it, were living better than ever before. From some of the great houses nothing could be saved. Castle Lacken, which was occupied by its owner's wealthy agent and therefore specially hated, was completely gutted, even its flooring was carried away. 'It is shocking to see families accustomed to ease and affluence arriving here with nothing left but the clothes on their backs as was the case with Sir J. Palmer's agent, Mr Waldron, whose losses amount to £4,000.' As no shops existed, every such house bought large supplies of groceries from distant merchants and stored enough to last for many months. Much of it was rescued by the palace. The French officers were surprised by the excellence of the wines and brandies they were able to save from ignorant palates, and of the great flocks of sheep and cattle that were driven away to the mountains a part always strayed into the cathedral precincts.

'The choicest beef and mutton from grazing grounds that feed the boast of the Dublin markets, excellent wines and spirits extracted from the cellars of his very good friends the neighbouring gentry ... were received, at first with groans and lamentations over the times, and at last with great equanimity, as a misfortune that could not be helped.'

This polite form of loot was shared by the bishop's family and friends with the French, who had from the very day of their landing been on better terms with their opponents, the loyalist gentry, than with the Irish Volunteers. Ill-feeling between them and the Irish had been growing all the time, and when the news of Humbert's defeat reached Killala, they were prepared even to fight their Irish allies, to quell what seemed to them like mutiny.

As professional soldiers whose supreme commander had surrendered, their duty was to give themselves up and rejoin their army as prisoners of war. But for several days there was no one for them to surrender to. The Irish were angrily opposed to any such plan and during those days, while the little French garrison waited resignedly for the English to take over the town, they grew more active, determined to defend it and to advance to meet the king's troops.

The courage of the volunteers at this moment would have gone down in history as unsurpassed had their decision been taken by an authorized army of any nation. They decided to fight when all prospect of French leadership was lost, when few of them had even firearms, in the knowledge that no quarter would be given by their enemy whose strength lay in cavalry, the most dreaded force of all to foot soldiers fighting without cover of artillery.

As it was, their only reporter was the bishop. He saw their determination as a tragedy, which certainly it was, but beyond that saw nothing but folly, nothing of their hopes of liberation, of the strength of spirit which made hundreds leave their homes, some walking sixty miles across roadless bogs and mountains to join the forces camping in his grounds. His earnest wish was that they should disperse to the safety of their scattered houses, and escape the vengeance which he foresaw as certain retribution. Instead, new recruits kept coming in, seven hundred and fifty in one day. 'Careless of the future,' he wrote, '... they thought of nothing by living merrily, as long as they might, upon the property that lay at their mercy.'

The French refused to issue any more arms, either to new or old recruits. The Irish said that if they were not thought worthy of being trusted with the ammunition brought from France, they had resolved to form a strong body of pikemen. 'They therefore desired permission to seize upon all the iron they could find in the stores of Mr Kirkwood.' Colonel Charost persuaded them to melt down their own pitchforks and any other farming tools they had. So Kirkwood's iron was saved, so was an ash planatation of the bishop's, which they wanted for handles. Pikes had been the most effective weapon throughout the rebellion, especially against cavalry. But Charost 'despised the service of pike-men against regular troops'.

On 18 September, ten days after Humbert's defeat, the pike-men threatened mutiny against the French, saying that they would imprison all Protestants in the cathedral and hold them there as hostages against the arrival of the king's army. On the 20th, two thousand pike-men, dismissed by Charost the day before, came back to camp on the castle meadows and the customs-house was attacked in a search for tobacco. Next day after breakfast, Charost, with the bishop as interpreter, went into the Main Street to confront a large force who were threatening to plunder the town. At four o'clock, just before dinner, a message came from an eye-witness that the king's army were advancing in great numbers, and by two roads, from Castlebar.

'Dinner was laid on the table, notwithstanding. In the midst of it, in rushed Thomas Kirkwood, a young officer of yeoman cavalry, with news that the attack on our front gate was commencing by about a score of armed men. Such a number did not frighten us. 'Stay 'till they get to a head,' says the commandant. We drank away, till they had increased to near fifty. Then the commandant took his hat, and marching out with his two officers fully armed, he steps forward to the pike-men, orders them to retire from the musqueteers, divides the latter into three platoons, and sets them directly to go through their exercise. Occupied for some time with these movements, they had not leisure to apply themselves to worse, and thus were easily persuaded at last to disperse.'

Early next morning, on Saturday the 22nd, 'the loyalists were desired by the rebels to come up with them to the hill on which the needle tower is built, in order to be eye-witnesses of the havoc a party of the king's army was making as it advanced towards us from Sligo. A train of fire too clearly distinguished their line of march, flaming up from houses of unfortunate peasants . . .'

The army was advancing from the north and south making the usual indiscriminate reprisals on its way. (At the village of Carrowcarden a group of loyalist Protestants poor enough to be indistinguishable from other working people were killed off by mistake.)[2]

'The peaceful inhabitants of Killala were now to be spectators of a scene they had never expected to behold – a battle! a sight which no person that has seen it once, and possesses the feelings of a human creature, would choose to witness a second time. A troop of fugitives in full race from Ballina, women and children tumbling over one another to get into the castle, or into any house ... continued for a painful length of time to give notice of the approach of an army ... The two divisions of the royal army were supposed to make up about twelve hundred men, and they had five pieces of cannon.'

The size of the rebel army on that day is impossible to know. Hundreds had taken the French officers' advice and gone home in good time, hundreds had fled after skirmishes with the enemy on country roads, but hundreds of others flocked into the town, even on the day of the battle – 'passing under the castle windows and running upon death, with as little appearance of reflection or concern, as if they were hastening to a show'. The bishop guessed that there were only eight or nine hundred in the whole rebel army by then.

Even this number would have put up a damaging resistance if they had been able to shoot straight. They took up good positions behind stone walls, covering the approaches to the town and their very first volley on each side of the first advancing column was strong enough to break it. But their bullets flew over the road above the heads of the enemy and only killed two, a corporal and a private. A hand-to-hand fight ensued, in which they were hopelessly outnumbered, and after twenty minutes of it they retreated pell-mell into the town, leaving dozens of dead and wounded on the way. The rest was street-fighting, mostly in the main street the far end of which was blocked by one of the fiercest of the king's Irish regiments, the Kerry Militia, whose zeal was enhanced by the traditional enmity between their county and the distant one of Mayo.

It was almost unheard of to attack a town with cavalry, but a Scottish regiment was ordered to gallop down the main street from the other end, pursuing the rebels and driving them into the Kerry's; and between the two they were cut to pieces.

It was 23 September. As on 23 August, when the French seized the town, the fighting was thickest at the top of the street by William Kirkwood's house. It was soon over, but no truce was allowed and surrender even if it was accepted meant certain death. So house after house was broken into by men trying to escape through the back or hide.

Of course every civilian on both sides was in terror and tried to stay indoors. But Andrew Kirkwood, a relative of William's and about his age, had for days been obsessed by presentiments of death, and worked himself into a frenzy. He spent the whole evening before the battle instructing his wife on how to manage his affairs and as soon as the firing began he rushed with 'a purse of guineas' in his pocket from his own house, which was in a comparatively safe position, to William's.

'Some of the defeated rebels, however, did force their way into houses, and by consequence brought mischief upon the innocent inhabitants, without benefit to themselves. The first house, after passing the bishop's, is that of Mr Wm. Kirkwood, the magistrate so often mentioned. Its situation exposed it on this occasion to peculiar danger, as it fronts the main street, which was raked entirely by a line of fire. A flying rebel had burst through the door, followed by six or seven soldiers: they poured a volley of musquetry after him, that proved fatal to Mr Andrew Kirkwood, a most loyal and respectable citizen, while he was rejoicing at the victory, and in the very act of shouting out "God save the King".'

Killala was secured by the king's troops in less than an hour but 'the hand of slaughter was still in pursuit of unresisting peasants through the town' late next day. 'Some houses were perforated like a riddle, most of them had their doors and windows destroyed.' The bishop pleaded for mercy for individuals where he could – and persuaded his own 'pot-valiant' butler to flee the country – but the king's officers could not often control their own troops, who plundered Protestant and Catholic alike. 'Their rapacity differed in no respect from that of the rebels ... except that his Majesty's soldiers were incomparably superior to the Irish traitors in dexterity at stealing.' The French were sent away as prisoners in time to reach Humbert and his staff who were at Dover waiting for a ship to France. The bishop's gratitude to them had been reported to the high command. O'Donnel's body, which had been dumped between potato ridges early in the fighting, was brought back on the bishop's orders and buried in the churchyard. In Killala the king's troops quietened down. For a few weeks parties of them were sent into the mountains to burn houses. Then the last flicker went out. In November Wolfe Tone's tragic capture at sea disturbed no one on land. And in County Mayo, the allies of France were unheard of again. A peaceful winter began, and a fearful famine.

Chapter Six

As I bicycled on towards Connemara, I thought more and more about Phoebe. In those days when a regret came suddenly over me, or a memory that made me angry with myself, I would utter a horrible inarticulate cry or shout something that even to me seemed unrelated to my thoughts, like 'where's the moon?' or 'I was in the garden, fool!' It was involuntary, like a laugh or groan. If there was anyone near I could muffle it, but now I still had nearly ninety miles of mountain roads to travel and my cries and nonsense leapt out uninhibited. When I stopped for a drink, and at night, my resolution to leave Woodbrook wavered.

Except near the few towns and villages, I was alone all the time. In the daytime I often longed for someone to talk to. At night when people talked to me, I was too tired to heed them. This, and the long distances I covered by bicycle, makes the journey unique in my memory. On a bicycle in those days you used to feel that you were travelling fast. Only once or twice in a whole day would a car pass or meet you covering you with dust, if the road was dry, and with white mud when it was wet. You could pass the quickest trotting horse and trap if the driver did not stop you for a conversation, and if you had the luck to catch one up when you were tired it would tow you along beside it. But what I remember best is the solitude. Something like fear of the supernatural overcame me in a thunderstorm by the shore of Lough Corrib. The blackness of the huge stretch of water was unworldly and the mountains changed shape.

Even nowadays it is one of the most impressive journeys in Ireland. The steep ways wind over four mountain ranges, mostly treeless, and the valleys glitter with lakes. Here and there on the lowlands there are plantations of pine and fir trees, very dark patches, usually marking the site of a gentleman's demesne. I passed several, but only remember the name of one because I had heard of it before – Lough Mask House, where Captain Boycott lived while he was Lord Erne's agent.

It is difficult to imagine that these mountains, like the Scottish Highlands, were once densely populated and I think it was very difficult for the few survivors of clearances and famine to keep to their old houses, while generation by generation neighbours went to emigrate or to the towns. I met one who welcomed me as though I was a rescue party that had found her in the desert at last. I had taken a short cut, somewhere through the hills of the Joyce Country. It was marked on the map as the worst type of road, which is usually quite good on a bicycle, and it saved me fifteen miles, though not in the end fifteen miles' worth of time. The track started steeply but smoothly enough for me to push my bike up it with ease. Then at every turn it grew more and more stony, until suddenly coming round a corner within sight of the summit, I saw that it had ceased to be a track at all. It was like a dried-up waterfall, a steep rocky bed between precipitous walls. The day was hot, the place sheltered, the rocks dazzling. I carried my bicycle over my head, or on my shoulder when I needed a hand to pull myself over a rock. Once I fell and the front wheel got bent. At the top I was exhausted and terribly thirsty.

I sat down there and made a cigarette, looking about me for a spring or stream. I saw none. But the way before me, sloping down from the top of the hill, had been cleared of rocks and was even grassy in patches which gave me hope of a smooth way to the road below. I tried the front wheel. It turned all right, with only a small scraping noise against the fork. I began to wheel it down the hill. Then I smelt turf smoke and suddenly, so close to the rocks that it seemed part of them, there was a house, its thatch thick with flowers and grass. The woman of the house was at the door with a baby in her arms. I went towards her at once. 'Ye frightened the life of me,' she said. She thought I had passed the house earlier without coming in and was on my way back and when she heard I had climbed the rocks with my bicycle, I could not tell whether she thought me super-human or mad. She had lovely black hair, supposed to be in a bun, but rather loose, and a strong and happy face with curious, clear eyes like a child's. I sat down by the fire and she gave me buttermilk in an enamel mug. Her husband was out on the bog she said, cutting turf. Her mother lived near Maam Cross about five miles away. She had written a letter to her mother 'two months since, and no one came to bring it to her'. This was for her the God-sent happiness of our meeting, for I had told her I was going in that direction. She had not sent the letter by post, because the nearest post-box was beyond her mother's house and for either she would have to wait till the next fair took her husband that way. She wrote a postscript to bring the letter up to date and I took it and said good-bye. It was as though she lived on an island no bigger than her house.

Her mother welcomed me as though I had saved a life, and as I sat down to tea – a large spread done specially for me because her husband and sons had not yet come home – she read the letter out in a rapid monotone. It said the baby was well, etc.

Maam Cross was only a few miles farther on. When I reached it that evening I did not know I was there. I had expected to find a town, or at least a straggly village with a church. But 'cross' is the ordinary word for crossroads and that is all it was, that and a lonely pub near a signpost. But even before the roads were made it was an important place for pack-animal traffic. Then as now you could not reach Westport or Galway, or Dublin for that matter, without passing through it and it is surprising that it did not become a market town.

The pub was built about 1825 by Alexander Nimmo, the Scottish engineer who reclaimed waste land and made roads and harbours in West Connaught which was almost inaccessible to travellers until his time. He built it as a house to live in for himself and his staff while they were working on the roads from Galway, but died before work was completed beyond that point. Maria Edgeworth and her friends, travelling along the newly famous Nimmo road in a huge heavy coach against everyone's advice, expected it to continue westwards. It did, but grew worse and worse, and several times the coach sank into holes as big as itself. After Maam Cross, as they entered the wildest part of the country, they found themselves accompanied by a 'tail' of sixty or a hundred men and boys who removed the horses and manhandled the coach whenever it got stuck.[1]

I had a pint or two in Nimmo's house and, isolated though it was, immediately felt as though I was in a city parcel office. All kinds of packages, crates, tools were waiting to be collected by people or taken away by bus. People came miles to Maam Cross because of the bus.

I think it was this inn, though it may have been one in the village of Maam some miles away, that became famous even in England as the scene of one of Lord Leitrim's angry acts, for which the mid-Victorian newspapers reported him as having refused 'fire and water' to the Viceroy of Ireland, Lord Carlisle, who was then at the most trying stage of an official progress through the comfortless west. Maam was in one of Leitrim's estates and the landlord of the inn, a man named King, his tenant. He commanded King to bar his door against the Viceroy and to fill all the rooms with local people, also tenants of course, who were ordered to spend the night there at Leitrim's expense.[2] And this was done. King feared Leitrim even more than Lord Carlisle and, though the rooms had been booked for him and his retinue long before, he sent them away hungry in their coaches with tired horses. There was nowhere else to eat or sleep for another twenty miles.

I could have stayed in the inn, but had very little money left and the evening was beautifully warm and dry, so I cycled on a bit and slept in the booking office of one of the disused railway stations that stood every few miles near this road. Most were occupied by families, with hens walking up and down the platforms. Mine was a ruin.

This road to Ballynahinch, on which Maria Edgeworth's party had suffered such annoyance, was the first easy road I had been on for days. It was tarred and comparatively level, so I went fast and easily next day. To reach Roundstone you have to turn left before Ballynahinch, and that road though stony with pot-holes every yard ran mostly downhill towards the coast of Bertraghboy Bay. I got to Roundstone earlier than I thought I would, and that was fortunate because for a long time I could not find a boat to take me over to the island. But I enjoyed my waiting time. It was the only beautiful village I had seen in Ireland. In the orderly arrangement of its houses and the design of its curved harbour it was more like an English fishing village of the old kind.

The harbour wall made almost a semi-circle high above the water and as you leant on it you could watch everything that took place on the water and the quays below. Small houses and shops were behind you across the narrow street. There were many men leaning on the wall, of course, and after leaning by one then another to choose the likeliest helper, I said that I wanted to go to Inishlacken. That was the name of the island where the house was. Without thinking it over at all, he pointed down to a small rowing boat on the sand below us. The tide was low. 'Take that one.' That was all he said.

I climbed down the steps from the quay and pushed it into the water. It was as light as a large laundry basket. Our lake boat was wide and the handles of its oars could not touch each other. These overlapped. I could row well but had not learned to keep one hand above the other. My knuckles were bleeding before I landed on the sandy beach of the island. I found the house, very near this beach, single-storied with the usual three rooms but no furniture in it. Its thatch was thin and its white-wash green with lichen. The top half of the door had lost its latch and swung open. It was in a beautiful position, alone and unfenced on a grassy slope, looking out across the bay. I decided to take it. It was the end of my journey. Afterwards it seemed symbolic of all my aims that I should arrive at an empty house on an island.

If there remained in my mind any doubts about returning to Woodbrook, they were dispelled by lack of money. I reckoned it would take me three days by the shortest route, via Galway, and by the time I had sent Ivy a postcard saying 'yes' to the cottage I had only half-a-crown left. In Galway it was raining and the cheapest hotel was five shillings for bed and breakfast. The landlord let me stay on credit and lent me a few shillings next morning.

I began to feel excited about my return. To be near Phoebe seemed enough, whoever else swam with her on the lake, and my book came to life in my mind again. So did the farm and horses. I cycled with fanatical strength all that day but the bent wheel slowed me and once going down a hill two spokes came loose and entangling themselves in the fork upset me. I was cut about a bit and wasted time extracting spokes from the wheel. I stayed out that night but was too excited and sore to sleep. I had enough money for food and drink, but it took two hours next morning before I reached a village, and on the way I was stopped by one of those hallucinations I sometimes have. I forget what it was – a hedge on fire, perhaps – but whatever it was it held me up because such visions make me stay still until they dissolve.

I arrived at Woodbrook at dusk, after everybody's usual bed-time. There were no lights downstairs, but one in Phoebe's bedroom, and I ran up hoping, I suppose, to be greeted as though I had climbed Mount Everest. But Phoebe's head was under the covers and I only got a muffled 'Hullo'. The windows were wide open and her father was dancing round the room with a tennis racket in his hand, trying to drive out a bat. There were many bats in the attic and she was always afraid of getting them entangled in her hair at night.

A few days later, on 1 September, we all set out for Round-stone on a lorry: Charlie, Ivy, Tony, Phoebe, Trevor-Roper, the driver and me. It was the grocer's lorry, an open one, and we had furnished it comfortably, stacking our bedsteads and table behind the cab and laying the mattresses on the floor. We also had several kitchen chairs which James Currid placed in a semi-circle, as though for guests by a hearth. We could see the country from these – the mattresses were too low – and surprisingly, the jolting of the lorry did not upset them. The day was sunny and even hot when we stopped for a picnic. The moon had changed and everyone said the good weather would last. The hay was saved and the oats not ready. No one had anything to worry about. Perhaps Charlie guessed how near war was, but we left long before the postman came and the last paper we had seen was that of the 30th. If he was worried he did not say so. And my moroseness had completely disappeared. It was a glorious and happy journey, all along the narrow dusty road that I had come home on, through Tuam, Galway and Maam Cross, but now with a lot of laughter, somersaults on the mattresses and that kind of thing. We were taken out to the island with the furniture in a large open fishing boat – a wooden one with an engine. The island was idyllic too, at least for us who did not have to work there or stay the winter. And someone had whitewashed the little house inside and out.

In these surroundings, without papers or anyone from the mainland to talk to, we were quite unprepared for the news that war had broken out, and I for one did not believe it, or tried not to. We had not even heard of the invasion of Poland, which happened on the day we left Woodbrook, and I remembered how at the time of Munich everyone's mind was prepared. At that time I believed with a dreadful certainty that war would begin within a week. So when a man from the mainland said that a friend had heard this on the wireless in a pub and that the first air-raid had struck London, I hoped he had got it all wrong. It was about seven in the evening when he brought us this news, and next morning it was confirmed without a doubt, except that the air-raid was nothing but sirens sounding a false alarm. The gloom and the confusion of plans among our party was intense. Should Trevor-Roper return to England at once? He seemed to wish to. Should I? Would Charlie, so long retired, go back to the army? I hoped he and my father were too old. My father was much his senior. Charlie said nothing about that and Phoebe nothing at all. The rest of us spoke of private matters because all else was unmentionable – the destruction of the world that had been predicted.

On the beach, alone with Phoebe some days after that, we saw seabirds, many of them huge and unknown to us. It was only slightly windy and the sun shone all the time. We walked round the whole shore of the island in about three hours. For once we were alone. All her zest had returned and we scrambled over rocks, wading through pools and picking up stones and bits of wood whitened by the sea. She threw scraps of wet seaweed at me. Once she stood still, pointing: 'Look at that!' I pretended to see it, as I often did in those days, to save shame and time. But she knew, and said it was a small flitting bird, quite unlike a seabird, and she thought I might know its name.

When we came to a sandy beach, we undressed and swam. The wind was high enough there to make rolling breakers and white horses out to sea. It was exciting.

We got dressed and sat down watching the waves till suddenly she looked at me and said, 'Thank goodness you're short-sighted.'

I said 'Yes'; but afterwards thought how dishonest I was to lean on that.

I was in a muddle about war, especially this one. I had when younger believed in absolute pacifism, that is to say I thought even Nazism could be conquered by passive resistance, and that to wait fifty years for that was a lesser evil than the kind of war this one would be. I also had, or thought I had, no patriotic feelings towards any country at all, and felt especially cynical about England and France which had looked on, their right wings with approval, as the Nazis tried out their new weapons in Spain and won the civil war for Franco. At Oxford we had also heard rumours, not confirmed in print till after the war, so far as I know, of huge sums poured by British and American industrialists, and by European bankers, into the Nazi funds. They helped to put Hitler into power and to keep him going until at last they were afraid of the devil they made – a devil that they once hoped would protect them against the bogey of communism. Also, someone had told me that anyone as short-sighted as I was would spend a whole war cleaning latrines. But like everyone else I knew that if the Allies won, fascism would stop for a while at least in Europe.

The island was so pure and simple, and our life there so unmuddled, that such thoughts slid quickly away. I remember it as an energetic, peaceful holiday and I think it was mostly happy for the others too. It certainly was for Tony, who was still at the age when a sandy beach gives full-time work with very short breaks for meals.

On September 12th Phoebe had her birthday dance. It was the only one she had ever had away from home and all the guests were unknown to her. Scores of them rowed over from the mainland, and as there was only room for a few in the house they filed in past the barrel of Guinness with mugs in their hands and out through the back door. They thought me very 'innocent' and Phoebe made fun of me afterwards, because I worked hard all evening with scarcely a moment for a drink myself, filling mugs for the same men, the only heavy drinkers there, who came round again and again, in at the front door of the kitchen and out at the back.

We stayed on the island for about three weeks. We were driven back to Woodbrook in the same lorry, but the mood was different. Everybody felt subdued.

Chapter Seven

The life of Woodbrook altered very soon and became entire, complete in itself and concentrated, as I suppose it had been in the old days. From now on the whole family lived there all the year round and the little social life there was took place within a radius of about twenty miles. For shorter distances the lack of petrol made us go by pony and trap more and more, to friends who lived near enough and for shopping in Carrick and Boyle. I suppose there was a good reserve of clothes, but any needed were bought locally once more, never in Dublin and only once or twice in Sligo when other things brought Ivy there. I can't remember buying any, except gum-boots and clogs, but I suppose I must have had new trousers when my knees showed through. I do remember one tough pair which Ivy got for me in Sligo. I had ragged elbows, but so I did in London years afterwards. Charlie's way of dressing never altered. His clothes, however old, had no holes in them except when he put a lighted pipe in his pocket.

Work on the farm became continuous. Till then, while most of the land was pasture, the men took occasional work elsewhere. Now we had to plough up the old pastures for grain crops and some of the meadows that gave the best hay went too. Ploughing, sowing, harrowing and harvest took the whole year.

All this, enforced by the Compulsory Tillage Order, reduced the income of the farm once again, for in our damp climate, where animals thrived, grain fetched a small price. We had never sold it before, but now we had more oats than we needed for our stock and were obliged to sow a fixed acreage of wheat as well. Wheat was a certain loss; even in a good year the grain never hardened, much of it became mildewed and raised no money at all. The demand for horses fell but the number we

239

kept on the land remained the same. Low though the rate of wages was, the total had been doubled.

The change in farming did not worry Charlie in the least, but to James Currid it was a disaster. He stood watching the fields turn slowly black beneath the plough as one might watch the demolition of an old beloved house, and once while he was giving me a haircut in the stable yard – his only time for confidential talk – he described the breaking up of the pastures as the ruin of Colonel Tom's and Colonel James's work and of their grandfathers' and great-grandfathers' before them.

Even without compulsory tillage we would have had to try wheat, when food became scarce, to get enough flour for bread. Ours was a bit musty at times, but eatable. The only nuisance was that the loaves went mouldy after their first day, so Winnie could not, as every countrywoman used to, make several days' supply at one baking.

All this meant that I, and Trevor-Roper until he had to go to England to enlist, were always working on the land except at lesson times and that Phoebe and Tony added poultry-keeping to their usual occupations, for we bought a large number of light Sussex hens and some ducks, reared chickens and ducklings and sold eggs that were collected by lorry. And it meant that everybody got to know each other better – we who lived in the big house, the Maxwells and those who came daily to work at Woodbrook.

When I say food was scarce I do not mean that we went short of anything necessary; no one keeping poultry and dairy cows could; but poorer people did and the very poor, especially in the towns, were reduced to a level of subsistence as low as any the oldest could remember. The shortage of bread was the worst for them, especially in the summer months, 'the meal months', for though diet was more varied than in Nanny's youth people depended on potatoes. The bread ration was meagre and the tea ration declined to $\frac{1}{2}$ oz. a week per person.[1] Tea with bread and margarine or butter had for years been the basic diet of the poor. Tea, or rather tea that was strong enough, was the only missing thing I longed for. A large pot of it had always been left stewing on the kitchen range all day and I used to help myself on my way in or out. I preferred it to freshly made tea. But now Winnie had to use old tea leaves several times, and she even put baking powder into the pot to extract the last tannin from them. The tea leaves turned white at that stage. Everything had always been bought in large quantities of course and it was only after rationing took effect that Ivy persuaded us all to light the fires without sugar. Before then we used to fetch sugar from Carrick in hundredweight bags.

I suspect that even after rationing we were favoured by John Lowe. The lorry that took us to Roundstone was his, but it was misleading to call it a 'grocer's' lorry because you could get everything else in his shop as well – ploughshares and coulters, even whole ploughs I think, exercise books, rat traps, clothes, tar, paint. His shop smelt beautifully. I used to imagine a recipe book for smells; there was a delicious mixture at Joe Fryer's forge too, and at the mill in Boyle; but John Lowe's shop was for the epicure. At the back there was a bar where you could sit drinking and the mixture wafted in to you together with the smell of the stables he kept for his customers' horses. We had all been frequent visitors for years and I suppose we numbered among his 'good customers', by which I mean not those who paid their bills, but those who took cartloads of stuff away. I had something to do with Charlie's accounts in the war. It is laughable but I tried. It was not so much the blind leading the blind but the worried leading the unworried into a morass that both would have reached unaided. I saw that he owed John Lowe about £500 when the war began; before rationing I mean. Lowe probably thought that the way to recover a debt without losing a customer was to let him have more and more things. Most of the things were for the farm, so rationing did not reduce the growing debt much. Or perhaps he was kind. I remember him as a generous hearted man. I used to like talking to him in the bar when he had time to stay and he had a strong personality that made everyone think he was in the shop even when he was not. I think he was a very large man, but it is so long ago and my visits to Carrick were rare. He was kind to the poor in small bits of largesse and he chose Christmas presents thoughtfully according to each customer's likings. All the shopkeepers gave Christmas presents, a bottle of whiskey or port, a ham or something, to everyone according to his station, and this continued throughout the war. Meat, I think, was never officially rationed though its high price stopped almost everybody eating it. The bacon and cabbage which old Michael Maxwell liked so much, and still called by the same name, became salt and cabbage for most people, except once a week when it was flavoured with a rasher. The Maxwells were more fortunate than many in having their own pig.

Anyone would think that a neutral island would at least have a supply of fish, but there was none inland and never had been in my time, except now and then some uneatable salted pieces: no fresh fish at all even on Fridays for rich or poor. I have read attacks on De Valera's government for neglecting the fishing industry and I am sure they were true in respect of exports, but the home market may have been impossible to develop, for no one liked fish. They thought it poor stuff fit only for fasting on, and even in Sligo or Galway where there was a choice on Fridays most people preferred eggs.

It did not occur to me then, but I now think of my pre-war attitude to the world, and even to England, as a microcosm of the attitude of the majority of Irish people to that war. I seldom saw newspapers and when I did I was either bored or plunged into despair and went back to the book I was reading. In the 1930s I took no more notice of the I.R.A. bombing in England than of ordinary murder reports – in fact it was more futile and less provoked than private murder – and though several of my friends had fought against Franco and others were writing and demonstrating against Hitler and Mussolini, I did nothing.

Ireland's neutrality was something more positive than that. An alliance with England would for one thing have caused civil war, and for the same reason it was impossible to introduce conscription in the six counties. But just as I, if I had been born later, would have been called a drop-out, so Ireland became a drop-out from the world. Professor Lyons has described a psychological effect of her neutrality in words that make me think of my life in the thirties.

'It was as if a whole people had been condemned to live in

Plato's cave, backs to the fire of life and deriving their only knowledge of what went on outside from the flickering shadows thrown on the wall before their eyes by the men and women who passed to and fro behind them.'[2]

Ireland had chosen the cave and I had chosen mine. The choice made people angry.

The flickering shadow I remember best was the news of the German victory that led to the fall of France and to Dunkirk. It had been a showery month of May and the day was dark and glaring by turns. We were working in the field near the gate-lodge, and Trevor-Roper and I had come back early after dinner and were sitting with our backs to a huge elm tree that grew inside the fence near the bottom of the avenue, waiting for the others. Tom was the next to arrive and when he saw us he almost ran. We half got up, thinking that he needed help, that a bullock or colt had fallen into a drain which was the usual cause of haste. But he did not shout or beckon and we sat down again. When he drew near he said 'England's finished' and told us what had happened. 'Hitler's taken France,' he said, 'and in a few days he'll take England.' It was a horrible shock to us. Trevor-Roper said 'Don't be stupid!' and, guided I suppose by precedent and the nationalist education he had had, spoke with calm, utter confidence in England's recovery. I stood up and walked towards where we had been working, overwhelmed by patriotic emotions that I thought I had discarded at the age of fourteen when I gave up Scottish Nationalism and learning Gaelic. Our instinctive response had nothing to do with anti-fascism which I thought was the only good reason for going to war.

Charlie bought one of the few wireless sets obtainable in Carrick, an ornate and heavy box that might have done for a dog's coffin, and when its batteries were strong it blared out the news two or three times a day. I am told that the news was more severely censored in Ireland than in England. No one but Charlie listened to it unless they happened to be in the room, but all through the war years he would switch it on and sit by it; then, even after listening to the most dreadful and dramatic events, would switch it off with a sigh and exclaim, 'No news.' He meant no decisive news, no glimpse of final victory. I was not in Ireland when the D-Day invasion was announced, but I am sure that was Charlie's first real piece of news.

The Irish Government and newspapers referred to the war as the 'emergency' just as older people spoke of their War of Independence as 'the troubled times.' Perhaps Ireland began the fashion for euphemisms that so many countries adopted later – Ministry of Defence for Ministry of War, Deterrent for H-Bomb, 'helping the police' for being forced to answer questions.

Phoebe worked hard at one thing or another all day every day except when church interrupted Sunday mornings – too hard I now think. She was eighteen then and I was twenty-six. I regret how little I remember of her, during that early part of the war, of what she said or felt. Her lessons with me continued as before but now that she had reached, rather late, the matriculation stage, I was little use to her except in history and English. Someone else had to be found and the search was exceedingly difficult. The ninety miles between us and Dublin was a prohibitive distance, and many months passed before Tom Crowe, an undergraduate of Trinity, began to spend his vacations at Woodbrook.

It was the farm and vegetable garden that gradually brought us together again, in a new sort of companionship. We both took pleasure in the transformation of the farm, in the extra people who came to work and the continually varying colours of everything in sight. The whole landscape which she had known all her life in shades of green now changed into patchwork, never constant and beautifully irregular because each field had always been a different shape bounded by a wandering stone wall or hedge. The black of the ploughland in winter could be seen from wherever we rode on the Hill of Usna and in spring and summer the wheat added yet another green to the many different old shades. At harvest time wheat straw was pale or brownish, usually with black spots on the grain, and it was stiff and upright, a contrast to the supple yellow oats.

Phoebe's enthusiasm consoled James a bit. Like a faithful family servant of a hundred years ago, he found most of his pleasures vicariously. If Miss Phoebe had a good hunt, he had a good hunt – he who had waited with his lame leg by the stables to start two hours' work on her sweating horse when she came home. If the major sold a polo pony it was he who followed its history. When I think of him I think also of Thady Quirk, the Rackrent family's steward. Castle Rackrent was published in 1800. James and Thady both worshipped their masters but got their own way when they wanted to. James would make a big show of obeying the children, and it was funny to watch him placating Tony when she was quite small and then secretly restoring to its status quo whatever she had asked him to alter. But not even Phoebe, far less Ivy or me, could persuade him to allow the cattle any of the best hay for winter feed. He would say 'yes' and let a little go to them if any of us was there to watch but keep the rest of it for the horses as he always had in the past. I cannot remember Charlie taking part in that endless argument. I am sure he kept away because he agreed with James.

Phoebe and I tried to learn about up-to-date methods of farming. There could be no very up-to-date method with the ancient implements we had, but the Department of Agriculture published an excellent handbook explaining what might be done without departing far from tradition and, except for the chapter on bees, which I decided was of academic interest only, we followed it as far as we could. I became a figure of fun to the Maxwells with my newly gobbled theories and of course in almost everything their traditional knowledge was effective. The only entirely new thing was silage. We tried it for the aftermath, which would have made a second or even third crop of hay, had there been sun. We dug a slanting pit to the measurements given in the book and pressed the wet grass in, but of course had no molasses. I don't think it succeeded. It smelt foul.

Even the vegetable garden gave a new outlet to Phoebe's zest. There had always been one in front of the house, though from the ground-floor windows and front door you saw nothing beyond the lawn, except the little valley where the 'canal' flowed towards the lake, and some rushy grassland rising to Hughestown Hill. It had never had anything in it that Phoebe

245

remembered except a few cabbages strong enough to overcome the weeds. It was in a sunny and beautiful place, sloping away from the house to the south on a decline that would have shocked County Dublin gardeners, but was good for us because its soil was heavy and even a cliff would not have drained too much water off. Tony and Phoebe had always loved its secrecy. It used to be the first place we searched when either of them was 'lost', for the lawn which had been levelled, in the eighteenth century I suppose, had turned it into a ha-ha; you could see beyond it, not into it – an ideal place to lurk. Now it came to life, again with the help of a book, and bore carrots, parsnips, leeks, onions, lettuces in summer, and savoys and brussels sprouts throughout the winter. Those must sound commonplace to anyone outside Connaught, but in the part of Ireland I knew the potato reigned supreme, with cabbage plants as its subjects in an inferior plot nearby. Even on the sandy soil of Inishlacken and the Connemara mainland, we had found it impossible to buy carrots or parsnips. In Connemara many gardens were hedged by fuchsia bushes, beautifully red in flower, but no small flowers were to be seen, and between Carrick and Sligo I cannot remember even one house with roses, nasturtiums, marigolds, wallflowers or michaelmas daisies about it. I have read that these paucities originated in the old colonial system. I think that is true of vegetables. But even the internationally educated Irish people I knew later had a gap in visual sense peculiar to their country; it seemed as though their choice of pictures, distemper or wallpaper happened quite by chance. Perhaps the dearth of flowers in the gardens of poorer people was caused by a similar blindness. Most of the simpler seeds and seedlings could be bought in Carrick or Boyle, but were bought only by the Anglo-Irish and their gardeners.

We also often explored the roof again – Phoebe and I again on that old playground of the past, hers and mine, hers and Tony's and every young person's who came to stay. It was a gently sloping slated roof with leaded valleys and, once you got up there, not at all difficult to move about on in rubber soles. James had had a bad time on it for years, in his nailed boots, and probably cracked as many slates as he repaired, but now that he was too stiff to go up there at all he would stand anxiously at the foot of the first ladder until we came down. The first took us to the flat roof of the drawing-room, then we hauled one of the shorter hay ladders up behind us and reached the slates from there. The roof and its valleys seemed to stretch a great distance, its intersections and varying heights making each part invisible from each like the folds of a mountain range and this made it difficult for us to remember the positions of the rooms below and find the source of each leak. The old ones were clearly marked by pieces of string – for string had always been James's first resource in repairing the Fiat's engine or the roof. He was expert in finding the source of a leak and would fix a string to it and lead the water down on to the lead. This works well until the string rots or frays. The black bitumen paste we used was not much better. In the attics above Ivy's bedroom and Phoebe's new one he used pie-dishes in the old days. Ever since Ivy first came to Woodbrook there had been a recurring drip above her bed. When she told James, he would climb into the attic with nothing but an empty bucket in his hand, come down a minute later and the drip would cease for weeks. At last she asked him what he did up there so quickly. He had emptied the pie-dish which had overflowed and replaced the end of the string that led the water into it.

Of course, one could only attempt to mend the roofs in fine weather, so the times we spent up there were always beautiful, in the sun or wind and above the trees and the wide hilly land, the lake and the Leitrim mountains on one side, and on the other Cootehall and the wooded uplands of Ardcarne and Rock- ingham. Before each spring we tried to keep birds from nesting on the drawing-room chimney with wire netting, but some large ones – I never learned their names – built nests on top of that. Except for Winnie and the girls, there was no one at Wood- brook who had not tried to mend the roof. Even tradesmen from Carrick, summoned at its worst trials by storm, did no better than us and in the end we devoted ourselves to palliatives rather than cures. Phoebe and I worked out a good arrange- ment of jam-jars in the rooms below, where pools on the flat roof dripped on to the windowsills of the dining-room and drawing-room, and I usually remembered to empty them. The inner wall of the drawing-room was more difficult to protect. When water came down there it was absorbed by hundreds of leather-bound volumes of the *Racing Calendar*, that ancient memorial to the glory of Uncle Tom.

The market value of horses had dropped suddenly of course and it continued to decline until it was almost impossible to find buyers at any price. Hunters could not be sent to England any more and Ireland was full of them. Working horses would have paid but, typically, we only bred one to relieve Carnaby who was old and lame – not even a pair for our own farm. Polo ponies were the best hope, and here there seemed to be a heaven-sent chance, for Charlie's younger brother Billy was the captain of Ireland's polo team and could introduce his brother to every player in the country. He came to stay, and immediately bought two lovely three-year-old fillies, half-sisters of Castor and Pollux, perfect chestnut images of those two. We put them on the train to Dublin, some days after his train, and they did well. But unfortunately Billy forgot to pay and no one felt able to remind him. 'Never mind,' said Charlie, as he always did when funds dried up, 'one day we'll see another White Knight in the paddock.' And so we did, this time in a too literal sense, for the cart-horse filly born that year was the last of the White Knight's strain to live at Woodbrook. She was the last born to the old mare Pella whose ancestor, the thoroughbred Pella, had given birth to the miracle foal. Our Pella was a large heavy hunter, bay and over seventeen hands.

The filly was named Pellette. Her father, a Percheron government stallion, was a superb showing of the Department of Agriculture's most understanding work, of its understanding of ordinary people. It placed pedigree rams, boars, bulls and stallions here and there all over the country and chose local people to manage them. The animals were subsidized and the stud fees small, and of course they were sought out and their progeny extolled. Each became the pride of its district.

Pellette took after her father in rounded strength and in colour: she was a beautiful dark grey with a white blaze and two white socks. Her fetlocks were not hairy like Carnaby's and

Jim's. She was kind like her mother but never grew as steady as a plough horse should be, because of the tinge of thoroughbred in her. Real horsemen, like schoolmasters, pretend to have no favourites, but that is impossible. Tom and even James had theirs. Pellette became one of mine as she grew up, and somewhat ashamed of myself I would give her a handful of oats between meals. I was present at her conception and at her mother's death, and she was linked to those two dramatic moments indelibly; her beautiful liveliness and growing strength, and her practical coarseness, compared to her mother's, made me think of her as a living causeway from the solid past over our depression to the altered and enlivened Woodbrook we believed we were working towards.

Chapter Eight

Jimmy Maxwell did most of the buying and selling of cattle, sheep and pigs at that time, and was so good at it that even the toughest Dublin dealer feared him. He and I went together to many fairs driving herds of animals along the roads and new herds back. Each fair day was an adventure for me, starting before dawn if the distance was great and ending after dusk; each fair day separated me from the enclosed life of Woodbrook and isolated us, making us stick together through the difficulties of getting animals over cross-roads in the right direction, and the rest, with only one dog and not a specially good one to help. Phoebe's and Tony's Welsh sheepdogs had never been trained to work. We stuck together at the fair itself too where even any old friend of Jimmy's was a rival for the day. In the eating house, where we all sat at a long table, talk was general, often teasing or bawdy, and there was a lot of laughter. But in the darkened bars over our black pints of porter our heads would be together as he confided in me. Everyone about us spoke in murmurs, mostly in twos or threes. Only some who had finished their deals spoke in normal voices or laughed and pushed each other about.

Jimmy was as worried as any of us by the financial troubles of Woodbrook and repeatedly asked me whether I could not persuade the major to get rid of all the riding horses except one for each member of the family. He perfectly sympathized with Charlie's life-long interest and spoke of those few as essential. But he explained that one horse eats as much grass as three bullocks and that all horses are bad grazers, so choosy that they leave clumps of the grasses they dislike which grow rank and coarse, unfit for cattle.

That was what he murmured to me in shadowy bars. He could never have murmured it to Charlie.

I think I mentioned it in a half-hearted way, but it was even more difficult for me than it would have been for Jimmy because I felt as Charlie did. I could not imagine what his life in the place would be like without horses and as for keeping one for him to ride I knew he would be bored within a year even with a three-year-old. Horses seemed to me an essential part of Ivy's and Tony's life too. And for Phoebe it would have been like draining the lake away – that unprofitable stretch of water.

Jimmy's warnings were true. As the market for horses faded out, the export trade in cattle to England prospered more and more. But Woodbrook's land had never been separated from the house, never a business anyone went out to attend to as something separate from home-life. The fields were part of home-life just as much as the drawing-room was. The drawing-room piano did not pay. A full-sized loom would have taken up less space and cloth was much in demand.

Only the bank manager dared pronounce a warning out loud.

Charlie was not extravagant. He had never in all the time I knew him spent anything on himself, except for tobacco which was now becoming almost unobtainable, and, incredible though it was in an Indian Army man, he scarcely drank at all. A bottle of whiskey, usually a present from his brother's distillery, would last a whole year. He would take a token sip after a deal, or with guests, and that was all. His leisure hours cost nothing more than the price of paints, brushes and canvases. But the bank manager had clearly had instructions from Dublin to find out what economies were possible. He took the unheard of and daring step of asking Major Kirkwood to call on him at Boyle.

Ivy went with him and often afterwards described that brief, historic meeting. It began with the usual bonhomie, moved through the 'hard fact' stage of figures divided by lengthy awkward pauses, and arrived at the helpful suggestions, which Charlie did his best to respond to at first. The only economy he could think of was to cut down on employees, excluding of course any of those who had always worked on the place, but none of those remaining was a luxury. There was no gardener, not even a proper stable boy. James Currid worked almost single-handed in the stable yard. Then came the final pause as the bank manager gathered strength to say, 'But excuse me, Major, I believe you run more than thirty pleasure horses on the land!' 'What are pleasure horses?' said Charles. The meeting was at its end. But all was well. That old philanthropist, the Land Commission, rescued the bank manager soon enough. Several pieces of land near the boundaries of Woodbrook were sold without making a noticeable difference to the place.

The Land Commission was the focus of most landless people's hopes and became even mine a few years later. It divided the land it bought into small farms, gave a building grant to each occupier and allowed an easy system of repayment for both land and grant. Its policy, I now hear, was mistaken from the economist's point of view; large farms would have produced more; and it is said to have prolonged that traditional curse of Ireland, the subdivision of farms between the sons of each family. But psychologically it was right. Except for casual work in England, and except for the permanent jobs of servants, in houses, stables and gentlemen's gardens, which were mostly hereditary with full keep, no one liked earning wages. They wanted the gamble of working for themselves. Their ancestors had for generations paid exorbitant rents to keep the right to that gamble and done the requisite number of unpaid days of labour for their landlord as well. Gladstone's Land Act of 1881 created the Land Commission as a court of arbitration to fix fair rents and to administer 'loans from public funds to tenants who wished to become owners of their farms'.[1] By an Act of 1903, the purchase of land by tenants became its principal objective and that basic policy, although altered in detail, continued under the Free State government and that of the Republic. So the Land Commission and Charlie had come into the world together. Charlie was born the year after it. It was the most successful of all the belated reforms the English tried. It ended the worst aspects of the landlord system before the end of English rule. But characteristically it was accompanied in the

252

same year by the most violent coercion act known till then.*
Through the Commission's agency, Willy and Jimmy Maxwell
obtained their own farms and built their own houses on land
that had formerly belonged to the Kirkwoods. But Jimmy continued to work full-time at Woodbrook until he got married
and both were always willing to come for spring or harvest
work.

I think my enjoyment of fairs was the same as Jimmy's, the
same as any countryman's, though more intense because I had
been brought up outside their tradition. Everything startled my
interest. I could have taken nothing for granted even if I had
tried. I was known as 'the Englishman'. Even in England
strangers think I look odd, and it was clearly impossible for me
to become one of the community. But most people's approach
to me was genuine – friendly or quarrelsome – and I did not feel
an outsider. None would have dared to tease Cecil King-
Harman or even Charlie, or thought of buying them drinks on
equal terms. When I went to the fair of Boyle with the Kirkwoods, which I did on the days it included horses, I felt separate
and did not like it much, though if Phoebe was there I enjoyed
her passionate likes and dislikes. Everybody goes by looks, but
her sense of character in a horse was quite uncalculated and
often true, not very different from her love or hate of a person
at first sight.

Every fair was for everyone an occasion for passions great or
small. The buying and selling which was the whole purpose of
the day had all the intensity of a private quarrel, but often
became like a gambling bout too, and the two protagonists
would be surrounded by excited onlookers, one of whom would
be asked in the end to arbitrate between them. It was close and
personal and always between two people only; nothing was ever
auctioned and a second buyer would never make an offer until
the first had walked away dissatisfied. Naturally it was slow. It
might take all day for a farmer to sell a large group of bullocks
– eight or twelve – because unless a Dublin dealer liked them
all, and their price, they were sold individually or in twos or

* The Crimes Act of 1882 which suspended trial by jury and gave
police summary powers of search and arrest.

253

threes in deals that took over half an hour with often hours of waiting in between. And very often a farmer would drive all his stock back home again at night hoping to get the price he wanted at another fair in another town later on.

And as all the onlookers at each deal were also prospective buyers or sellers up or down the street the excitement grew to a peak before midday, then declined and spread to the murmuring dark bars which when the fair was almost over became noisy and normally sociable.

For a people without motor transport, most of whom lived without even a pub within bicycling distance, the fair was the only form of community life. The two or three summer agricultural shows were out of reach of most. There was no entertainment at the fair – the few itinerant musicians, some of them good, were regarded as beggars as they were in the streets of Dublin, and as for flirtations with women, there could be none that went beyond a joke with an assistant in a shop that sold clothes. Bar-tenders were all men, except in one or two houses where the publican's wife came out to help. The comers to the fair were all men, except for one or two widow farmers. Other country women had no chance of leaving their lonely homes for the day.

I remember the fairs of Boyle and Ballyfarnan best because of the beautiful shapes of those two towns. Each has a river and an elegant bridge. Boyle has a steep hill rising up from its river in the centre of the town to a wide space of street called the Crescent which is like a half moon, the straight side lined with small shops with dwellings of one or more storeys above them, the curve made by private houses all eighteenth-century in style, and washed not only white but pale blue, pink and yellow. A few of these were shops with bars. They all belonged to working people. Yet their roofs were slated. The thatched roofs of Boyle remained only in the poorest quarter – Irishtown.

Both sides of this long hill, as it widened from the bridge to the Crescent, and one wooded side of a street that turned off it towards Woodbrook and Carrick were lined with blue and red-lead carts, cattle, mostly black or the dark grey of the Kerry, sheep unpenned in little clusters on the pavements, horses held by their owners or tethered to lamp-posts or trees if they were quiet enough. The asses, which were numerous but seldom for sale, were usually tethered to the wheels of their carts, but some would stand for hours at liberty and not wander, which made me envious when I thought of the business I had with our pony Willy-Winkie whenever there was a long wait at the mill and I wanted to go for a drink. Pigs are always the wildest and usually remained with a net over them in the cart that brought them to the fair. Some men managed to drive their pig along the road for miles with a string attached to one hind leg and an ash-plant to guide it. I have often watched them, and once tried it on the avenue. I don't know how they do it.

In the way that memory works after so long a time, I have pressed several fairs into one as I think of Boyle. Those animals would not appear together on one day. On fixed days every year, in various towns, the fair would be for horses, cattle, sheep or pigs, but never exclusively so. I never saw horses at a sheep fair, but a few cattle and pigs would usually be there in the least popular part of the street. But whatever kind of fair it was, the animals all stood on the pavements with their noses to shop windows or the doors and windows of houses. And the townspeople hated it even though they did more trade on fair days than on any other day of the year. In Boyle there were one or two grand shops with plate-glass windows which had to be boarded up against the cattle and the streets became ankle deep in sloppy dung.

My favourite bar in Boyle was John Cryan's – bars had no name except the owner's – and I suppose I liked his because I liked him and his wife; but it was unusually bright and when its doors were open you missed nothing of what was going on outside. It is on a corner. His grocery shop opens on to the main hilly street, with the Royal Hotel, where judges and generals and travellers had stayed since the eighteenth century, beside it, the river below that; and his bar opens on to the side street that leads to the Carrick road. This was the street where the horses stood on a fair day, and from John Cryan's bar you could watch what went on. He had stools at the grocery counter too, but to drink there among people who were doing their shopping was exclusive, something like a saloon bar in England at that time. His real bar was only about twelve feet long and five wide, and was perfectly simple, ornamented only with advertisements for drinks that no longer existed such as D.W.D. – Dublin Whiskey Distillery – on a large mirror imprinted with red, black and gold, or drinks long unknown like Buchanan's Scotch Whisky, which had chosen for its advertisement a large framed picture of two white dogs fighting in a basket and a black one looking on. He had also cut out and framed a picture of horses from a Dublin Horse Show poster. However crowded John Cryan's bar was, it was peaceful.

It was there that Jimmy told me he was going to marry Molly Kelly. The Kellys lived within three hundred yards of Woodbrook's gate-lodge and of course we knew them well. Molly was about my age, and the nicest girl I had ever seen about the place. So I was envious when he told me. It was an abstract kind of envy. I only knew her to say hullo to as I passed the house and I looked on marriage as a ghastly fate that overtook people in their middle-age. Yet at that time I yearned for many things which if they had been given to me I might have spurned.

I was drawn towards the unfamiliar everywhere I went. In Boyle I saw a tall and ragged farmer whose tattered hat and faded thick top coat distinguished him from the rest. 'A mountainy man,' said Jimmy, half affectionate, half derisive, as one might say 'a country bumpkin'. Mountainy was a word used by valley-dwellers for anything uncouth – old-fashioned clothes, rough manners, a lean and awkward cow. Jimmy and his like always shaved before a fair day and changed their working clothes for a blue suit. Farmers from the mountains wore heavy old-fashioned clothes, often ragged; few had real beards, but many let their hair grow long and came to the fair with a week's growth of stubble. In gait, manner and speech, they seemed like people from another country. I wanted to leave whatever company I was in and go with them.

In Boyle there were few such men and those kept away from us because the stock we sold was too dear for them, but at the fairs of Ballyfarnan the majority of sellers were 'mountainy men'.

Imagine then my longings and excitement when I first saw the street of Ballyfarnan enlivened by these people. The town itself was beautiful, high in a valley between mountains north of Woodbrook on a narrow, rushing tributary of the river Shannon, and I loved it too because of what I had heard of Carolan who spent most of his life there; I imagined him drinking in this place or that.

Jimmy and I went to the sheep fair of Ballyfarnan to buy ewes as part of the new policy, if that is not too grand a name, of improving and enlarging the breeding stock that grazed on Usna. We set out on bicycles at first light, before dawn, with that silly cattle dog of his running beside us and jumping into fields after rabbits and hares, so that we often had to stop to whistle it back. We had only a short way to go on the tarred road – the main Sligo road that led past Woodbrook's gate to Boyle – and soon turned off to the right downhill to Cootehall. From this turn, by the forge, the twisty way was white between stone walls with single trees and sometimes a hedge, up hill and downhill, turning back on itself and on again like a maze, until at last we freewheeled down into the long street of Ballyfarnan that curves towards its river. I think this street was the whole of Ballyfarnan. If there were side streets, I forget them, and certainly if you looked through the few narrow archways on the east side you saw fields and hills behind the houses. The houses were all long and low, and most of them were thatched. All, I think, were whitewashed. In front of each house, all down the long street, were sheep in small flocks of ten or twenty, pressing against the doors and under the windows. It astonished me to see that it was possible to keep them together and each group separate without pens, but so long as their hindquarters were towards the open street they stood still with boys and dogs to mind them. If one tried to break away, a tap on the ground with a stick would usually turn it back, but if it did succeed its companions would follow, of course, jumping over each others' backs and running up the middle of the street till someone turned them towards their owners.

We leant our bikes against a wall and walked the whole length of the town to the bridge at the lower end and back again on the other side of the street, looking at sheep. I should have needed a notebook to remember a tenth of what Jimmy remembered. He knew all the owners of course, and the kind of land their sheep had grazed on, but when it came to buying I saw he remembered not only the flocks but individual ewes. We bought twenty ewes in separate lots, here and there.

Often he would start with a rude question – 'What's them, at all? Goats off the mountain?' – and when he heard the asking price would shake his head as though he pitied the seller's ignorant hopefulness. 'Ye'll come down a bit before the evening or ye'll be driving them the long road home again.' If he really thought the price too much he would walk away, for it was a breach of etiquette (which I once made from ignorance) to make too low an offer ('You broke my price!' the man said angrily to me on that occasion and would have no more to do with me). But if the price was nearly right, Jimmy and the seller would settle down to their duel and a crowd would gather. At the height of the bargaining Jimmy would hold out his right hand, and when the seller refused to slap it walk away as though the deal was over. Someone, but never the seller, would call him back; there would be cries of 'Divide! Divide!' – meaning split the difference that remained between them – and when that failed, 'Can no one help them out?' A helper-out would be chosen and in those final minutes the outcome depended on his persuasive powers. Having fixed on a price he thought fair, he would catch Jimmy by the wrist and pull him till he was near enough to catch the seller's wrist with his other hand, then try to clap their hands together. If their palms touched the bargain was sealed. Neither would ever go back on it to change it, and only the luck money remained to be fixed, a much quicker and usually more light-hearted business, though I have seen as much trouble taken over luck money as over the deal. The 'luck' or 'luck-penny' is a bit given back by the seller to the buyer to make the purchase lucky. Its proportion of the price is roughly set by tradition. The buyer cannot fix it, but if the seller is mean about it there is a quarrel.

All payments were made in cash. I forgot which of us carried ours at Ballyfarnan, but I know I have never had so much money in my pockets as on a fair day, and it was astonishing to watch dealers paying out hundreds of pounds in notes in the rain and wind, or counting hundreds in a crowded bar. Robbers could have flourished on the farmers' long, lonely roads home, but in all the years I was at Woodbrook I never heard of robbery at or after a fair.

Buying was over by 11 a.m., and after a few pints we went to the eating house, a thatched one with small windows and a long crowded table. It was raining a bit but the door was open, and the light and talk and the girls that served us made it lively. Plates of meat and gravy were put before each person and with our forks we speared potatoes from huge dishes set along the table and peeled them with our knives on to our side-plates. Irish cooking is said to be the worst in Europe, but I cannot remember it as good or bad, just beautifully filling. There was very little meat but unlimited potatoes and these I think the Irish do much better than the French, but I did not care in those days. I was hungry.

Then came the slow walk home, wheeling our bicycles at the pace of the flock we had bought.

Chapter Nine

Some time in the winter of 1940 to 1941 I visited London, intending to enlist if they would take me. They refused, and a fortnight later I was back on the platform of Carrick-on-Shannon station feeling as though I had been away for a year. I was alone on the platform; the station-master and porter had gone in out of the cold. Again I smelt the beautiful air, renewed for me, sharp with frost, more intensely nostalgic than before. During a wakeful night on the crowded train and boat I had thought of all sorts of ways in which Phoebe and I might meet, the places where I would find her, what we would say, hoping it would not be at the midday meal with all the others there. My train had been late and Charlie was late in fetching me which gave me hope that they would have finished eating, that I would find her alone in the garden or Shanwelliagh. Then I heard the familiar sound of the old Fiat and ran down the steps to meet it.

Charlie did not ask what had happened in London. All the way home he talked optimistically about the farm as he drove me along the empty, icy road, but when we reached Hughestown Hill and caught our first glimpse of the house he told me that James Currid was ill, and perhaps would soon die.

I had only a small bag, so he drove straight into the stable yard, not to the front door, where immediately we saw a savage fight between James Currid's two dogs. His little sealyham was turning the spaniel – four times its size – on its back and by the time we reached them it had set its teeth in a death grip on the spaniel's throat. I had saved the spaniel several times before by holding a lighted cigarette near the sealyham's nose; the smoke made him relax his jaws. But I had no cigarettes.

Phoebe came running from the garden to greet me, having heard the car, not the dogs, and I called to her for a soda-water siphon, our other remedy, which she brought from the house. She squirted it at the sealyham's nose. He let go at once, and I pulled him off and shut him into James's room. The spaniel's white throat – he was liver and white – was rather bloody and an ear was torn but he was no worse than he had been many times before. He walked away growling. Such was the nature of my reunion with Phoebe, which I had imagined in so many forms all night on the train and boat. She called the spaniel back and bathed his wounds. She told me James had asked to be taken to his own house some days ago and been put to bed there. He had never lived in it till then, having always preferred his little room beside the stables, and now it seemed he had gone there only to die. The room seemed dead to me already as I put the sealyham into it, stale and unused.

James loved his two dogs but had never been able to unite them in friendship. The spaniel was floppy and sycophantic. It would lie on its back as you approached, wagging its tail apologetically. The sealyham was muscular and rigid, and growled even at people it knew well. James was the only one allowed to stroke it, or pick it up in his arms. He had given up trying to let the two live together years before. The sealyham he kept imprisoned in his little bedroom. Phoebe and Tony were sad to see it there, staring out through his window at the horses which gazed calmly over their half-doors, and this little form yapping and dancing in a frenzy when any of us crossed the yard. The spaniel roamed about all day, sniffing people's boots or licking their hands and sometimes clumsily chasing rabbits which it never caught. Imprisonment, of course, made the sealyham fiercer still.

I thought of the dogs as two sides of James's character – the loving, obedient one which did everything it could to help me and the Kirkwoods, and the stern private one shut up in a room which no one was ever allowed to enter, hating the people who passed by, mean with praise, refusing to marry.

I was told that women liked him in spite of his gloomy ways, but he was cautious to an absurd degree, which cramped his private life. His gloomy manner was easy to mimic and everyone made fun of him behind his back. But it was his inverted optimism that infuriated Phoebe. 'You came off very lucky,' he would tell her as soon as she regained consciousness after a fall from a horse, following her as she limped home with stories of how so-and-so had been killed or crippled by just such a fall.

His house and few acres of land on which he grazed bullocks were by the Sligo road not far from the Kirkwoods' boundary. He had bought and furnished it with his share of racing profits, thirty or forty years ago, and it had stood there empty ever since, an ideal place to marry into, but lonely and hard to manage for a bachelor.

In those old days of thoroughbreds, it was necessary for someone to live in the stable yard. There were two or three rooms with windows facing the horse's boxes from which every sound could be heard. James had chosen one of these to spend his life in and stayed in it, having meals with Winnie in the house until his last illness began.

Charlie and Ivy visited him frequently while he was ill but it was Jimmy Maxwell who nursed him. He had no friends outside Woodbrook and no relatives at all, except one niece who came at the end from Co. Sligo where he was born. Till then Jimmy stayed with him. He asked for his dogs some days after my return and they stayed there too, the sealyham locked up and the spaniel loose as they had lived all their lives. I did not visit him, nor go to his wake. I am sure he did not want me at his bedside, but found out later that people thought my absence from the wake unfriendly.

I did not know the social importance of my mistake, but as I sat in the drawing-room alone on the night of the wake, with Tony asleep upstairs and every adult in the district except me gathered round his corpse, I knew I was wrong to have separated myself from them all. It was fear that kept me away, a private squeamishness. I had never seen a dead person. And it was curiosity that made me wish I had gone.

The Kirkwoods were home before midnight and it was clear that the experience had been as strange to them as it would have been to me. Religion, not class had kept them away from wakes, though of course those two dividers were still one in effect, and for the same reason they were not expected to stay long.

Charlie said nothing when he came home except, 'Poor James', which was, according to Jimmy, all he could say when he last saw James alive. He had called at the house an hour before his death, laid a hand on his forehead and said 'Poor James, poor James.' Jimmy did not see in this gesture the sympathy and sorrow which we knew it expressed. He merely thought that James, far gone as he was, did not want a hand on his forehead. It was difficult enough for me who lived in the house to recognize Charlie's emotions. One had to see his feelings in his face and gestures, not wait to hear them expressed. The only verbal expression he made beyond those two words was to say on the evening after the wake that he could not remember Woodbrook without James, which in fact was not so for he often spoke vividly of his early boyhood with Billy, but it was essentially true because James had arrived some years before he went to Sandhurst and memory pushes the marks it makes backwards or forwards regardless of dates.

I wished Ivy had been the one to stay at home instead of me because in addition to the natural fear everyone feels in the presence of a corpse, this way of 'seeing off' the dead, of 'giving him a good send-off' as people called it, shocked her. It was not the thick smoke of cut-plug or the whiskey – there was not much whiskey for lonely old James and no dancing or games – but the habit they had dressed him in. She disliked intensely all ornamental ritual and because he had been attached as a layman to some uncommon order, his habit was not the usual plain monkish brown. She said he had coloured gloves on and a pointed hat. It seemed to her a mockery. She felt that something had been imposed upon James that he would have protested against if he could. Twenty years later she was similarly shocked by that part of the Orthodox Christening service where the priest holds the uncomprehending baby up to look at several icons in turn.

The sober one-night vigil held for James was itself a tiny vestige of a custom that shocked Protestants all over Europe and seemed to the Catholic priesthood too to make a mockery of death. But the purpose was, on the contrary, to honour death, to exalt the dead person's spirit by the most lavish and gay party that friends and relatives could provide. According to tradition, it would be James, not his friends, who was hurt by my absence, for I should have been one of his hosts. The corpse is the only guest, and that is why there can be no wake if the body has been placed in a mortuary or chapel. To drink to someone's memory is quite a different thing.

Within old Michael Maxwell's lifetime, people tried to make the dead person join in as nearly as possible. A pipe would be put in his mouth, or if he had been fond of cards his friends would sit round his bed to play with him, placing the cards dealt to him in his hand. In some places the corpse was lifted up and made to dance among the living dancers, presumably between two people who held him under the armpits. 'In Norway, as the corpse lay in the uncovered coffin in the kitchen, while the meal (the last meal in its presence) was being eaten, old women would address the deceased saying "Now you will take this last meal in our company." '[1] That expressed the ancient intention of the wake which survives in a dull, restricted form in Ireland to this day.

'In the old days the wake of an old person was a far merrier and more enjoyable occasion than even a wedding.'

The two-night wakes for old people used to be the most boisterous, because they gave time for word to get around to distant places and on the second night the corpse house would be packed, with crowds outside it. The lively entertainment – rowdy games, song and dance, trials of strength, horse-play – boiled over on the second night which was why the clergy ordered families to bring their dead to rest in the chapel on the evening before the funeral.

Two-night wakes became quieter and gradually died out. The last Willie Maxwell could remember had no dancing or singing, only verbal games which involved a good deal of laughter and shouting.

It was in 1920. As each person arrived at the *corp* house, as Willie called it, he went into the *corp* room – a bedroom leading off the kitchen – knelt down and prayed, then said to the nearest relative something pleasant about the dead person he had known. Then, in the kitchen, two men would greet him – one with pipes and tobacco and the other with whiskey. The clay pipes – chalk pipes, he called them – were the very same as the broken ones I sometimes turned up while ploughing with the name Curley of Knockcroghery on them, a village near Roscommon Town. They were very cheap and roughly made, with tiny bowls, and were mostly bought for wakes where great numbers and large quantities of tobacco were given away. A horse and cart with two 'kishes' of them packed like eggs travelled round the country selling them. Some publicans gave one with your first pint of porter. For a century, from 1820 till 1921 when the Black and Tans burned Knockcroghery and its little factory down, these pipes were three a penny, and in 1920 what Willy calls *corp* house tobacco was 'fippence a half' – a half quarter, two ounces – whereas the tobacco most people used was sixpence. You could smoke as much as you wanted all night. One of the relatives would spend all his time cutting tobacco and handing it round on a plate and if you needed a new pipe – they were easily broken – he would give you that. You would always get as much whiskey as you wanted too, and at some wakes they had Guinness's porter or even stout as well. The rosary was said about midnight, and after that until about three in the morning most people left in twos and threes. At one time, everyone would take a pipe home and keep it in a special place in memory of the dead. About eight or a dozen would stay till dawn in the old tradition of keeping the corpse company, and these had breakfast of tea and bread and butter.

The corpse was excluded from most of the games, though often when people were pelting each other with potatoes or bits of turf, or splashing water from the bucket on the dresser, they would treat it as one of the company, pelt it and sometimes knock or jostle it on the floor by mistake. This fitted in well with the ancient idea of the dead taking part with the living but once, at a tumble-down house near Lough Key when he appeared to take action without help, all his entertainers ran away and left him alone in the house. He was a poor old man named Tom Mac Shera who had been afflicted all his life with a terrible hump-back that pushed his head almost down to his knees. It was impossible to lay him out in the ordinary way so they tied him on to the kitchen table with a rope round his chest and one round his knees to get him to lie as flat as possible. At the height of the festivities some mischievous boys crawled underneath the table and cut the chest rope. The old man sat up.

It was the pre-Christian tradition of much of all this that alarmed the church, for the resurrection celebrated at the wake was two-fold – the new life of the soul on its departure for the other world and the creation of new lives on earth to replace the dead body. A dance once habitual in Silesia, Germany and Hungary clearly expressed the concept of reincarnation. A young man or woman, according to the sex of the dead person, would be chosen to represent the corpse and lie on the floor. If he was a man, all the girls in the room would bend down to kiss him in turn, then sing and dance in a circle round him. The game 'kiss in the ring' played at Irish wakes was similar.

Everywhere and most recently in Ireland, betrothal or marriage, real and mock, was staged at the wake. Kissing games often ended in love affairs; sometimes a boy and girl who had felt shyly drawn towards each other would be thrust into each other's arms outside the house by a game like 'Postman's knock' and disappear for hours. In a game called 'The cure for a sore head' a man supposed to have a sore head demanded as his cure that so-and-so kiss so-and-so and both the boy and girl chosen were allowed to complain that they had not been kissed properly and demand to be kissed again.

Matchmaking and marriage games occasionally led to fulfilment. Willy remembered hearing of a game called 'marrying' in the olden days 'and if you and a girl leap across the twig [broom] in the wake house, you were supposed to be married, and I often heard it was a legal marriage' – that is, it was considered binding by ordinary people. I believe it was more usual for the girl to leap across the broom towards the man when he called her name. He would then place a real or makeshift ring on her finger. In some places one of the men would dress up as a priest and 'marry' one pair after another at the wake.

I suppose there is no evidence of how many wake night matches were taken seriously, probably fewer and fewer as time went on; probably the games were gradually slightened, like 'ring-a-ring-o'-roses', until the sexual meaning was so disguised that none of the players knew of its existence. But some were certainly effective in bringing young people together up till the second half of the nineteenth century at least, so much so that the priests of that time felt it necessary to continue the repressive campaign the church had ineffectually tried to conduct since the seventeenth century. The priests of the nineteenth century succeeded where their forefathers had failed simply by forbidding eligible girls from attending wakes unless they were relatives of the corpse. It was an easier task for them, because notions of 'morality' had changed to suit their purpose.

The ancient intention of the wake was to pacify the dead, to please his spirit well so that he would renounce all intentions of coming back to the world to molest the living. But why should he molest them? It is said that he 'might return to take revenge on those who had succeeded to his property'. It is said 'that the dead were always anxious to take living persons off into the other world' and there are 'thousands of stories about people who, in their youth and full vigour, were frightened at night by some ghostly spectre, barely succeeded in returning home, took to their beds and died within a short time'. Such precise fears were certainly there in the past. But every living person to this day fears the dead; the instinct, far deeper than reason, is less explicable than the one that makes us jump at a sudden loud noise which we know will do us no harm. Anyone who has 'seen' a ghost fears it, even if it is the spirit of a loved and kind friend. Willie loved Miss MacDonald, who had befriended him for so long, yet when her spirit appeared to him on the avenue he ran home trembling and went to bed.

James Currid, though often severe in reproof, had never harmed anybody so far as we knew, but for years after his death some were afraid to go into the stable yard at night; and I, after hearing ghostly stories of him, feared him too, though only while I was doing something he had disapproved of in his lifetime like taking the best oats for the cart-horses, oats that had been in the bin for two years. These oats were stored in a barn beside his bedroom, an eerie place at any time with high rafters hung with scraps of harness and machinery that in winter cast moving shadows grotesquely from the flame of my hurricane lantern. The second-year oats, which he tried to keep for hunters, were held – those for immediate use – in a circular waist-high bin made of zinc. You could not see into it, even in daylight, because of the shadowy nature of this barn and whenever I dipped my scoop there I would make as much noise as I could. James had once plunged his hand in and caught a rat which bit into his finger and clung till he shook it off. In rainy weather he used to cut my hair just within the entrance to this barn or in the harness room opposite. In fine weather, I brought a chair from the house and he did it in the yard in the open air. But even in the open he blew on my neck and ears as though he was grooming a horse.

He cut all the men's hair, including Charlie's. He was good at it, but said he had not learnt it, and these were the only occasions on which he could bring himself towards an intimate conversation with any of us. Our backs were to him and he would stop blowing and hold his scissors up when he wished to speak. It was while he was cutting my hair that he told me so much about Aunt Nina, Colonel Tom and his famous horses – Paddy Maher, Apollo Belvedere, Phaeton, Knight of Usna, The White Knight and the horse whose name I cannot remember that kicked and broke his knee. He spoke of his days at English race meetings and of how when he landed at Dún Laoghaire with horses during a foot-and-mouth scare he was nearly suffocated by a conscientious customs man whose duty it was to fumigate horse-clothing. 'You'd better go in too,' said the man, pushing him into the gas chamber. This story marked the utmost limit of his gaiety.

His private life remained private even during hair-cutting. I longed to know about the girls he courted and why, with his house and money and rather good looks, he had never married one. But if he had 'a cure for women', which everybody said he had and laughed about, he took his secret to the grave together with his cure for horses which no one, not even the vet, could explain. Whenever I dared to question him about his love-life, he would blow down my neck with all the power of his lungs and resume his snipping, breathing in through his nose and out through pursed lips with a regular whistling sound. It was a way I had learned from him. Most horsemen used it. It keeps the dust and scurf away from your face and the rhythmic whistle is pleasing to the horse.

Chapter Ten

Neddy died soon after James. It was winter but the ground was soft enough for digging graves. His death marked another memorable point, even nearer to the end of Woodbrook's life as we had known it. And though no one said so his death was a portent like James's. He had been a wonder for miles around us because he was a Spanish ass as tall as a mule, whiter and stronger than the local kind. Children came specially to pet him and visitors to the Maxwells or James or Winnie searched him out where he was grazing on Shanwelliagh and stood to stare. I think some worked him secretly on farm work when the Kirkwoods were away, but except for that his only labour was to pull the old bathchair or carry the children while they were too young for ponies.

Neddy was buried in Shanwelliagh where he had grazed all his life. He had a grave to himself dug by many hands and was covered first with lime then with clay, then with topsoil, over which the grassy sods were replaced. By summer there was no sign of his grave except the remains of a flimsy monument which Tony and Phoebe had put up, and having been buried alone he was more privileged in death, as he had been in life, than most of the people who crowded Ardcarne churchyard, whose graves were soon lost, whose bones often came to the surface and were jumbled in the long grass. There were specialists in every district, men with good memories, old sextons and others, whom people engaged to identify the graves and even the skulls of relatives. Like the gravediggers, they were rewarded with whiskey. James Currid was buried in Ardcarne churchyard. I did not go to his funeral and have never looked for his grave.

His death increased my responsibilities and Phoebe's and

Charlie's in the stable yard. Until then my only fixed task was to feed the cart-horses in the early morning, to allow them time to eat and rest before they started work. Now someone had to look after the grain barn. I decided how much oats to take to the mill at Boyle, how much to be rolled and how much crushed and whether the wheat was hard enough to make flour. All calculations worry me and these did. Phoebe helped me to clean the harness, which in wet weather, especially after a hunt, kept us side by side for an hour or two. That made me like the tedious job. I cleaned the boots by myself, also in the harness-room where in winter I made a good fire to boil the pigs' potatoes on. I used to spend far too long on Phoebe's riding boots.

Tommy taught me to plough. I never became good at it but of all the crafts I have ever learned it is the most delightful. A single-furrow horse plough is beautiful even rusting among weeds in summer, but when you take it to the field and yoke two horses to it it seems to come to life again, unexpectedly but gradually. The coulter, a knife that cuts the surface of the earth, is always out of place to start with. You need spanners and a heavy hammer to put it right. And then with the rope reins in your hands which also hold and balance the handles of the plough you call to the horses and flick the reins against their flanks. As they pull, the coulter, share and mouldboard rip the earth and turn it over in a black wave making a crisp, hissing sound as though a sea-wave continued without drawing back, and at the end of the first furrow, as you lay the plough on its side to allow the horses to turn, you see that the mouldboard and the ploughshare and the tip of the coulter are bright silver after a year of disuse. I thought of Persephone sometimes.

My pockets would be filled by the evening with pieces of pottery, iron and wooden kitchen utensils that had been covered by grass since the Famine and sometimes, as Nanny had said, the horses would be pulled back with a jerk as the coulter or share struck the foundations of a house. I specially liked a certain kind of clay pipe which Tom called 'Danes' pipes' – they were much more delicately made than the Knockcroghery pipes; the pieces of stem were finer and smoother, the bowl even smaller, more slanted and not much thicker than the shell of a goose's egg. Most bowls were broken, but not all, and thinking them lucky I kept a collection of them in my bedroom. I laughed at Tom's belief that the ancient Danes had used them, but have recently heard that they did smoke certain herbs in pipes.

Tom took such pride in his work, and in the appearance of Woodbrook, that he never allowed me to plough within sight of the road. Phoebe agreed with him. She always hid her paintings if they seemed to her tentative or amateurish. But the pleasure she took in work well done was sometimes enhanced by its originality. So, when she proposed to paint the farm carts in untraditional colours she was taken aback by Tom's displeasure. The colours she chose were pleasant and not gaudy. As she mixed the paints and I pulled the carts out of their shed, I knew very well that Tommy and the rest would disapprove, but was quite unprepared for the passion he got into. She had tried them out on planks of wood to show him and as soon as he arrived described her plan excitedly, shaping the cart in paints on the plank. He was silent. Then when he spoke he could not control his voice. He ended by saying that if she used those paints he could never again drive to town. Phoebe blushed and looked utterly ashamed, all her high spirits cast down. And perhaps it is her look at that moment that makes me remember the incident vividly. There was no protecting her. I was helpless.

She would not have gone against his wishes in any case; but we both knew there would be no coal fetched from Carrick station, no timber carted, no sows taken to the boar. We got out the usual red lead at once for the shafts and the conventional blue paint for the body of the cart. Phoebe's original colours found their expression on the trap. I was the only person who drove the trap to town.

None of the new activities disturbed the order of my life at Woodbrook. In fact they gave it a sense of permanency which I had not felt before. The Dublin bus and the afternoon train by which in the fields we told the time no longer made me feel nostalgic. My restlessness seemed to have been smoothed away. And when I was invited to teach the children at French Park and stay there one night a week I did not want to do it. Ivy and

Phoebe persuaded me, partly because they still thought I should earn some extra money which, as before, I did not need and partly because Ivy's friend Vicky, whose son and nephews needed lessons, could think of no one else who lived near enough. She and Ivy had got married at about the same time – Vicky to Francis French, Lord De Freyne, who died in 1935 leaving her with four daughters and a son, the youngest, who was about fourteen when I went to them to teach.

The boy was called Francis, and having grown up as the only boy among three sisters I felt the most experienced sympathy with him. Girls are so much stronger and more mature in childhood and usually bossier. He was rather delicate and they were bright and bouncing to say the least and then, like me, I am sure he had been teased at school for having too many sisters. It must have been much worse for him because he was not only the youngest but through no fault of his own the publicly prized heir to the estate and the seat in the House of Lords. Also the names of his two nearest sisters, Patience and Faith, were a joke against him that no one grew tired of. Faith, whom I knew better than the others because she came to my little class for English, was according to this silly joke the thing that led at last to a male heir. The two older girls, and sometimes even Patience, were often impatient and cross with him as I soon got to know through having meals with them. I gave lessons every Wednesday afternoon and again on the Thursday morning after staying the night. Patricia, the eldest, fetched me by car from Woodbrook and drove me back next day. She was a year or two younger than me and the car was a year or two younger than the Fiat, a bit more roomy but no grander. Their financial troubles had long been similar to the Kirkwoods'. It was said that they did not even own the family estate on which they lived, that their father had had to raise money by selling it to the Land Commission and that ever since then they had paid rent for it.

Theirs was the usual story of decline in fortunes but more striking than any other I had heard because they had been in the country so long and their riches had until the nineteenth century been vast. They were Norman by origin.[1] Sir Hubert de

273

Freyne, the first to settle in Ireland, had accompanied Strongbow in the invasion of Leinster in 1168, acquired large possessions near Wexford and was presumably forced to swear fealty to Henry II. His descendants – the Frenches and the ffrenches whose name we distinguished by stuttering – were among the old colonists whom the Tudors feared as having grown 'more Irish than the Irish' – the only colonists who might have made the system work. They were middle-class people not aristocrats and several made their money not from land but trade. In the direct line that led to Francis and his sisters, there was a succession of Mayors of Galway, presumably all merchants, one of whom grew extremely wealthy by importing salt. He became mayor in 1538 and was called Seán an tSalainn – John of the salt. Irish had long been their native language and remained so until the eighteenth century, by which time the salt, translated into land and greatly nourished by the Penal Code, had made gentlemen of its inheritors. John French of French Park who died in 1734 was known by an Irish name – Seán An Tiarna Mór – the Great Lord.

It was he who built the house I knew, so beautifully and spaciously, in 1667. It was his private blacksmith who made the two graceful pairs of gates for which the place was famous – the entrance gates by the roadside, with the date 1704 shaped in wrought iron and the stable-yard gates which seemed like the entrance to an inner palace. And yet his estates were not exceptionally large at the time. His father had left him only 6,000 acres. It was not until 1708 that he began to merit his title – 'the Great' – by acquiring one after another the lands and houses forfeited by Catholics in Counties Roscommon and Sligo. The family had of course turned Protestant at an expedient moment. They resumed their old religion some years after the Catholic Emancipation Act of 1829. In 1839 Arthur French of French Park was created the first Baron De Freyne.*

My clearest memory of their house is its autumn and winter look – the red Virginia creeper exposing gradually as its leaves

* He was the first to spell the family name De Freyne with a capital D.

fell bricks of a duller, deeper red with pale ones here and there, not quite even in shape if you looked closely and worn by weather – seventeenth-century bricks. Some of the walls were four feet thick, and all the space between the brick and the plaster that faced the rooms was filled with turf which had originally been packed there in the brick-like shape that everyone uses as fuel. Even now, when it had crumbled to dust, it was a perfect insulator against heat and cold but the fear of fire was more intense at French Park than at Rockingham or Strokestown, the two other great houses I knew. Strokestown was almost the same shape, but it was an eighteenth-century house, built of stone. It looked grander and solider. I thought French Park far more beautiful because of the lightness of its brick. Its gates were lighter too, very high and wide but the ironwork delicate.

The house itself was like a generous curved gateway, its principle block with the front door in the centre being set well back from the wings which were joined to it by long low passages curving forwards like arms. The house embraced you in its shelter long before you reached the front door. The main part had three storeys and the wings two. The passages, though they were only the height of the first floor, had delightful windows, small near the ceiling and large near the ground. At the end of the passage leading to the east wing was the billiard room where I gave lessons, beyond it the family chapel. Much as I liked it all, and in spite of the gay and noisy games that filled the billiard room after lessons, I felt apprehensive there between the dim chapel and long curved passage.

It happened too that my first visit took place shortly after James's funeral; and my muddled emotions about death were stirred again by the experiments of a spiritualist. Lily, the family governess whose teaching I was supposed to supplement, was absolutely hooked on raising the dead.

I might not have been alarmed in any other house but here in winter, while paraffin was severely rationed and few lamps lit, the stage was perfectly set. The dining-room was large and long in daylight, but at night its shadowy limits were undefined. The dining-room table, with its huge white tablecloth, was an island from which we could barely make out the dark portraits of ancestors we knew to be hanging on invisible walls. After dinner someone would carry the lamp through the hall where our shadows ran up the walls and down again among more ancestors – in oval frames these – and lead us into the drawing-room, where in spite of a great fire of logs and turf large areas behind my back remained in sinister darkness. Here we would play cards or parlour games at first. Then late in the evening Lily would preside over spiritualist rites. There was nothing unusual about them – table tapping, table turning, sliding wine-glasses etc. Often it was like any other game, exciting or funny. But when it worked it frightened me. The card table did seem to rise from the floor and turn. The wine-glass apparently moved without being pushed. Questions were answered by ghosts of Lily's friends, and she made alarming comments on it all. The girls took it as a joke with thrills, but I went to bed, carrying my candle up the freezing stairs and down the long empty passage, watching each shadow and trying to believe she had deceived us.

Douglas Hyde, the poet who was then President of Ireland, was often there and I am sorry now that my ignorance prevented me from listening to him properly. I did not even know he was president, such was my disregard of current affairs. I did know he was a good poet, but his best work was said to be in the Irish language, hidden from me, and I was too shy to tell him how much I liked his translations in *Love Songs of Connacht*, the only book of his I knew. Besides, dinner seemed to be the only time for talk. There were many people at a large table and I was never near to him.

And so it happens that my only memory of this great man is ludicrous; I wish I had had more sense. It is of a game he played with the girls on all fours in the drawing-room. He was over eighty but had no difficulty in getting down on to his hands and knees and as soon as they were ranged opposite him on theirs he would hold a bar of chocolate between his teeth like a cigar and they would crawl towards him and bite off as much as they dared. It was somewhat messy because he had a bushy white moustache that drooped over the chocolate and his lower lip. I watched this parody of kissing with a horrible selfish sympathy, thinking of the years between Phoebe and me.

Yet here was someone who, if I had only opened the way, would have taught me more than any man I met in all my time in Ireland. He was born in 1860, at about the same time as Michael Maxwell, and though he was the son of the Protestant rector of Frenchpark, he had been brought up on the old culture that made Michael's stories so poetical and his conversation so rich. But even in childhood he was closer to the best of it than Michael because he first heard it in Irish, which was still the natural language of the Frenchpark* district while, less than twenty miles away near Cootehall, it was dying rapidly. Of course it was not his own language, but by chance illness prevented him from being sent away to school in Dublin and after lessons at the Rectory in Latin, Greek and the usual subjects he spent all his spare time playing with Irish-speaking boys, going fishing on Lough Gara or shooting with their fathers on the bog; or sitting at home with them in the evenings. He was good at languages, but must have made a conscious effort to learn this one without any pressure from adults.

Because of this upbringing his approach to Irish scholarship was unique. His familiarity with the songs and stories people knew by heart showed him that the content of the manuscripts was once known to almost everyone, literate and illiterate; that in ancient and modern Irish 'all that is of most value as literature was the property and in some sense the product of the people at large.'² And then, his love of other languages and literatures let him see his own country's in relation to the world: besides the classics he knew Hebrew and translated from French, German and Italian.

There was an unusual width in his patriotism too. He was an ardent nationalist but did not share the narrow-mindedness that often goes with it. What he opposed was the thoughtless acceptance and even aping of English ways which led not to an English character in Irish life but to no character at all. His famous statement in *The Necessity for De-Anglicising Ireland* could

*The house was called French Park; the village, Frenchpark.

have been taken seriously by many countries that gained their independence after his death: 'When we speak of the necessity for de-anglicising the Irish Nation we mean it, not as a protest against imitating what is best in the English people, for that would be absurd, but rather to show the folly of neglecting what is Irish and hastening to adopt pell-mell and indiscriminately everything that is English simply because it is English.' He thought that during the nineteenth century Irish people were ceasing to be 'Irish without becoming English'.[3]

As to the history of the country, in which I was so interested, here was part of it in the room with me. Like Michael he had lived through the frightening and I suppose inspiring half century that led to the War of Independence. He had played a principal part not in the war, but in the artistic renaissance that preceded it. He was a fountainhead whose separate streams flowed through the work of Yeats, Lady Gregory and Synge. His re-introduction of Irish literature to Ireland led also to a new literary movement in the old language. And through the Gaelic League, which he founded in 1893, he tried with remarkable success to make the arts available to everyone as they had been long ago. The arts were all Irish and the ideals national but, perhaps because it had a real ideology behind it, the league fulfilled a social need much more effectively than any rural institute or working man's club. That was not its primary intention, of course. Its aims were 'to preserve and revive the Irish language, literature, music, dancing and games, to encourage Irish art and industry', and soon social centres were formed all over the country to which people came for fun or learning. He insisted that it should be non-political, that it would welcome members of any religious sect or any party. Only a few Orangemen joined, but there were many Unionist members, and revolutionaries signed on with them beside the names of Lord Castletown and The O Conor Don. When, after twenty years, it became involved in politics he withdrew from it.

The choice of Douglas Hyde, son of the Anglican rector of Frenchpark and descendant of one of the Elizabethan 'undertakers', as the first president of Ireland seems extraordinary, but it followed an old tradition by which the people had chosen men like Tone, Emmet and Parnell to lead agitation for reform and independence.

The choice expressed also, though not intentionally, the almost perfect social and religious toleration that had allowed a Protestant minority to live in peace in the twenty-six Counties since the foundation of the Irish Free State. During the years of the Free State Douglas Hyde had remained aloof from government affairs. His abhorrence of party politics made him refuse to stand for the Dáil. Early on he had turned down the offer of a safe seat. So his acceptance of the presidency under the Constitution of 1938, came as a surprise to his supporters. He was able to accept because this new office, although potentially an influential one, was far above the spite and treachery that controls parliamentary life everywhere. So far as I know, he never used the presidential powers. Perhaps the need never came, but anyway he was old. He died in 1949 at the age of eighty-nine.

He spent all his leisure till then at Ratra close to Frenchpark village and was expected like one of the family to come as often as he wished to, to the De Freyne's house. He was one of the family distantly. His great-grandfather, Protestant vicar of Killarney, had married Sarah French of French Park. And like so many descendants of the colonists he was connected with the Kirkwoods too.

Chapter Eleven

I wonder whether Lily felt about my visits to French Park as I felt when at last the Kirkwoods found another tutor for Phoebe. We were neither of us supplanted. We did not have to give up teaching, but for us both, perhaps, it was as though the rough road we had led our pupils happily along for years had been shown to have too many turns in it.

What I remember best about Tom Crowe's arrival at Woodbrook is my intense relief. Phoebe's matriculation exams were approaching and I believed he knew a straight way there, which turned out to be true, for she did get in to Trinity College, Dublin, a year later and never would have reached it without his help. My jealousy about the teaching business was slight, with a strong twinge now and then when I saw them go into Aunt Nina's room and shut the door behind them – and, surprising though it seems when I remember the state I got into about Trevor-Roper, I felt no personal jealousy at all. My liking for Tom Crowe was sudden and instinctive. He had the quick kind of intelligence to which I respond, though mine is slow. He said funny things shortly, then left them alone; he was consumed, as I was, by irrational curiosity about matters which seemed to many people dull. He could not hide much. You could see him in confusion one minute and next minute not. Such qualities were Phoebe's too in her different way, and maybe it was because of them that all three of us got on well together. They often went out alone for hours on bicycles to places that remain distinguished in my memory because she was with me when I first saw them. They often played tennis together, which I could not play. But none of that distressed me. When they were with me I was happier than I had been for years. Phoebe's anxieties became intense and often she seemed depressed. She knew her school work was below matric standard. She practised the violin several hours a day as before and had horrible scars on her neck under her chin, which she said was because she held it badly. She looked after a hundred of the grown-up hens and ducks and all the incubator eggs and brooder chickens. And she never gave up painting. Always in the background were the family debts.

I helped her with the poultry. The incubator was in her father's room on a table under the window opposite his bed. It was of the latest kind, using very little paraffin and showing only a dim light. We shared the delight of opening it and watching the chickens break out of their shells, and also the horror of the deformed ones and those which got stuck. The brooder, or hover as some people call it, was in a corrugated iron hut attached to James's old room with one window facing the stable yard. I think it had been a stable-boy's room in the old days, like James's. The brooder, which we had placed in the centre of its wooden floor with a wire netting fence about it, acted as a mother to about fifty chickens after they were hatched in the incubator. The heat it gave them came from two paraffin wicks which had to be adjusted carefully to keep the temperature right. Like an ordinary lamp, if you filled it too full it would flare up, not at once but some minutes later. Phoebe made this mistake one afternoon, and went away to see to something else. I was in one of the boxes grooming a horse. I smelt the rank smell, then saw black smoke streaming over the yard. I could not see the brooder house for smoke, nor even the kitchen door. There was no one about. I filled buckets from a rain-barrel and put the fire out. But all the chickens had been burned to death. The tank which stored all our paraffin was only three yards away. For me it was exhilarating, an achievement, but for Phoebe doom. She ran to me at the last moment and helped to clear up the mess. No one could extinguish her guilt.

Tom Crowe was not at Woodbrook then. He was an undergraduate at Trinity and only came to us during the vacations, twice only I think, a long summer one of three months, and six weeks or so at Christmas during the same year. It was the year that I named in my diary 'The year of the Skull and Bones'.

Like the 'year of the Bees' it took its name from the events of one day or rather one evening which spread like a spillage of indelible dye, seeping outwards, backwards and forwards over the year. The day was still and sunny, very sultry in the afternoon with heavy clouds on the horizon that never obscured the sun. It became sinister after the event and spread its fear back to the brooder fire and forward to the advertisements in the *Irish Times* that Woodbrook was for sale.

I have said before how I mostly remember the angry or sad moments of the past, but now it strikes me too as extraordinary how I forget the disagreeable aspects of people and of the weather. The summers at Woodbrook were mostly rainy, but the ones I remember seem fine. This had certainly been fine, for all the hay was in early and the fields near the house deserted, but on the Bottoms, the aftermath had grown sufficiently to give cover to the corncrakes whose crake-crake, crake-crake came from various distances along the canal bank more distinctly than ever because of the still air. If I go on about that sound too much, it is because I think of it every time I think of Woodbrook, just as one thinks of waves after staying by the sea. It was continuous. It was mysterious. The bird was always hidden under cover as it craked. Its very harshness was romantic and became nostalgic. It accompanied many incidents that touched my heart and it has a special place there now because I believe I shall never hear it again.

Tom Crowe and I agreed later that no one could write the truth about the end of that evening and be believed, but I think he will have to write it sometime just as I must now because it had a fearful effect on both our imaginations and of course on Phoebe's. And then he took part in the whole episode and I appeared only in the last act, not knowing what had gone before.

He says that during their French lesson that morning they had read a story of Maupassant about death. They did not speak of it at dinner so far as I remember or if they did it meant little to me not knowing the story, but afterwards alone together in the garden they thought and spoke of nothing else and decided to visit a churchyard and look at old graves. Naturally they chose Kilronan, probably the oldest one except for Holy Island in the most beautiful setting of all beside Saint Lasair's well. There was nothing macabre about the expedition. They set out on their bicycles light-heartedly with that lovely sense of freedom that the narrow twisty roads gave on long fine summer afternoons. They came back in high spirits too and at supper said they had been to Kilronan and 'everywhere for miles'.

At about eight o'clock, when we had finished eating, Phoebe and Tony left the room and Ivy, Charlie, Tom and I stayed at the table having coffee I suppose, or rather 'Irel', for real coffee was impossible to obtain. We began to hear a distant sound of jubilation, voices chanting to a drum, Tony's voice clearly distinguishable in spite of the high weird shriek she was achieving. It was not a bit unusual to hear such sounds. Improvised dances and melodramas came spontaneously to the girls. And we sat on talking until we had finished our coffee. But when Ivy and I, who left first, came to the turn in the passage where it led into the hall we saw that the dance was unusual, or at least that its props were. There was a human skull on the floor and Tony was dancing round it flourishing two arm-bones above her head. There was an old drum nearby which she had been playing from time to time with the bones for drumsticks. Phoebe was near the skull and obviously enjoying herself. She had been dancing, and clearly the Dance of Death and all its abandoned movements, its chanting and shrieking and insistent rhythm, had been created with her help.

My glimpse of it only lasted seconds, until Tony saw her mother's pale and rigid face. Ivy had turned pale at the sight of it. She said nothing but Tony was paralysed. She lowered her arms not to a natural position by her sides but half-way so that the bones took awkward angles a little way from her chest: white shirt, dark skirt, bare sunburnt legs and feet: her face, an appley pink and brown below a straight fringe with straight hair hanging down each side of it, straw-gold and shining, looked puzzled and alarmed. She stood with her feet apart, one each side of the skull on the dull red patterned Persian carpet. Phoebe was also quiet and still as though she knew something terrible had occurred but was not sure what it was. She looked at her mother, then at me. She had a fairer skin than Tony, though her hair was darker, and her face seemed to me translucent. She was wearing trousers, pale fawn ones, and an old bluish shirt of mine which she had pinched. She had thrown off her shoes, and stood there in her dirty bare feet quite unconscious of how lovely she looked. The expression of her eyes which I remember best during those seconds-was of childish bewilderment, but immediately it changed to understanding and she took a step towards her mother as soon as she saw what the matter was.

But for Ivy there was no time to be lost. She told Tony in a voice that frightened us all to come upstairs with her. Tony placed the bones on the carpet carefully and went. Ivy took her gently by the wrist, not the hand, and they walked upstairs together faster than was natural. We had all been standing near the foot of the staircase where it led from the hall. That was the last I saw of Tony and Ivy till next day. I looked at Phoebe but she had withdrawn her attention from me as she often suddenly did. She said 'Where's Tom?' 'In the dining-room.' She picked up the skull and bones as though they were dishes that someone had left on the floor and put them out of sight in the 'office'. I stayed, wanting to ask her about them, but she only smiled and said 'Better find Tom'. I went upstairs to read on my bed.

I could not read because the voices from the upstairs bath-room, only a few yards away at the end of the long passage, were inescapable and more impelling than any book. Tony was protesting then crying. Ivy sounded mad, like my idea of Lady Macbeth. She was saying, 'Wash it. Wash it! Wash it all out. That's not enough, wash it! Now some clean water. Wash it out again.'

I left my room as this was going on and went to look at the horses, then gave more straw to the pigs though they did not need it. It was close and thundery as it had been all day, but the sun now low in the west was still glaring. There were heavy clouds all about but they stayed away from the sun – oppress-ive. I was oppressed too by the inescapable outcome of that innocent game.

Phoebe found me in the cow-yard. She had been searching for me but not calling as she normally would. I was sitting on a shifter or some other cart by the hayshed rolling a cigarette. I was glad I was rolling one. It gave me a chance to keep her alone with me for a minute and let me question her. She said she and Tom had picked up the skull and armbones in Kilronan graveyard and brought them home in her bicycle basket. 'But that's not the point,' she said. 'How can we get rid of them – take them back or what?' I didn't know what to do. But Phoebe's reply to that was 'Tell Tom what we should do.' Tom, she said, had the skull and bones in the ballroom (the loft) and was waiting for me. As we went through the little iron barred gate into the stable yard the sun went down, the clouds gathered over the tall elms behind the harness room, and when we had climbed the steps and shut the door behind us we found the ballroom almost in darkness. There was only one heap of grain on the floor. Tom was at the far end by the fireplace leaning on its mantelpiece over which one of Phoebe's landscapes was hung. In a few days we would clear the grain away for her birthday dance.

Their taking of the bones had not been in the slightest ghoulish. They had been looking at an old tomb whose heavy slabs were out of place, as most are at Kilronan. The stone at one side was broken and among the fallen rubble they saw these bones. Tom took the skull up to look at it and Phoebe the two bones. They thought they 'might as well bring them home'. But now in the darkening loft we were all three afraid of them and spoke in whispers, though no one was near. Should one of us bicycle back to that graveyard and put them there? Ardcarne was nearer and had plenty of skulls lying about in the grass. But we were afraid of being seen. Where could we hide them? Bury them? We felt a superstititous fear of keeping them at all and then the only land soft enough for digging was in full view of the Maxwells' house. The tillage fields were out of the question because of next year's ploughing – 'skull found at Woodbrook – search for rest of skeleton – gardaí inquiry – murder hunt, etc.' We began to laugh a bit or nearly laugh, and then I remembered with some disgust a place where I had buried the burnt chickens and often the corpses of trapped rats, the only place where digging deep was quick. Just as I thought of it and they agreed it was the only possible place, the sky darkened, changing dusk to night, and brilliant lightning through one of the circular windows lit up Phoebe's face.

We waited for the clap of thunder, which was not a fearful one, then left. Phoebe ran across the yard to reach the kitchen door before the rain began. But it was only a few large drops; the clouds thinned out a bit and Tom and I walked through the yard, me with a spade, he with his secret underneath his coat, past the kitchen window where Winnie smiled at us from the sink and into the side garden, which was bordered in one place by gloomy pine-trees. The place was hidden by shrubbery. It was unwelcoming even for hens, which never wandered there looking for a nest. The children never played there because the ground was soggy. The trees were tall, their flaking bark gave them a dead metallic look near the bottom and from below you never saw the green of their tops high above, only a few scraggy twigs sticking out with brown pine needles like fish-bones. It was the only part of Woodbrook I disliked. I believe I was the only person to go into it and usually I went in the very early morning before anyone else was about, after the horrifying job which gradually ceased to horrify me of taking the rats from the traps I had set the night before. The ground was soggy because it formed the 'soak-away' for bathwater. The cess-pits were several yards farther down its slope, but did not seep to the surface.

No one would watch us, which was partly why I had chosen this nasty place. None of the family wandered here and no men ever came this side of the yards after work.

I dug. Tom kept on suggesting how deep I should go. He seemed to think it was better to make the hole oblong like a human grave. He spoke seriously and practically. He said the earth did not look like earth, which was true because it came out in porous blocks like wet sponge cake but black. I had always hated this earth. I have never seen anything like it since, or before I buried the first rat. I made the grave oblong and laid down the spade. The skull and bones were on the ground beside us.

Tom took up the skull with both hands. It was almost as dark as night beneath the trees. I picked up the armbones and was waiting to place them in the grave as he stooped over it when a tremendous flash of lightning lit his pale hands up with the skull between them, its black eyes and chopped off nose, and he halted, stooping. The thunder came next second, close, against our ears, against our hearts, so that we cowered as though being shot at. It rumbled away, but was followed at once by another crash and another, and all during the cloudburst that began with it lightning and thunder continued. All during the burial as I shovelled the earth back and Tom trod it firm we and the spade and the stark pine-trees were shuddered at and lit from second to second. These ghastly trees were thin on top and we were drenched. We were aghast and years later when we often met after parting from Woodbrook we spoke of it incredibly, thinking of the storm scene in *King Lear*.

It was not the first time that a skull had been taken from Kilronan graveyard. If any of us, even Ivy, had known more of local history, we might have escaped the guilty feeling of doom. Skulls were believed to have healing properties, especially for epilepsy, and Carolan's served this purpose for years before it was stolen: 'small fragments broken off were ground fine, put in water and swallowed as a cure.' Milk would be boiled in it and given to the patient and 'from the frequent use made of it in this way, the edges were much burned.' It was evidently not rare to find skulls so used in the eighteenth century. Francis Grose, Robert Burns' friend, who travelled in Ireland to make his beautiful engravings, visited the Abbey of Cloontuskert, also in Co. Roscommon, and wrote, 'A skull is here shown, in which milk was boiled and given to a man afflicted with the epilepsy. It exhibits strong marks of the effect of fire and, being very black, has an unpleasant appearance.' Grose was a boy about seven years old when Carolan died near Kilronan in 1738. About thirty years later the grave was opened to make room for a body of a priest and Carolan's skull was tossed out by the gravedigger. A man called Dillon, afterwards Lord Roscommon, who was looking on picked it up, borrowed a gimlet from the local carpenter, made a hole in it, 'tied a piece of green silk ribbon in it [presumably to distinguish it from other skulls] and laid it in the small square recess in the wall ... of the chapel. One of the O Conors, Mrs MacDermot Roe, who loved his memory, her family having taken him into their house as a child and looked after him there for the rest of his life, renewed the ribbon frequently.'[1]

About the year 1798 someone stole Carolan's skull, probably a gentleman riding from Carrick-on-Shannon to Sligo, who finding that 'a very great part of it had been scraped away by the peasantry ... thought it no sacrilege to put what remained in his pocket and rode away'.

Communities such as Kilronan and Ardcarne were as closed in those days as in mine. There were many more people in each but they knew each other intimately and most were related in some way to each other. It is certain that whenever a skull was used as a saucepan, many older men and women remembered the face and hair that had once covered it. So it looks to me as if no one, not even the monks of Cloontuskert, saw anything profane in disturbing bones that had once been reverently laid to rest.

Chapter Twelve

Goldsmith in his essay called Carolan the 'Last of the Irish Bards', but he was much more famous as a musician than a poet. And the real bards had harpists and reciters to perform their work, whereas he composed and played his own harp music and sang or spoke his own words. On the day of his death old Mrs MacDermot Roe spoke of him as 'the head of all Irish music' and the extraordinary grandeur of the wake she gave him showed how widespread his popularity had been: 'The respectable people coming so numerous, the place got so thronged that they were obliged to take up all the houses in Ballyfarnan; the lower orders of people with shades [? tents] in the fields, with caggs of whiskey; a cagg each side of the hall door, harpers going on constantly without and within, and Mrs MacDermot Roe herself attending to the country women at their going and desiring them to cry over her poor gentleman well.' It was a four-day wake.

He had been educated first with her own children by their private tutor, then by one of the O Conors of Ballinagar who was living poorly near Ballyfarnan because his family estate had been forfeited to John French, the great landowner. When he went blind through smallpox at the age of eighteen she appointed a harpist to teach him music, and as soon as he was qualified three years later she provided him with money, a horse and a guide and started him on his life-long travels from one gentleman's house to another.

In Irish gentlemen's houses at that time the harp held the place taken by string ensembles elsewhere. Ordinary people had the fiddle and the pipes for their music. The lavish hospitality of the gentry, both Protestant and Catholic, was noted and sometimes ridiculed by travellers. In the country no music could be heard unless at home. So a good harpist, being invited to the same big houses again and again, could always live well. There were many of them. 'The Big House ... with its numerous retainers and dependants, formed the social unit: a sort of oasis in a desert of poverty, which was a centre for the distribution of hospitality, and also of charity to the poor.'

During my early years at Woodbrook I felt I belonged to a remnant of one of those old social units, no longer an oasis, for oppressive poverty was rare and the Kirkwoods' fortunes waning, but a sort of nub of life for everyone about the place, whether they worked there or lived in the house or not. Charity was seldom given as charity; we were too far from Boyle or Carrick to know many of the very poor; but when anyone came to the door wanting money or things he would get them, and a meal if he wanted it as well. Charlie was much criticized by the country people for allowing tinkers to graze their horses on the Bottoms at night. They used to pitch their tents on the roadside verge near the gate-lodge, open the gates and close their horses in. Charlie would never let anyone turn them away, even though there was no fence between the Bottoms and the garden. But the same country people who resented the tinkers always came to him for help, and this naturally close relationship was a survival from the old tradition of The Big House. If there was an accident – I remember a terrible one to a little girl – Ivy was the first person to be sent for; the doctor and ambulance were too far away. If a bullock fell into a drain in the middle of the night, no one was afraid to knock Charlie up, and he would get dressed and go to help to pull it out.

Then, the custom Charlie's parents held to of not paying servants was a survival of the old Big House polity. Old Mrs Kirkwood could not have started it and would not. She and her employees thought in terms of food, drink and presents and just as she advised Charlie to hand the servants money in sealed envelopes, so Arthur O'Neill, the eighteenth-century harper who left memoirs, said 'the different gratuities I generally received were handed me in a private manner'. By 'generally' I take it he means not always, and once after spending several weeks performing in houses 'where I was well received and used' he named the town Moneymore 'Moneyless' because performing there he found himself 'uncommonly short of money'. Both he and Carolan refer frequently to hospitality, rarely to money. In fact Carolan so far as I know never mentions it. In his songs dedicated to patrons, if he says how they treated him at all he praises or curses the drink they offered. His satire was feared by the stingy.

I don't think attitudes in the Big House had changed much two hundred years later. Styles of living had, extremely, and got nearer to each other, the gentry being poorer and the poor not starving. But at Woodbrook certainly the attitude to money had not changed. Many of the landlords were prodigal and the people attached to their houses showed a curious disregard for money, for spending-money, I mean; money from cattle or dowries was eagerly sought and kept.

But together with that, those who worked in the Big Houses, even in my day, thought nothing of taking any chattels they might need from time to time. I was told that even in very large houses where dozens of temporary servants came and went money left lying about was never touched; things only were taken, not to be sold but for personal use, and their removal was not regarded as theft either by employer or employed. Perhaps it was understood that because of the miserable wages paid, where any were paid, justice could be done in this way.

That was certainly so in the case of Charlie's mother and a maid who had spent all her youth at Woodbrook. She had worked in the house without wages from the age of fourteen, and in her late thirties, about 1920, she got married. Ivy remembers her but not her name, and remembers her wedding well to which with her parents-in-law she was invited. It was a fair distance away and some days before it a strange horse and cart arrived at Woodbrook's kitchen door and was loaded with an astonishing number of cases and trunks, some of them bearing the family initials and old P & O labels from India. Ivy's father-in-law helped to load the cart and as it drove off down the avenue he went into the house with Ivy and began to reprove his wife. He said 'I know we must give her a generous trousseau, but that leather case I had in India . . .' 'I never gave her that. Why didn't you ask for it back?' 'How could I?' The wedding presents old Mrs Kirkwood had given to the maid, though good ones, would not have filled a governess-cart. As guests at the wedding, in a little house in the mountains, they ate off their own plates, the same pattern as I remember with the Kirkwood's crest on them, and with their own silver. Relationships were cordial. It did not occur to the bride to conceal what she had taken, and though the Kirkwoods were secretly startled and annoyed it would never have occurred to them to be so rude as to call attention to it. When they reached home that night, they found linen and much else missing, but again said nothing.

So, when Winnie was about to be married, and a motor lorry arrived, Ivy and Charlie watched it being loaded with a kind of amused curiosity. Charlie helped. There certainly were many cases, but then Woodbrook had been her home since childhood almost, for nearly a quarter of a century. And all was well. I was out on Usna when the lorry came, but I have a poignant memory of her departure from Woodbrook a few days later. I naturally wanted to say good-bye to her and wish her well but mistook the time and almost missed her. I met her cycling away down the avenue at high speed. She had an alarming way of throwing herself off the bicycle, both feet at once, as though she was jumping out of a car that would not stop for her and then, running with it, she held on to the handlebars until she forced it to a halt. This she did when she caught sight of me and was breathless.

She said a lot rapidly, emotionally, in a natural mixture of regret at leaving Woodbrook and excitement about her future. She must have said it all before two minutes earlier at the door but it was coloured by her personal feelings for me which were at that moment affectionate and strong. I was flooded and tongue-tied by the nice things she said. In the end we exchanged good wishes formally and she rode off.

I don't know why I felt so sad. We had never felt close to each other emotionally. In my bad moods I would wish her at the other end of the world and I should think she found me a nuisance very often, especially when she was busy in the kitchen. But for ten years, at any time of day, I had had cups of tea, standing by the range talking with her as she worked, and on her butter-making days I never passed the dairy without going in to take a turn at the churn. Nor did any other man of course; it would be unfriendly and unlucky not to. Sometimes I kept on churning long after she wished to resume it because I loved the moment when the butter came, the change in rhythm, the thud, thud, thud, of solid lumps created in the liquid. And to watch her washing new butter was beautiful – in the water I had drawn from the boiling well.

I think she felt as I felt on the day I left school, longing to leave and then thinking back on my years there and the people I would never see again. For me her departure was another part of Woodbrook chipped away. Her clutch on my thumb had been relaxed.

I did not go to her wedding. Ivy and Charles went and were entertained in the good old personal way at the bridegroom's parents' house in County Leitrim. People had begun by then to have wedding breakfasts at hotels in Carrick or Boyle where after a while the guests bought their own drinks, but at Winnie's there was enough food, drink and music to last all night at home. Indeed hers was said to be as good as the best of the old-time weddings, the only joy missing being the race from chapel to house after the service, in which the whole congregation used to take part, driving their traps and sidecars so recklessly that there was often a crash.

Several of Winnie's guests had cars and had saved enough petrol for the occasion, and she and the bridegroom were driven by a chauffeur in a hired limousine. It was into that that Ivy and Charlie were ushered, to their astonishment, after being welcomed with drinks at the house when the service was over. The bride and bridegroom got into it too, and the chauffeur drove off. 'But where are we going?' said Ivy. 'We going on our honeymoon,' said Winnie. 'Dash my buttons,' said Charlie. 'You don't want us on your honeymoon, Winnie!' 'Who better, Major?' she said. And they drove on. But a 'honeymoon' as it had come to be called was nothing more than the old-time wedding tour on which the bride and bridegroom sometimes with honoured guests were driven round the countryside for an hour or so. Even Charlie had not heard of it. They returned from the honeymoon to the wedding breakfast and the music of three good fiddlers who held their fiddles in the traditional way below the ribs instead of the chin. If only Phoebe had been taught that way she would have had no scars.

When her parents came home from the wedding it was Phoebe who showed them the servants' quarters, not giving them time to sit down before they explored that part of the house now unoccupied for the first time in generations – the kitchen in working order as usual with a good fire in the range, the dairy with crocks of cream nearly ready for skimming, the servants' hall without a fire in its fireplace, the bedrooms without new tenants. There had been no maid for some time; we had competed with each other in sweeping and so on, and watching Charlie at it I had learned the origin of the phrase 'sweeping things under the carpet'; he used to lift the corner up, and leaving my dustpan aside I took quickly to this method. They wanted to find a new cook but no more maids.

By then I had been several times to Dublin to see house agents and put advertisements in the papers. We all knew Woodbrook had to be sold and there were repeated threats from creditors – chiefly banks – that if it was not sold soon it would be taken at an immediate and tiny price. None of us appeared to think of this often but, when one did, gloom spread to all.

Numerous and hopeful buyers came to see the place. They liked the house and a distant view of the land and got on so well with Charlie that we thought each time that the whole estate was sold for the advertised price. But Charlie never went with them to walk the land. He said, which was true, that the Maxwells knew it better and after taking them over the paddock and one or two near-by fields he always summoned one of the Maxwell brothers to show them the distant parts. None made an offer, and at those times we were all depressed in contradictory ways, hoping it would be sold next time or that a turn of luck would make the sale unnecessary.

Ivy of course began spending money again. She and Phoebe

saw the emptied servants' quarters as a virgin forest and after making clearings began to knock down walls, install french windows and the rest, letting light and air into corners that had never known them.

At the same time, she revived the social life of the house by inviting people to stay, students from Dublin whom she had never seen before, old friends she had been long separated from, and for a while the whole of Lord Longford's repertory company, whose tour included Carrick-on-Shannon and Boyle. Every alcove of the dining-room, drawing-room and hall was provided with a makeshift bed and mattresses were laid on bedroom floors.

During the last weeks of the year the house pealed with voices and feet running up and down stairs. Home-made plays and pantomimes were concocted all over the ground floor, dancing never ceased and the fields, usually deserted in December, were dotted with people walking here and there. I remember two of the guests as being outside all day whatever the weather, though like wild creatures they kept apart and never invaded one another's territory. They both became involved in perilous incidents. Leslie Summers, the younger of the two – the boy who kept his tame crow in the downstairs bathroom – had brought a large lurcher with him and was continually running with it after hares. He had come from England on leave from the army and had bought the lurcher, he said, to relieve the boredom of route marches on which he had frequently to lead his platoon along monotonous roads; the lurcher led them all over the countryside instead. He never parted with it, not at meal times nor at night. He was terribly lean and excitable and fell in love quickly with a pretty blonde girl whose lack of regard for him almost caused a fire. Nothing in those weeks resembled the familiar life of Woodbrook which is why, I suppose, his unhappiness that evening impressed me so sadly; nothing intense had till then been so brief. His love had no chance at all of running its course. Only ten days remained before his return to the army and the chances were that with his rash daring courage he would not survive many months.

At tea he suddenly said, 'Why am I picked out for misery?

Look at you all!' People laughed. Phoebe said something nice to him, to which he replied, 'Look at David enjoying his cake!' He left his and blundered out of the room with an ungovernable gait that endeared him to Phoebe and me at least.

She and I were in the stables by good chance when he set out to avoid us all by spending the night in the hay. It was a dark, cold night, but still, and we were putting blankets on some of the horses. We heard the click of the cow-yard gate as he went through it with his lurcher and saw a lamp in his hand. But of course it never occurred to us that it might be a house lamp with an open flame; on any normally breezy night he could not have taken a step outside without its blowing out. We did not want to intrude on him and he had climbed the ladder to the top of the hay barn and began to make his bed before we saw the hay alight. We ran but he had put it out before we reached him. And that was all.

Gerard McLarnon, Longford's leading actor, whom we called Gerry, was even more eccentric and I think as lonely. While the others were making up their amateur plays indoors, he spent the whole day on Usna or Shanwelliagh rehearsing his part for next week's theatre; which was Lear on the day I remember. Whether he was rehearsing or not he always appeared to be in a passion, his gestures wide, hair and clothes disordered, his pale face burning or blanching. I have never known anyone who showed so much interest in what others said, whatever they said, and this was flattering though he did not know it. I believe there was nothing and nobody that did not interest him. His friendliness was warm and open, and his features were as ragged as his coat. He was broad and strong, but not very tall. No one could help looking at him even in a crowd, and alone on the high rocks above the lake, with a gale blowing black clouds above him, he looked to me from a distance like a prophet in the wilderness. To Peter Corrigan he looked like a parachutist.

As Gerry spoke to everyone he saw, it was surprising that Peter did not know he was staying in the house, that they had not met in one of the yards or gardens. Peter lived with his parents nearby and had recently started work at Woodbrook as a willing but clumsy factotum – house-boy, gardener, stable boy and so on. He had very big boots, handed on by someone else, and when anyone was cross with him for one of his silly mistakes Ivy said his whole character sank into them. He was about eighteen but of so boyish a nature that we and the Maxwells were alarmed when he joined the Local Defence Force – the equivalent of the British Home Guard – and was issued with a rifle. The Germans had dropped a bomb or two on Dublin by then and their next thing was supposed to be an invasion by parachutists. Peter was trained to look out for them and, fortunately for Gerry, less well trained to use a rifle.

To Peter, King Lear on the high rocks appeared to be signalling by semaphore to his comrades on the Leitrim mountains on the far side of the lake. Gerry's voice was clearly audible, though the words were not, because, said Peter later, he had no education in German. He shouted to him to surrender, but that word was blown away behind him and Gerry did not hear. He fired one shot, then ran for his bicycle to report the danger to the Gardaí at Cootehall.

These incidents seem commonplace to me now that I know they could happen anywhere when people find themselves in unfamiliar situations. At Woodbrook at that time they were dramatic because manners had so long remained unchanged. Even in my early years there, no visitor would have carried an open lamp to the barn and even during the civil war no one would have mistaken an actor for his enemy. The whole, long, exciting Christmas party seemed to me, looking back on it next March when I and one servant were alone in the house, something unnatural, even forced. The reason Ivy created it was kind and clear. The children, having spent their winters in England in the past, had been isolated since the war began. They enjoyed it and learned a lot about the outside world from it, especially Phoebe who was the same age as many of the guests. Tony was in ecstasies of joy and jealousy most of the time.

The house party built itself up to a climax by Christmas Day and was revived again on St Stephen's Day when the Wren Boys led by Tommy Maxwell came into the house with their music.

Then suddenly everyone left.

It would anyway have been difficult to get back to normal. But now that the life of the house was uncertain, no one knowing how long the family could stay, we even churned the cream half-heartedly as though we felt there would be no one to eat the butter. And then, as though to confirm the abnormality, there came a spell of unprecedented cold – first a heavy frost which made riding or driving impossible, then at intervals several beautiful falls of snow such as we had never seen before. I could not remember snow lying everywhere for longer than one morning. Now it stayed for weeks, turning the hill of Usna into a mountain with peaks where it drifted, smoothing the rugged grass of the Bottoms to make it look like a snow-covered lake except where the spiky tips of rushes showed through, bending the boughs of the copper beech outside the drawing-room window, covering the top of each black twig with an uneven coping of pure white; black and white trees, grey and white houses, and everything else pure white.

It must have been Phoebe's last memory of Woodbrook, this purity. She left with her mother and Tony soon after it began. Someone had lent them a flat in Dublin and Ivy accepted because the matriculation examination was in June and tuition in Dublin was easy to find. Also everyone thought it might be easier to sell the place from there. They intended to come home for the Easter holidays. Phoebe thought so, but I did not believe they would manage it. I thought I would never see her at Woodbrook again.

Charlie brought the Fiat to the front of the house in the early afternoon. Her eyes seemed to melt as we said good-bye at the door, but with the usual business of seeing to suitcases and keeping the dogs out of the car I hardly saw her. I think she had stockings on – a rare thing – and a yellow jersey underneath her overcoat. I could describe the cases more exactly. Charlie drove off jerkily, and an arm waved. It may have been hers, but her coat and Ivy's were almost the same colour and the one window of the car that would open gave room only for one arm. The sun was dazzling on the snow. A few minutes later I watched the car climb Hughestown Hill and disappear.

The drawing-room fire needed making up before Charlie's

return, but I would not go into the house just then and followed the dogs all over Shanwelliagh to the lakeside. The snow was untouched until we marked it and absolutely silent, the sky the palest possible blue, almost white, the air pellucid, but no living thing to be seen for miles except a herd of bullocks huddled and still against a hedge. When the dogs ran over the hill I did not follow them and suddenly felt that extraordinary sensation of imagining myself the only person in the world. Other people have described it to me and I had had the experience once or twice before but never so convincingly. It lasted a few seconds, then was broken by the whistle of the Dublin train leaving Carrick station. I went back to the house to mend the fire.

As soon as I lay down in bed that night my mind searched restlessly over the past, and every experience I had shared with Phoebe came back to me, turning round and round upon me with nostalgic joy or regret. I could not sleep. For a long time I kept worrying about something she had said; what had she meant by it? What exactly was it? And then about a poem she had written as a child which I had copied into my diary because I liked it. I got up and took the old noteboooks from my trunk under the bed; they were not formal diaries, just hard-covered pocket books into which I wrote everything haphazardly, some-times with a date, often not. This made my search long. But I found the poem and tore that page out. Then, flicking through the rest, I came on scraps of sentiment and slapped them away half-read. I shied away from the irrecoverable past and stacked the notebooks on my bedside table – one of those cupboards meant for chamber-pots – put out the candle and tried again to sleep. But it was useless. Phoebe bicycling, fallen off a horse, climbing into the boat from the water, riding to hounds in front of me, painting alone, practising alone as I passed by the window, doing her homework in a circle of light from the lamp that turned her hair gold, Phoebe in the horsebox and with Heath's *Practical French Grammar* in the summer grass by the tennis court – all these images turned round and round in me and many had gaps between them which needed urgently to be filled. I lit the candle and searched the books again, and sud-denly they enraged me. I wanted her, not my old thoughts of her.

299

I put on my clothes, took the books under my arm and went downstairs to the kitchen. It was about three in the morning but the embers in the range were still red. I took the ring off quietly so as not to wake Sally who now occupied Winnie's bedroom across the passage, and starting a blaze with a few sticks from the morning's kindling I burnt the books one by one. I think it was the most destructive thing I have ever done. I think it was mad. And whatever the unconscious motive – purification by fire, killing that part of my spirit to let it be reborn, burning the tangible signs of the past to set imagination free – the outcome was the opposite. It brought me no relief; it aggravated that tortuous searching state of mind; and next day I had an awful sense of loss. The loss of Phoebe was alleviated by the certainty that I would at least speak to her again. The loss of the books was final.

I thought about that night's madness many times later and still do. It was cataclysmic. It was like a child smashing beloved possessions in a rage. Its wastefulness affects me to this day, for besides the introspection and all the private cries and poems that disgusted me that night, the books were full of details about what happened, the people and places I knew. I know now why it turned sour on me at the time; it was that I only wrote emotionally or about Phoebe when I was in a bad mood. While I was happy with her, I left my diary alone òr wrote in it what happened at the fair.

Charlie and I spent the rest of the winter together with this girl to cook for us – and Peter to help in the stables. It was all right but a bit embarrassing at meal-times, for neither of us was good at talking without the family there to set us off and we both thought we should try. Charlie used to groan a lot and say 'Well, I must say' as an exclamation complete in itself – there was nothing new in that, but no one to laugh as there used to be or finish the sentence for him absurdly. I thought up things to say which were of no interest to either of us. But after supper it was pleasant in the drawing-room. We both read and occasionally spoke of what we were reading or read bits out. With the help of John Lowe, he had rigged up a bright electric lamp to save paraffin. It was fixed by clips to a car battery.

He seemed depressed very often but was optimistic whenever he spoke about the house and land. Half the time he thought the sale would be averted and because one of the hunters was in foal by a thoroughbred, and beautifully healthy, he said 'B'God. David. why don't we go out and look at her! She might bring us another White Knight. In May, don't you know.' We went out and looked at her.

Long before May, Ivy wrote that she and the others had decided to stay in Dublin for Easter; it was something to do with moving to a house when the loan of the flat came to an end. She asked Charlie to come, and in May soon after the foal was born he let all the horses out on grass. It was earlier than usual, but the weather was mild and the grass unusually forward. That afternoon he left for Dublin.

Chapter Thirteen

I got used to living alone and might even have enjoyed it in a smaller house without so many rooms shut up, their beds, chairs, tables draped in white shrouds. 'Sally' stayed on with me of course, but my very doubt as to her name shows how separate we were. I don't think she disliked me any more than the hens which she also fed but she had nothing to say beyond the usual greetings as she laid my meals on the hall table, none of the warm response most country girls give to almost any inanity one utters. She led a full life outside the house when her work was done, going out every evening after six, which was possible now that I had tea and boiled eggs instead of the large late meal. I have never hated eggs so much as I did in the summer of 1943, eating them morning, noon and night and wishing I could send them to England. I might have eaten them more cheerfully in the proper place, Aunt Nina's room, but the dining-room table was shrouded, and to use it alone, so large and far from the kitchen, would have been absurd. The hall was particularly gloomy in wet or windy weather when I had to keep the front door shut to stop the rain from coming in. I sat in the drawing-room sometimes but did most of my reading and writing in my bedroom, Phoebe's old one, where I still kept two of her paintings on the wall.

I spent more and more time outside the house, and as the daylight lengthened the harness-room became my real home. I had always liked it, especially in the winter time when the blazing fires we used to have kept us warm with the door wide open. There was a beautiful battered table made of unstained oak planks, a chair, a couple of milking stools and saddlery on all the whitewashed walls. I knew there was a camp bed folded up in the coach house and one day planned to move in completely.

But the only excuse for my presence at Woodbrook now, at least from Charlie's point of view, who paid me, was as a caretaker, so I continued to sleep in the house. The stables were empty; people used the yard only as a thoroughfare, except for Peter who sometimes weeded the cobbles and me who had to go to and fro from the harness room anyway, because it was there that I boiled the pigs' potatoes.

I had company there in the evenings when I wanted it. Men would come to light their pipes or dry out from the rain and I grew to know several well who had till then been casual acquaintances. Chance had made me a host, like the smith Lord Leitrim sacked from his yard at Mohill, for all I had to offer my guests was what any blacksmith offers – a good listening ear, some talk and a fire. I saw more of the Maxwell brothers than ever before.

Jimmy and Tom were naturally my best friends; we shared so many experiences, good and bad; but now that I was alone they expressed their feelings to me intimately and I saw how much they had withheld in the days when they knew I would be returning to the Kirkwoods in the evening. For instance, they were as bitter about the horses as the bank manager had been. Even Tommy, who was such an expert horseman, thought it mad to keep them now that the market was finished for ever as he believed it was.

I never heard one of the Maxwell family say anything else against 'the Major'. It was this matter of horses alone, the essential matter of Woodbrook, that caused a judgement to be made. The hostility openly expressed to me was slight; probably none of the brothers was conscious of the deeper ancient one that lay beneath it. But some time later when I asked Tom whether he knew what it was that in the end put every buyer off – the hawthorn bushes on Shanwelliagh that had continually to be cut back, the spreading flag-lilies that encroached on pasture, the thistly places we had not attended to enough, the beds of rushes on the Bottoms? – he shrugged his shoulders. Then he said simply, 'Woodbrook belongs to us.' He said it naturally and quietly as though the whole world knew it, as though it could cause me no surprise. Of course I knew what he meant but pressed him to explain it, which he did unemotionally by saying that his family were living there before Cromwell put the Kirkwoods on this land. We had one of our old pedantic arguments then – I mean the half angry, half joking kind we used to have when we were eighteen about murder or Protestants going to hell – and I reminded him that the Maxwells had come from Scotland with James II long after Cromwell. But he was thinking, as many people did, of heredity through the female line; his mother's family the Feelys had always lived on this land. So had thirty families, I said, half a dozen of which had survivors living within half-an-hour's walk of the stable yard – notably the Conlon brothers of Newtown who could claim the same right to Woodbrook. But he believed in his family's right through their mother's line with calm certainty. Besides, no one else had the money to buy the place.

His eldest brother, called Michael after their father, had emigrated to America as a young man. He had saved money. They had written to him. It would take time.

In spite of their affection for the Kirkwoods the Maxwells misunderstood their way of living as much as the Kirkwoods misunderstood theirs. Being musical themselves, they were sympathetic towards that, though I guess that if Charlie had been a musician and played the piano in the daytime they would have thought him mad. Jimmy put down Charlie's love for painting to shell-shock and to all he suffered in the Turkish prison camp during the old war. He spoke very kindly about it, saying how young 'the Major' was then and 'how any young man being through those troubles might be a little soft and out painting the skies and that kind of thing'. On most fine afternoons, all the time I knew him, Charlie was out in the fields or garden with his canvas, paints and folding stool. So was Phoebe, as I said to Jimmy, but he thought it a suitable pastime for a young girl. The occasion of this conversation was a letter from her with messages for him in which she told me of a Dublin painter who liked her work and hoped to get one or two of her pictures shown. She had started a new and more crowded life, richer in many ways.

Willie's farm was near the railway line, a couple of miles

from Woodbrook house on a piece of land that Charlie had sold to the Land Commission. He was still at home in the sense that he had not moved across the old 'mearing' of the estate. He lived with his wife in a new house, built with his own hands on a Land Commission grant, under the shadow of a modern ruin called The Rookery because of the great colonies of rooks that built their nests on the top of its ivied walls and on the trees that had been planted when the walls were built to make the grounds pleasant. But no one had ever lived in the house or walked the grounds. The house stopped growing and the trees continued. The house was almost finished, on the orders of one of the nineteenth-century Kirkwoods who found our Woodbrook house too small, but as Willy said, 'No one was able to put the roof on it, not the best tradesman that was sent for from any town could keep the roof on it. It would be up one evening, perfect, and in the morning fallen down.'

Willie believed that the Kirkwoods were not meant to put a house there, that because they had chosen the wrong site a supernatural power interfered every time the work was near completion. His brothers acknowledged the supernatural only when it fitted in with Christian teaching, whereas he accepted it openly. In his soul he was much nearer to their father than to them. He sometimes spoke of fairies as 'fallen angels' and more often as 'the gentry'. The places they frequented were 'gentle places' and once he spoke of a field where they were so thick on the ground that the cow had to snout them away to get a bite at the grass. His way of talking was poetical. His images enriched me. It was as though marvellous visions that come to most people only in dreams formed part of his waking life. Often he made a fairy story into a joke but he never dismissed it or looked for a factual explanation. Nor did I. But all the same I interpreted factually the business of the Rookery roof. I thought the people round about had hated the notion of having a big house there and had pulled the roof down whenever the workmen had gone off for the night. Everything else I had heard convinced me that country people however oppressed could, if they survived eviction, get their own way.

I got lost one night near the house. I had a natural explanation for it but Willie had one which interests me more because perhaps it shows his instinctive knowledge of the subconscious mind. What happened to me was simple. There were four pet lambs, almost fully grown, in the paddock beyond the tennis court at the end of the flower-garden. I was as familiar with this paddock as with any part of the house. When I opened the front door after dark that night there was one of the lambs nudging my knees like a dog. It followed me into the paddock and after shutting the gate I began to search for a hole in the fence. As I walked across towards the other side, I lost my way. I walked here and there and in circles for about two hours, sometimes sitting down to gather my wits, sometimes walking straight ahead, as I thought, but never reaching fence or wall, always wandering as though in endless space. I became frightened. At last I lay down on the grass. It was damp and cold. The lush smell of Ireland soaked me as it had on the day of my arrival eleven years before. I slept for a bit and when I woke walked straight back to the house without doubting the direction I took.

During the next few days I told several people about this experience. They laughed when they heard I had been led astray by a pet lamb. I mentioned my peculiar defect of eyesight called night-blindness by the London oculist who said my pupils took hours to widen in the dark when other men's took seconds, which made me entirely blind whenever I left a lighted place for a dark one. But no one I spoke to took this for a reason. 'Going astray' was a common thing to them. Anyone who had not been astray knew someone else who had. Some said certain fields were known to have 'a stray' in them, meaning a lost soul I think. One man said you would be lost if you walked over the grave of an unbaptized baby and a very old man at Cootehall believed it could only happen in a 'gentle place'. He said the 'gentry' would put you astray.

Willie Maxwell had twice been astray on the Hill of Usna, every curve of which he had known since childhood, and been severely frightened. Once he had been brought back to his sense by wading across 'a big, big river' which next day was not there. He said it was 'some mist that comes over your eyes'. He said 'if you had a coat, wearing your coat, and that the linen wasn't torn in it ... take off your coat and turn it and put it on you, that you'd come back to your eye-sight.'

Most beliefs of that sort are parables, and this was one for me. I needed to turn myself inside out and cross a river for, ever since the Kirkwoods left, my indecision about the future had been growing until at the time I went astray my mind was in a state of utter confusion, obsessed by worry that kept me from sleeping properly and from reading or writing at all. Had there been no choice but to go back to England and teach, I should have calmly hated the prospect. But there were choices, Ivy's letters gave several in Dublin, offering new and as it seemed to me exciting ways of earning a living. Charles and she and their relatives would help. Then I knew I could find a tutoring job with some other family in Ireland. All plans seemed repulsive and exciting by turns. The only agreeable one was to borrow money and take a small farm nearby, something that I could run myself. It could have been done on a bit of land we all knew with a tumble-down house that was repairable. It was useless for cattle or grain crops but had a potato garden. Pigs, which I knew how to keep, might keep me on it.

Tommy laughed at the idea. He was right, as it turned out, not to take me seriously. But I was serious enough for days to go to see the Kirkwoods' lawyer in Boyle about it. I had known him for twenty years. He had a fatherly way of making me turn against his kind advice. It was Jimmy who convinced me I was wrong. He knew I could rear pigs: he had taught me; but he believed I was too 'innocent' to sell them, and this he knew because we had been together so many times at fairs. Also I guess that he and Tommy and the lawyer were shocked at the idea of my 'coming down in the world' as they thought it. The lawyer thought that, though he had heard 'no word but kind words' about me, I would never be accepted in the community as an equal and he warned me that no legal rights I might obtain would help me there. Which I anyway knew.

Now I stopped thinking about plans, and when at last I made up my mind what to do it was as though someone else had decided for me. I wrote three letters in the harness room one evening, one to Phoebe, one to Ivy, one to my mother, saying I would go back to England, and as the postman would not call for them till dinner time next day I had no choice but to sleep on them. The postman gave me one more chance to go back on it. He had no change. I had only a ten shilling note and no cigarette tobacco. No stamps. I let him take the letters and promised to pay him next day.

It was quickly arranged. Charlie wanted to come down anyway and as soon as he arrived I could go.

I felt at once as though I had stepped on to a moving train. The invisible driver would keep it going whatever my regrets; and the result was that on the day before departure, which is usually the most distressing, I hardly thought or felt any emotion except an impatient longing to see Phoebe again. Charlie had come back more talkative than I had ever known him, full of accounts of her activities in Dublin: how, if she had passed matric, she would go to Trinity in the autumn, her painting, her parties, her music, her small parts as an actress in the Dublin theatre. (Most theatres employed a number of amateurs.) And how the whole family loved the small dower house they had been lent in a large home park at the foot of the Wicklow Mountains about twelve miles from the city. For those last few days, we could converse at meals. Their life and especially hers came out of him in vivid snatches which my imagination put together.

Despairing of a quick sale, he had let about a third of Usna to the Carrick Golf Club as a course, the long slope opposite the starting point of the old racing gallops, from the road as far as the quickset hedge of the Newtown 'mearing' through which we had so often ridden after searching for the gap, and excluding – as I was glad when I found out – the Giants' Graves. A new fence was being made in a straight line over the hill regardless of natural bends. Charlie liked the golf course – or perhaps it was his enviable positiveness that made him say so – and played golf on it by himself before it was ready, getting out his old clubs from the 'office', and on my last-but-one morning persuaded me to play with him. I was bad at golf. I longed to be riding with him instead, as in the old days. But he did not want to bring the horses in from grass. We could see some of them from the golf course and stopped to watch them. He threw his golf clubs down and called them to him with his old high-pitched 'cup cup cup', meaning 'come-up'. He petted them and gave them sugar from his pocket. One of the bullocks ate our golf balls when they landed near him.

At dinner time we went into the gate-lodge for drinks. No one had lived there for several months and the club had now acquired it as a bar, with Tommy Maxwell as barman when he could spare the time; the members were to call him from the fields when the course officially opened. Charlie did not really want a drink – he never did – but said we must launch the place and made it cheerful, encouraging Tommy and me to have more and more porter to his one. More and more happy-seeming small talk too, until as we were leaving Charlie said casually that a man from the six counties, now staying in a Carrick hotel, was coming about four o'clock to look over the farm and would Tommy walk the land with him. 'I will, Major,' said Tommy. 'I will, of course.'

In the afternoon I set out for Carrick on my bicycle to search and beg for enough cigarette tobacco to last me for the journey to London which, with the night I would spend with the Kirkwoods near Dublin, made at least forty-eight hours.

Near Carrick it began to rain, not very heavily but enough to make me feel uncomfortable and stare at the ground to keep my spectacles clearer, and as I sped down the hill towards the bridge over the Shannon, I suddenly saw white chalk marks on the road, so unusual a sight that I pulled up as soon as I could and walked back to look at them. Someone had chalked two words across the road in large block capitals but the rain had blurred them, leaving only a few letters legible. The last word could have been 'Woodbrook'; one or two o's and a k at the end were clear, and the first word began with a B. I leant on my bicycle trying to decipher it. I was fascinated as by a puzzle. It was possible to count the letters of the second word and the more I looked the more certain I felt that they spelt Woodbrook. Then suddenly it seemed that the first word was 'Boycott'. I rejected that for Boyle with two letters after it – Boyle at ... Boyle it – but came back to Boycott as the only word to make sense. It had been written so that no one coming from Carrick before the rain could have missed it, and hard as I tried to disbelieve my guesswork it shocked me into gloom, despondency and fear. It could only mean 'Boycott the sale of Woodbrook' if my guess was right.

It rained all night and I woke frequently. The water from the stable roofs and ballroom sounded like a pebbly stream as it ran into the overflowing rain-butt by the woodshed and the rain on the trees near my bedroom window pattered inconstantly, now as light as the rush of hens' feet at feeding time, next minute in a roar. The heaviest sound came from the huge leafy horizontal branches of the copper beech which made an almost constant undertone and the lightest from the row of ashes directly opposite my window whose long thin leaves were higher than the house. By daybreak, the rain had stopped and while I was feeding the pigs the sun came out for a bit. The wind had moved towards the south, leaving warm dampness as it dried first the cobbles, then the surface of the mud. Everything I did, I did carefully and consciously thinking 'this is the last time'.

Tommy had given me a message from his mother in the evening inviting me to go and see her. I would have gone anyway to say good-bye, but I was pleased by her thoughtfulness and as I walked up the path across Shanwelliagh to their house the 'last time' thought was poignant. It was sentimental too. There are so many 'last times' in everybody's lives that they don't know of while they happen. But after the thought occurred to me at my last breakfast with Charlie in the hall I could not get rid of it. It made the morning sadder than it need have been.

I saw old Michael first with his two sticks in his usual morning place half sitting on their wall with his shoulders in the hedge that grew above it, but no smoke from the pipe that was in his mouth. He shouted when he saw me and raised one stick as a greeting. When I came up to him he cursed the Kaiser and we spoke for a bit about Lloyd George. It was impossible for him at his age to distinguish between the two wars but he had absolute faith in England's strength to beat the Germans and wished it would happen quickly. He talked of a horse that I had never heard of belonging to Lloyd George. It may have been

King George V's. I don't know. Then he took an old tin out of his pocket and said, 'D'ye see the class of tobacco they're giving out now from the shop?' It looked like dried bramble leaves with long strands in it, of coltsfoot probably, which is a poor substitute for tobacco. I knew at once that his sons had made it up to pacify him when none of the real stuff was to be found.

It was about eleven in the morning, yet no sign of cooking. The pots were at the side of the fire, the kettle, still singing on its hook, had been swung aside too and all the ashes swept back. The table smelt of new soap and was still damp in places after a scrubbing; all the delph on the dresser shone – those many coloured patterned jugs and dishes that are never used but commemorate occasions in the family history. Nanny had done a spring-cleaning for me on this special occasion. She was alone. She took my hand in both of hers as I came in. She dusted a chair for me and placed it by the fire facing the open door so that I could sit with my left elbow resting on the table, the pleasantest position in the room. She poured out a glass of whiskey for me, full to the brim, and a bottle of Guinness in another glass beside it. She took nothing herself and as usual did not sit down.

We talked for an hour and twice she wept. I turned back to wave to her from the wicket gate, and, strong though she was, she seemed for the first time to me tiny and frail as she stood in her doorway all in black. My departure was only the immediate cause of her tears. In the poetical language of an old lament she had been praising the Kirkwood family and mourning their departure of which mine was part. The whiskey and Guinness and the anecdotes she told which made me laugh were in my imagination Woodbrook's wake.

Charlie drove me to the station. I thought it a miracle that the Fiat had survived my stay at Woodbrook and he said it never ought to have survived James, whose repairs with a matchstick and string had always been good for one trip.

The platform was empty. I was thankful we had not long to wait, but the engine gave a peculiar stuttering squeak instead of a full blast whistle before it appeared on the bend. 'She's short of steam,' the station-master said and laughed. All the waiting time I had missed was transferred to the journey. We went very slowly with dreary stops at every station, mostly for re-fuelling, for the engine had used up its coal ration and was running on turf which burns quickly. Outside Mullingar it stopped for two hours while the driver and fireman dismantled a long fence, prising five rows of wire off and sawing up the posts to re-light the furnace which had gone out. We reached Dublin late in the evening, but luckily in time for me to catch the last bus to where the Kirkwoods were staying. I left my trunk at Broadstone station.

Chapter Fourteen

We were very shy when we saw each other though it was easy to
hide that evening behind the flooding talk, Tony's battery of
questions and giggles, Ivy with so much to tell and ask. But next
morning when we went out alone together to explore the park
we walked side by side like strangers who want to get to know
each other but dare not. 'This is the old path to the dower
house; that the new. This elm is rotten in the middle, but someone hopes to save it. The lily pond is where those weeping
willows are. Shall we go there?'

We sat on a stone seat beside the pond in the sun. There were
dragonflies, and lilies were flowering in groups here and there
flat on the dark water. The birds that sang were close together
and more numerous, judging by the sound, than those we were
used to hearing at Woodbrook, whose song even at dawn had
always been scattered, some of it near, some far away.

'Are there any corncrakes in the evening?' I said, which made
her laugh. She had not heard any. 'What will you do?' she said
with such a grave expression on her face that I laughed too and
put my arm round her shoulders and pressed my cheek to hers. I
told her about the book I had begun in the harness room and as
soon as I told her, the only person I ever could have told, I felt
hopeful. She looked happy and now it was easy to make her
speak about herself. Then I saw she really was happy. All the
sadness about Woodbrook had been covered by the full, varied
life that was opening out before her and as she spoke of Dublin
she showed me that her exile was a liberation. The work she
used to do alone was heard and seen by talented people. The
future was full of rich choices and the present crowded with the
excited gaiety that townspeople of her age and class took for
granted. It all shone through her eyes, a light, unhampered

mood suffused her face. She was absolutely beautiful, mobile, brown from the sun, elated, expectant, impatient like someone in love or a child that has made a discovery.

Perhaps she was in love. She spoke of boyfriends cautiously, nervous I suppose of how I might feel, but her gift for describing character left me with vignettes of a dozen men she knew well, mostly much older than she was. It appeared that the ones she liked best were oddities whom she called 'mad' in an affectionate way.

We were walking back to dinner by another way, closer to the mountains, and when she stopped talking I felt sick. I often do before saying good-bye, and it is especially embarrassing when it happens at a meal-time. But I wasn't quite sick and the meal got eaten. Ivy kindly made it seem that I was only going for a short time to England, that there would always be a room for me with them, that I must come back at the latest for the Christmas holidays – in other words that my life in both countries would be holidays, which, since the idea of permanence before it really happens always seems to me as bad as prison, consoled me.

I was blind when I kissed Phoebe good-bye. I kissed her on the forehead, and ran through the park to the bus-stop where I had to wait for half an hour.

Next day I was in London.

We wrote to each other frequently at first, and as always happens gave it up. Her life in Dublin and mine in London had nothing to do with each other and gradually I forgot her; I mean, for lack of knowledge I was no longer concerned with what she was doing now, nor could my work or friends be of any more interest to her than a stranger's. My frequent thoughts of her, and I suppose hers of me, were in the past only. But Ivy's letters never stopped and their extraordinary hopefulness encouraged me during the most difficult time I had had in my life up to then. I was completely out of place in London.

There was an invitation in each of Ivy's letters – for a holiday, for help towards a Dublin job – and at first I wanted to go, but the daily London round seduced me. So the first Christmas went by, and Easter and summer, and when at last I set out for Dublin just after Christmas 1944 I travelled with misgivings. The simple pleasure I had shown in my letter saying I would come turned into doubt and anxiety. It was Ivy, not Phoebe, who had invited me. Perhaps Phoebe dreaded, as I began to on the ship, that there would be nothing between us except the 'Do you remember?' kind of talk. Among the cold and hungry passengers I wondered who was travelling without emotional anchors. Many, I thought. They were all shrivelled. I felt shrivelled.

The Kirkwoods were staying with Phoebe's Uncle Billy in a high house near Howth Head, in the highest suburb of Dublin, with all the winds blowing at it and beautiful views from its windows of the city, the Liffey and the bay. You got there by tram. I saw it above me like a monument on top of a cliff and climbed its terraced garden, about fifty yards of path and steps, to arrive a bit late for breakfast. Phoebe was still in bed. I was shivering with cold. Peta, Billy's wife, pulled an electric fire near to my legs and gave me tea and eggs. Then the rest of the family came in to talk to me. I had not seen Billy for five years, when he last visited Woodbrook, and at first I thought he was Charlie, but a minute later when Charlie opened the door I knew them apart, though they looked like twins. They were both in their sixties. Ivy and Tony arrived, full of talk.

I was alone in the room when Phoebe came down to breakfast. The change of light as she opened the door showed her like a shadow for a second, and then the shadow was gone because she drew back and shut the door behind her without seeing me. I heard her running upstairs. I was not even sure it was her shadow I had seen, but when she returned I knew. She was in a long house-coat which covered her shoes, its upturned collar touching her cheeks. I had never seen her in such a dress before and was still uncertain that she was not one of several guests I knew to be staying in the house. The house-coat hid her except for her hair and the front of her face. But even with her back to me, I knew her as soon as she moved towards the sideboard to forage for breakfast, thinking herself alone in the room. As soon as she heard me get up from my chair she turned with such a beautiful look of surprise that I could not speak. The way she said 'David' made me laugh and hug her. She was tall, and these clothes made her look taller. 'Then the boat was early!' she said. It had been about two hours late. 'Has everyone had breakfast?' She sat beside me eating as though I was there every morning and her acceptance of me was the best thing about my stay. I asked her about her shadowy appearance and retreat. She had forgotten to switch her bedroom fire off. That was all.

I was there for three or four days, one of many guests who ran in and out of the garden and from room to room, as if on a treasure hunt; but they were only seeking each other out in the turmoil. There was a noisy dinner party every evening and one big, dancing, drinking night, sequels to Christmas. I seldom saw Phoebe alone, yet felt close to her and happy, because whenever we met in the crowd she just looked at me laughing.

On my last morning she walked with me to The Summit, the summit of the Hill of Howth, Howth Head, where the tram terminus was. The wind was strong and buffety, making talk impossible; in places where there were no houses to shield us we turned our backs to it in order to breathe; but the sun was dimmed only for seconds by flying clouds. As she ran before me down a rocky, grassy slope towards the cliff's edge I saw she had grown more lithe, not less, and I suddenly had a pang of nostalgia that stopped me as I ran, like physical cramp. It was the careless freedom of the way she ran that reminded me of her childhood, and instead of overtaking her I let her go from me, watching her. I thought quickly and bitterly against myself that it was my diffidence that had encouraged her to go from me in the past. I leapt and ran and overtook her before she reached the cliff.

We were out of breath. In a sheltered place behind a hump where we sat down her face was glowing, her eyes bright with pleasure. The whole of Dublin was spread below us, divided by the Liffey, the Wicklow Mountains, where we had last met, far off but clear, and out in the bay white horses as far as we could see, with breakers leaping and foaming backwards, fringing the rocky coast. There were many seagulls. The 'himp of holth' – the Hill of Howth – the man attached to Anna Livia Plurabelle, the River Liffey – we spoke of these images simultaneously; we had both been trying to understand *Finnegans Wake* since we last met. And during a silence a thought I had dreaded on my way from England came into my mind, that I would start some barren talk about the past – the hills we had climbed near Woodbrook, the 'do you remember?'

It was she who spoke of Woodbrook. It had not been sold. Her parents now wanted the Maxwells to have it, but there seemed no chance of their being able to raise the market price and no firm word of money had yet come from the eldest brother in America. She said, 'Wasn't it lovely, wasn't it!' She said it passionately, looking straight at me. It was she who said it. But I knew she knew that none of them except her father could wish to live there again. Her sadness was nostalgic, perhaps like the loss of a beloved book that helped to form her mind; however seldom you look into it you need it there on the shelf; to have Woodbrook and not have the curse of it, to enjoy it for part of the year as her mother had. Her sorrow was for her father who enjoyed no other life.

It was too cold to sit for long and we walked, talking of what we saw and other things. She was evidently happy and whenever I glanced at her face, so quick to change, so beautifully mobile as it always had been, I felt as I had felt by the lily pond, that she would surmount the worst of difficulties by looking forwards. Everything she said was positive. In the long distance, after the war was over, she hoped she could make her music good enough to allow her to enter the Brussels Conservatoire. Nearer were the opportunities that London might give for her not only for music, but painting.

Had I seen their London house, was it spoiled, would they live there again? People were in it; it could not be sold now and she was glad. I had walked past it several times. It needed painting like all London houses, but was unspoiled. The walnut tree was bigger, the high wall and gate the same. As I spoke of it I was thinking of her illness there, not of the lessons we shared and the tea and buttered toast.

We walked homewards down the hill with the wind behind us, the sun very low in the sky by then. Some seagulls were walking on the pavement and quickened their step to let us pass. Phoebe said, 'No one aims straight, do they?' I half understood her, but did not answer.

When I left for England that evening I said good-bye to her and all the family at their crowded front door. I resented it – this public end – and my mind was absent from the polite things I said concentrating on no one, least of all her who was standing in the background. If she said good-bye I did not hear it. I could easily have asked her to see me to the tram, but was unreasonably shy, thinking quickly that I would only say something stupidly regretful to her there and spoil the Hill of Howth, that I would come back to Dublin soon and we would find ourselves alone together without contriving it. At that moment both Billy and Ivy invited me to return, asking when my next holiday would be.

Picking up my bag, I waved and walked down the steps with my back to them. I had seen the lights of Dublin every evening during my stay, stretching down and along the valley and up the hilly streets, but now they struck me poignantly as something long forgotten or seen only in the imagination of child-like fairyland. It was many years since I had seen a city without a blackout. I was thinking of Easter, of how much longer the evenings would be then during my next few days with Phoebe, when, half-way down the terraced path, she ran behind me jumping the steps and caught my arm.

We came to the darkness of the gate. I don't think we spoke until we heard the tram faintly, starting off from the Summit. She said, 'Then you'll come at Easter, then?' 'Where will you be?' 'At Kilmacanogue, I expect. Or here. It doesn't matter.' She picked leaves from the evergreen hedge and bit one of them.

The tram was louder now. We heard it sliding noisily to its first stop. She looked at me. 'You'll have to go.' I took her hand but the tram was in my ears, nearer and noisier, the last one to catch the boat-train. It seemed to me that she shivered. I pulled her to me and whispered, 'See you at Easter,' into her ear. I kissed her ear. It was cold and smelt of a scent I had never smelled before. She leant against me softly, her hand on the back of my neck. I kissed her cheek, then heard the tram again. She put her hands quickly and gently over my ears and turned me towards her lips. She kissed me passionately and for a second I was startled and did not respond. Then we kissed. Her hands were away from my ears, clasping me to her as I clasped her to me, and I did not hear the tram until the driver put its brakes on and it screamed on a strident note descending to groan towards its stopping place opposite the house. I ran to it.

I thought of nothing but those parting minutes during the whole tedious journey to London. The parting was a revelation and a confusion too. Could people go back to each other after so long? I thought not. I longed to, but thought not. But at least there was Easter which might tell us, and thinking of that I calmed down.

Phoebe's first letter to me after that is dated New Year's Eve, three days after my return to London. It was written in pencil and began, 'Here I am feeling cross so I'm writing to you.' She had suddenly fallen ill and the doctor had ordered her to stay in bed for another week at least. She had had a high temperature, a headache and so on, but those were diminishing and her letter was impatient rather than distressed. The only sentence in it that in retrospect looks alarming is 'I'm far from being very ill.' If she had had 'flu, which was what I supposed, she would never have used those words. The rest of what she wrote was lively with events and people, keeping me in touch with what had happened to the house-party since I left. But a letter from Ivy next morning told me she was very ill. The doctor did not know yet exactly what was wrong.

I wrote to Phoebe every day in January 1945, and sent a book or two until I heard she was unable to read. I wanted to go for a week-end and see her but decided that would be 'stupid', using the word she used for the ill-advised and useless. She wrote on the 5th to say she had been moved by ambulance from Uncle Billy's house to a nursing home in the centre of Dublin and described X-ray processes, nurses and fellow patients with the same lively interest that had inspired her letter of New Year's Eve. Whenever I heard from her during the days after that I

319

was reassured. Whenever I heard from her mother, whose letters were more frequent, I knew she was seriously ill.

Then on the 18th they both wrote to me. I had the habit of putting Phoebe's letter unopened into my pocket to wait till I was alone, but on that morning it was not necessary. I laid them both on the breakfast table, poured out tea in a sort of ritual, and read Phoebe's first. Her writing was larger than usual and the lines unevenly spaced though straight, not very different from any letter written in bed, but noticeably different from her others. She thanked me for my letters and said 'I am still prostrate, but much better and I hope it won't be long before I am up and about again.' She could not read. A friend had sent her a wireless. She wrote about what she had heard on it and about happenings in the nursing home, some of which made me laugh as I read her letter.

Then I opened her mother's: 'Dear David, This is just to tell you that Phoebe is "holding her own", and to tell you to keep on hoping that she will recover. She is still very contented and comfortable and quite unaware she is so ill . . .'

Many days then passed without a letter. I remember my acute anxiety, my watching of the doormat for the post. It came at last near the end of the month on a foggy day, a single letter white on the doormat and the right shape. There were only a few words in the letter. It said what I knew it would say when I picked it up from the mat – that Phoebe was dead.

Epilogue

Woodbrook remained unsold until after the war when the eldest of the Maxwell brothers was able to travel from America and buy it for the family. When I heard this I thought it a just conclusion. But when I visited them twenty years later it seemed to me that fate had gone against the Maxwells in their turn. That beautiful place lay like a dead weight on their shoulders as it had done on Charlie's in his last years there. Only two of the brothers had remained on the estate, my two best friends, Tommy who lived alone in his parents' house – both had died – and Jimmy who had settled in the Big House with his wife. Their eldest brother had returned to America as soon as the deal was done.

It was in June 1968 that I went to see them. I hired a bicycle in Carrick-on-Shannon and timed my arrival at the house for evening milking time when I knew Jimmy would be home from the fields. I felt no nostalgia as I forced the bike up the avenue, rough as it had always been, unchanged, but when at the top I saw the huge torn roots of the copper beech that had been blown down in a gale I was as sad as I had imagined I would be. Then under a bush outside the gates of the stable yard I saw Winnie's butter-churn long cast away, worn out and obsolete. I leant my bicycle against the gate and picked it up. It was covered with green lichen.

The yard seemed derelict, the 'ballroom' windows broken, the stable doors unpainted, James Currid's room falling to bits, weeds and pools of water on the cobbles. There was no one about.

I walked out into Shanwelliagh to look for Jimmy or Tom but it was impossible to see anything through the bushes. I tried to find my way to the boiling well and was soon lost – high thickets everywhere. I heard cattle now and then and came across bullocks grazing out of sight of each other on the patches of grass that remained to them. Their once wide and open pasture had been spoiled, this time, not by horses but by white-thorn and blackthorn as in the years of the Great Famine.

I went back into the cowyard and found Jimmy milking. He knew me at once, before I spoke, and without stopping milking turned his face towards me with a look of astonishment and pleasure.

I suppose he was over seventy but except for its extreme thinness his face had not changed. It was only when he stood up from the cow and reached for his stick that I saw how bent his back was and how stiff his legs.

When I asked him how he was doing, he said he was ruined by the rates. He only had 150 acres of the original Usna – the rest was golf course – but the proportion of rates was as high as in the major's time and he was alone, moving slowly with rheu-matism, unable to run after cattle, crippled as his father had been, though less severely. And as he walked with me round the outside of the house, I saw that this was the reason for the bushes on the pastures and other signs of neglect. 'I had the last of the Woodbrook horses up to three years ago,' he said. 'Do you remember Pellette? A great mare.' We walked across a rubbly place where the drawing-room used to be. The two wings of the house, incurably leaky, had been a continual annoyance to him, especially as he did not use them nor any of the main rooms, and he had pulled them down, restoring the house to its original shape.

It was a sensible thing to do and yet it looked wrong es-pecially on the lake-side of the house where the dining-room – Aunt Nina's room – had been. There I looked up at Phoebe's french windows, black and empty, closed of course but ready to open into nothing. The place where the joists of the flat roof had joined the main wall had not been plastered over.

I looked through a front window into the hall and saw an old reddish sofa pushed against the wall, its back to the room, the remains of a carpet, a painting of one of the racehorses on the floor, propped against the sofa. I wondered how such things *came to be left there. They gave me a sense of abandonment* more forlorn than an empty room. *The hall and the so-called* 'office' like the whole of the upper storey had lain unoccupied for almost a quarter of a century.

Winnie's old domain, where Jimmy and his wife lived at the back of the house, was an oasis in a desert, and here in the warmth of their hospitality and talk I forgot the hollow rooms that lay above and about us. They had dexterously converted this part of the house into a three-roomed dwelling, tranquil and easy to live in, with bright curtains and patterned delph. Unfortunately they had had no children. There was no one to help on the farm. Tommy who lived one field away worked elsewhere.

Jimmy Maxwell's difficulties at Woodbrook were peculiar to him and the place, not at all typical of post-war Ireland. All over the country old settlers like the Kirkwoods had sold their demesnes and the few who remained lived like retired people on their home parks. One might think that the departure of so many influential people, with money to spend locally, would turn out to be harmful to rural society. It was not so. Woodbrook was an exception, a rare one I guess. Rockingham and French Park appeared to be prospering under their new and many occupants.

The demesnes of Rockingham, whose house had been burnt down by accident, and French Park, which had been pulled down on purpose, had been divided by the Land Commission and parcelled out among small farmers. The huge wall that surrounded Rockingham in my time had been knocked waist-high like others all over the country. The last vestiges of the Anglo-Irish landlord system had passed away.

Those remnants of colonial rule, such as the Land Commission, which touched on practical affairs were all beneficial so far as I know, but because I re-visited Ireland in 1968, the year in which the traditional 'troubles' were resumed – in the Six Counties this time – I was more conscious of the evils that remain outside the Republic. The situation in the north-east remains the old one – segregation, the inability of natives and settlers to live together as one society, the settlers' fear and their determination to hold exclusive power. This is now the cause of violence as it was in 1798.

It is as though the whole of Anglo-Irish history has been boiled down and its dregs thrown out, leaving their poisonous concentrate on these six counties.

Notes

Notes

Part One

Chapter 4

1 (p. 41). Baron E. De Mandat-Grancy, *Chez Paddy*, translated by A. P. Morton, Chapman and Hall, 1887, p. 110.

2 (p. 42). ibid., p. viii.

3 (p. 42). George Ewart Evans, *The Farm and the Village*, Faber and Faber, 1969, cap. 6.

4 (p. 42). George Ewart Evans, *The Old Rural Community*, B.B.C. Third Programme, 27 January 1965.

5 (p. 42). Baron E. De Mandat-Grancy, op. cit., p. 20.

6 (p. 43). W. S. Blunt, *The Land War in Ireland*, Stephen Swift, London, 1912, pp. 72–6.

7 (p. 44). See *The Country Gentleman*, 18 and 27 July 1908. Also Baily's *Magazine of Sports and Pastimes*, July 1908.

Chapter 8

1 (p. 71). Except where otherwise stated, all quotations in this chapter are taken from W. E. H. Lecky, *A History of Ireland in the Eighteenth Century*, vol. I.

2 (p. 71). Hansard, 12 April 1878.

3 (p. 74). Arthur Young, *Tour in Ireland*, ed. A. W. Hutton, George Bell, London, 1892, vol. II, p. 54.

Chapter 9

1 (p. 77). See Lecky, *A History of Ireland in the Eighteenth Century*, Longmans Green, London, 1912, vol. I, p. 285.

2 (p. 78). Isaac Weld, *Statistical Survey of Co. Roscommon*, published in Dublin, 1832, by the Royal Dublin Society.

3 (p. 79). M S. collection, Department of Irish Folklore, University College, Dublin.

4 (p. 81). Lecky, op. cit., vol. I, p. 149.

5 (p. 81). ibid., vol. I, p. 189 note.

6 (p. 82). Cf. R. L. Stevenson's *Kidnapped* cap. 22-3, how Cluny Macpherson, chief of the Clan Vourich, had almost royal authority as an outlaw.

Part Two

Chapter 1

1 (p. 103). Vol. 1, p. 3.

2 (p. 103). N. C. Macnamara, *The Story of an Irish Sept*, J. M. Dent, London, 1896, p. 97, whose source is Wm. Molyneux, *The Case of Ireland being bound by Acts of Parliament in England stated.*

3 (p. 104). H. F. Berry, *Statutes, Ordinances and Acts of the Parliament of Ireland*, (John to Henry V), Wyman, London, 1907, p. 433.

4 (p. 104). ibid., p. 435.

5 (p. 104). N. C. Macnamara, op. cit., p. 132.

6 (p. 105). Edmund Curtis, *History of Medieval Ireland*, Macmillan, London, 1923, p. 241.

7 (p. 106). Sir John Davies, *A Discovery of why Ireland was never entirely subdued*, etc., reprinted in *Ireland under Elizabeth and James 1st*, edited by Henry Morley, Geo. Routledge & Sons, London, 1890, p. 266.

8 (p. 106). Thomas Leland, *A History of Ireland*, Brett Smith, Dublin, 1814, vol. ii, p. 287.

9 (p. 107). W. E. H. Lecky, *A History of Ireland in the Eighteenth Century*, vol. 1, p. 7, quoting *Annals of the Four Masters*, A.D. 1582.

10 (p. 107). Edmund Spenser, *A View of the State of Ireland*, 1595, reprinted in *Ireland under Elizabeth and James 1st*, op. cit., pp. 143-4.

11 (p. 109). N. C. Macnamara, op. cit., p. 71.

12 (p. 109). ibid., p. 176 quoting *The Irish Land Question*, by Geo. Campbell, p. 30.

13 (p. 110). Constantia Maxwell, *The Colonisation of Ulster*, 1925, p. 150, reprinted from *History*, 1916.

14 (p. 110). ibid., p. 157.

Chapter 2

1 (p. 111). Burke, *Landed Gentry of Ireland*, 1958.

2 (p. 111). John O'Hart, *Irish Landed Gentry*, James Duffy, Dublin, 1887, vol. 2, p. 372.

3 (p. 111). Brother of Charles Coote, Vice President of Connaught. See *The Writings and Speeches of Oliver Cromwell*, ed. W. C. Abbott, Cambridge, Harvard University Press, 1939, vol. 2, pp. 123 and 131.

4 (p. 112). Edited by Robert C. Symington for the Irish MSS. Commission, Dublin, published by Stationery Office, Dublin, 1949.

5 (p. 112). See, inter alia, W. E. H. Lecky, *A History of Ireland in the Eighteenth Century*, vol. I, pp. 16–17.

6 (p. 113). ibid., vol. I, p. 31.

7 (p. 114). 1 April 1939.

8 (p. 114). E. A. D'Alton, *A History of Ireland*, Kegan Paul, Trench, Trubner, London, 1906, vol. 2, p. 156.

9 (p. 114). *The Writings and Speeches*, op. cit., vol. 2, pp. 154–5.

10 (p. 115). ibid., vol. 2, p. 124. (Letter to the Hon. John Bradshaw, President of the Council of State, 16 September 1649).

11 (p. 115). W. C. Abbott, op. cit., vol. 2, p. 47.

12 (p. 115). W. E. H. Lecky, op. cit., vol. I, pp. 104–5.

13 (p. 116). James Hardiman, *History of Galway*, W. Folds & Son, Dublin, 1820, p. 134.

14 (p. 116). W. E. H. Lecky, op. cit., vol. I, p. 105.

Chapter 3

1 (p. 122). MS letters of John Dunton, 1659–1733, quoted by Edward MacLysaght, *Irish Life in the Seventeenth Century*, Irish University Press, 1969, p. 358.

Chapter 7

1 (p. 154). *The Irish Sketch-book*, Chapman & Hall, London, 1843, vol. 2, p. 116.

Chapter 8

1 (p. 158). For this and all other quotations in this chapter see *Reports from Committees, 1850*, ordered by the House of Commons to be printed 14 August 1850.

2 (p. 161). Isaac Weld, *Statistical Survey of Co. Roscommon*, p. 249.

3 (p. 172). Cecil Woodham-Smith, *The Great Hunger*, Hamish Hamilton, 1962, p. 77.

Chapter 9

1 (p. 177). Occupiers of more than a quarter of an acre of land are not to be deemed destitute, nor to be relieved out of the poor-rates. *The 10th & 11th Vict.*, cap. 31.

2 (p. 181). Marston Garsia, *Criminal Law and Procedure*, ed. C. Hampton, Nutshell Series, Sweet & Maxwell, 1968, p. 33.

3 (p. 181). Cecil Woodham-Smith, op. cit., p. 408.

Part Three

Chapter 2

1 (p. 197). All these quotations are from the MSS. collection of the Department of Irish Folklore, University College, Dublin.

2 (p. 200). The *Freeman's Journal*, 13 April 1878.

3 (p. 201). The *Irish Times*, 3 April 1878.

Chapter 3

1 (p. 206). *A Narrative of Killala By an Eyewitness*, printed for R. E. Mercier and John Jones, Dublin, 1800. Except where others are named this book is the source in chapters 3, 4 and 5 of all information about what happened at and near Killala at that time.

2 (p. 209). William Carleton, *Traits and Stories of the Irish Peasantry*, Baldwin and Cradock, London, William F. Wakeham, Dublin, 1836, vol. 1, p. 314.

Chapter 4

1 (p. 212). W. H. Maxwell, *A History of the Irish Rebellion in 1798*, Bailey Bros., London, 1845, p. 259.

2 (p. 213). ibid., p. 259.

3 (p. 213). Arthur Young, op. cit., p. 249 etc.

4 (p. 215). W. H. Maxwell, op. cit., pp. 232 ff.

5 (p. 216). W. E. H. Lecky, op. cit., vol. v, p. 53.

6 (p. 219). Thomas Pakenham, *The Year of Liberty*, Hodder & Stoughton, 1969, p. 326.

7 (p. 219). W. H. Maxwell, op. cit., p. 328, quoting a MS. journal of a field officer.

8 (p. 219). Thomas Pakenham, op. cit., p. 328.

9 (p. 220). W. H. Maxwell, op. cit., p. 243.

10 (p. 220). Thomas Pakenham, op. cit., p. 327.

Chapter 5

1 (p. 223). W. E. H. Lecky, op. cit., vol. IV, p. 125, thought that in spite of this widespread belief the oath probably never contained these words.

2 (p. 226). W. H. Maxwell, op. cit., footnote to p. 247.

Chapter 6

1 (p. 233). See Maria Edgeworth, *Tour in Connemara in 1833*, ed. H. Edgeworth Butler, Constable, London, 1950.

2 (p. 233). For his letter to King see the *Irish Times*, 4 April 1878.

Chapter 7

1 (p. 240). See F. S. L. Lyons, *Ireland Since the Famine*, Weidenfeld & Nicolson, 1971, p. 551.

2 (p. 243). ibid.

Chapter 8

1 (p. 252). F. S. L. Lyons, op. cit., p. 68.

Chapter 9

1 (p. 264). For this and other quotations in this chapter, the source is Sean Ó Súilleabháin, *Irish Wake Amusements*, The Mercier Press, Cork, 1967.

Chapter 10

1 (p. 273). Burke, *Landed Gentry of Ireland*.

2 (p. 277). Douglas Hyde, *A Literary History of Ireland*, T. Fisher Unwin, London, 1899. Preface, p. x.

3 (p. 278). Quoted by Diarmid Coffey in *Douglas Hyde*, Talbot Press, Dublin and Cork, 1938, pp. 43–4.

Chapter 11

1 (p. 288). Donal O'Sullivan, *Carolan, The Life and Times of an Irish Harper*, Routledge & Kegan Paul, 1958; see Vol. I, Chapter XX for this and the references in Chapter 12 to skulls.